AF574148

Critics Review

Most of us only have the ability to go back in time by relying on our own recollections, but Mike Sciales takes us on a journey to long-ago in a style that is uniquely his own. His impeccable eye for detail and impressively sharp memory quickly transported me to our neighborhood, our classrooms, and a time when life was far different from today. Tagging along as he spread his wings beyond Syosset was an additional treat and truly a joy

Debbie Hornstein Meyer
Syosset High School
Class of 1971

"It's a good read!"

Mike Colangelo
Syosset High School
Class of 1972

As a local historian and author of several books about Syosset and Woodbury, I suspected that I would enjoy "Syosset Blues" for its 1960's Syosset references and not much else. Within a few pages, however, I ended up mesmerized by the author's incredibly descriptive writing style and his very 1960's Long Island sense of humor. By the end of the book, I had pretty much forgotten about the Syosset connection and was completely engrossed in Mike Sciales's stories of military life during the Vietnam era, the primary focus of his book.

"Syosset Blues" is a hefty-sized volume, so leave yourself plenty of time to read it, as you will want to indulge in every detail of every real-life character the author introduces along the way. And when it's over, you will likely find yourself wanting more, which Mike offers by way of his second release, "The Making Of A Combat Jag," the next volume on my read list.

Whether you are a Syosset Baby Boomer, a Vietnam Era vet, or just someone who appreciates good writing, "Syosset Blues" is a worthy addition to your library.

Tom Montalbano

I read Combat JAG first, and just finished this gem. It really doesn't matter the sequence, just get them and enjoy. Mike has the ability to put you right in the chapter, I felt like I was there at Moran's, just two bar stools away. Or riding 'shotgun" in his old 60's Ford Maverick across Canada, on the way to "The Base That Time Forgot". A story teller for the ages, grab a favorite beverage, and settle in for a great read!! "Shyster" I'm awaiting the next book.

Steve Lloyd

FOREWORD

SYOSSET is pronounced Sigh-Ah-set

For some years a number of folks have said, "You ought to write a book." The usual impetus for these pronouncements was drinking. While an excellent idea, my time was not my own and I lacked the technological advantages necessary to complete this.

In 1911, some aspiring writers asked Mary Heaton Vorse, a famous writer, the secret of her success. She replied: "*The art of writing is the art of applying the seat of pants to the seat of the chair.*"

The autumn of 2016 was colder than usual, a harbinger of things to come. One rainy afternoon in late October, I applied my seat to a comfortable chair and began to write. It began to snow in Boise on December 15, 2016. I repaired to my small office with a cup of coffee and my two dogs, Hamish and Charlotte, and began to cobble together the story. I'd come out at five.

January of 2017 was cold, snowy, and unusually foggy. Hamish had started looking poorly right before Christmas; he just looked tired. He still came upstairs every day and along with his sister, would just keep me company. The best dog I ever owned died at the end of that frozen January.

Record breaking low temperatures were compounded by record breaking snow falls in our valley. The snows came down, drivers made ruts, those ruts froze, and didn't unfreeze, until late February. Trapped, like Mary Shelley one wet summer centuries ago, I wrote all day long and well into the night during that, "*Snowpocalpyse,*" a once-every-five-hundred year event. That long winter finally ended in late March when the temperatures and the rivers rose, and I finished writing the great American memoir.

I've been re-writing, editing, and polishing ever since.

Mike Sciales
Dec 2018

The stories are true; the people are, or, like my childhood friend & under-age drinking buddy Joe, were once real. Joe died in 2017.

Acknowledgments

I once again must to thank my incredible wife of more than 30 years. She has been my sharpest critic, toughest editor and best friend. She kept me on schedule and we had a lot of fun.

Laurie, **you remain the best**.

Finally, thanks to all you Long Island Hillbillies; my friends, you lived the stories. I just typed them up.

They all did their part, any factual errors or omissions are mine alone. Nothing libelous to be found, I did change some names just to protect any delicate sensibilities. The events and remarks made were real.

DEDICATION

This book is dedicated to all those tough guys from Syosset, decent, ordinary guys who didn't ask for it, but stood up when called and did the job.

Villagers like Ted Swiencki, Kevin Keaster and Steve Nielsen, three genuine American patriots and heroes; and all those others from 11791 who served.

And for those Syosset heroes who gave everything.

PFC Gregg Eugene Lavery, 19, H Company, 2nd Battalion, 4th Marines, 3rd Marine Division, III Marine Amphibious Force, USMC. Died March 18, 1968, Quang Tri Province, South Vietnam.

Corporal Mitchell Harvey Sandman, 20, Company, 5th Battalion, 46th Infantry, Americal Division, US Army, Republic of Vietnam. Died June, 3, 1969, Quang Ngai Province, South Vietnam.

Major Henry James Repeta, 39, 42nd TAC Electronic Warfare Squadron, 388th Tac Fighter Wing, 7th Air Force, USAF. Died Dec 23, 1972

This is also for all the truly remarkable men and women who serve the nation. My friend, and mentor, the late Colonel Daniel P. Haas, my Staff Judge Advocate at RAF Upper Heyford, was one of those very good guys. I was lucky to know him.

Finally, and**,** especially, for **Technical Sergeant Nathaniel B. Edwards,** the **OBM**, who made everything else possible on that rainy night at Lajes.

Thanks Nate, I passed it along.

Table of Contents

Prologue

Two Roads diverged in a yellow wood,
And sorry I could not travel both
And be one traveler, long I stood
And looked down one as far as I could
To where it bent in the undergrowth;

Then took the other, as just as fair,
And having perhaps the better claim,
Because it was grassy and wanted wear;
Though as for that the passing there
Had worn them really about the same,

And both that morning equally lay
In leaves no step had trodden black.
Oh, I kept the first for another day!
Yet knowing how way leads on to way
I doubted if I should ever come back.

— Robert Frost

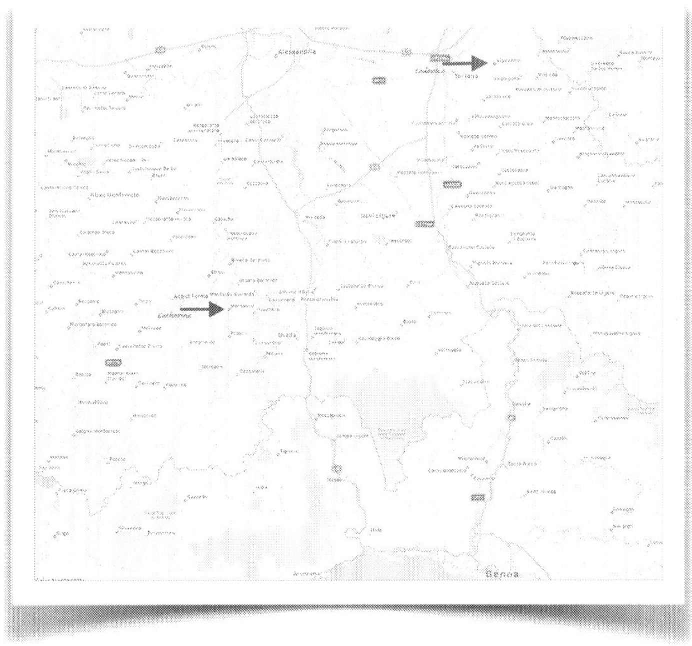

The Immigrants Tale

In 1887 Ludovico, my maternal grandfather, was born in the valley town of Viguzzolo, Province of Alessandria, in the Piemonte region, seventy-five miles east of Turin, Italy. His family was poor and jobs were scarce, so in 1911, with an empty stomach and dreams of a better life, he bought a third class "steerage" ticket, boarded the SS Florida in Genoa and began his voyage to the New World. Once he arrived in Little Italy, that teeming ghetto on the lower east side of Manhattan, he saw this was indeed a land of opportunity, but realizing just how homesick he was, vowed to work hard and save enough money to return to Italy and live like a king. He took work as a window washer on tall buildings, which was very dangerous, given the lack of concern for worker safety, but paid very good money.

In 1897, ten years later and two hundred miles south of Viguzzolo, but still in the Piemonte region, my grandmother was born in the remote mountain village of Morsasco, in a tiny one room dilapidated shack on a small plot of land. Catherine's childhood was spent with her siblings and parents, first working the family plot for their own food and later joining them and working as a farm laborer, barely eking out a living and never getting beyond the same peasant life all the previous generations had been born into.

So it happened in 1913, not long past her sixteenth birthday, with no desire to be herding goats until she married an old one, Catherine fled the grinding poverty and boredom of those mountains and took her first and last bus ride to the port of Genoa, forty-five miles away. She left her family and all she knew without a backwards glance when she embarked steerage on the SS La Provence, then the largest ship in the French Merchant Marine, for the six-day voyage to New York City. She easily cleared Ellis Island and began her life in the new world. She too moved into Little Italy and took up work as a seamstress in the garment district.

The soles of her shoes were barely dry from the voyage when she fell under the charm of the decade-older Ludovico, who simply promised her a better life if she threw in with him. He was a good-looking fellow, and, very strong from work washing windows on skyscrapers. They married shortly thereafter and moved into a one bedroom fifth floor walk up in a tenement at 91 Baxter Street, just off Canal Street, in lower Manhattan. Barely five hundred square feet, their new home boasted a kitchen and two rooms on either side for bedrooms. The bathtub also served as the kitchen table when a board was placed over it. The hall toilet was communal and shared with the other three families on their floor. Originally slotted to move into a place on the second floor, when my grandfather found out it'd be five dollars cheaper, he took the top floor apartment. Catherine walked up and down those steps twice a day, every day.

In no short order the union produced five children starting in 1917 with my mother, Julia, followed by her three sisters and one brother. My mother only attended school through the eight grade, it being necessary for her to join the work force, since small, nimble girls were much in demand at the clothing factories where they could scramble easily amongst the looms and other machines to untangle jams and oil the mechanisms. Children were often maimed or killed. She worked twelve hour days six days a week and handed her pay packet over to Ludovico, just like her mother and sisters did.

When she was fourteen, my mother took a job at a book bindery in the forwarding department where she glued backing on book spines before they were further bound. The job paid much better than working the looms, but she neglected to mention that to her father, who suspected nothing because the amount she always handed over to him remained the same as before. She secretly wound up saving a fair sum of money; her subterfuge necessitated by Ludovico's old world habit of beating his wife because he could, and he had extended this custom to her and the other children once they'd made it past their First Communion.

My mother turned seventeen in 1934, and when her father celebrated by giving her a black eye, his American daughter marched to the police station, where she swore out a complaint. When Ludovico got word that his daughter had put the cops onto him, in very short order Lodovico, along with her brother John and little sister Rose, fled the United States and returned to Italy, taking the over thirty-thousand dollars he'd squirreled away, gleaned from the sweat of others.

The average Italian worker's annual salary in 1934 was fifteen hundred dollars. The average salary in his village was much less. He would now be a "patron," a wealthy man who deserved respect. He could also get another wife, a good one who hadn't been corrupted by all those new American ideas. His foresight should have given him the life he truly deserved, but what he didn't see coming was Benito Mussolini, the Italian politician, journalist, and dictator, who'd been in office since 1922. Ludovico admired Mussolini; his old school ways had restored order to Italy, and even made the trains run on time for the first time.

Fresh back off the boat, Ludovico came home to the Viguzzolo a grand patron and, made plans for his new life. He would be a patron, a man attended to in his golden years by a strong son and beautiful young daughter who herself, as the daughter of a patron, would marry well and assure the family would prosper. This plan would evolve as they all lived happy lives in the fine new house he was having built. As the days sped by, he dreamed his dreams and storm clouds gathered.

In 1935 he watched with admiration as Mussolini reorganized the Italian Armed Forces, creating five Alpine divisions. He was less enthusiastic in 1938, when the forty-one year old gentleman of leisure and his sixteen year old son John were drafted into the Italian Army, and the Alpini, becoming mountain troops. They were posted to the Balkans where John was killed in 1942 while trying to disarm an unexploded bomb. That explosion tore off his arms and he lay bleeding and calling for help until he died. (Back in New York, my mother dreamed that her brother had been injured and could not use his arms and was calling to her for help.) His death was confirmed when Rose returned to the USA in early 1946. She approached some Americans soldiers who liberated the area and identified herself as an American. They turned her over to the Red Cross and brought her back to New York.

A now-shattered Ludovico survived the war, returned to Viguzzolo, and took up the life of a patron with no heir and no daughter to care for him in his old age. He drank more than he should have and died at age sixty-three after falling out of a lemon tree he was tending on the property of his unfinished villa.

Meanwhile, Catherine, who'd brought the DNA across the Atlantic, lived in that walk-up until she died in 1981 at age eighty-four. She spoke Mandarin Chinese because that's who moved in after the Italians left, and she saw all four American daughters marry, giving her ten American grandchildren. She lived long enough to see each of them graduate from high school and watched as each one went off to university and professional lives.

CHAPTER ONE

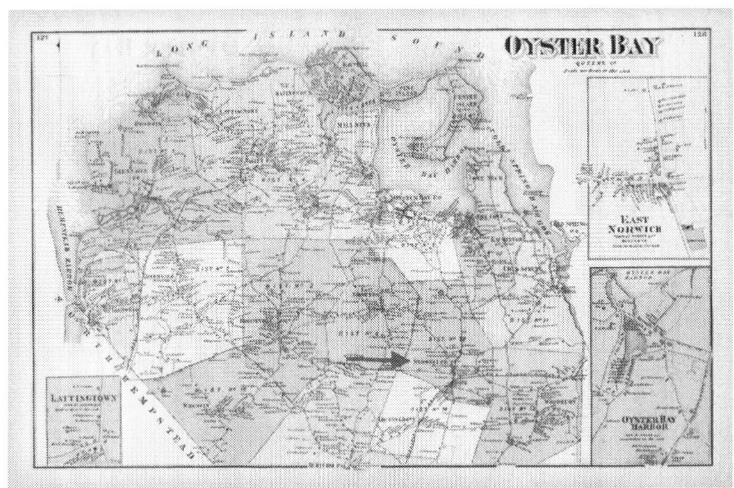

The Move East

Syosset, population 9,000, was one of nineteen unincorporated hamlets within the boundaries of the Long Island town of Oyster Bay, which was created in 1653. Oyster Bay contained eighteen incorporated villages and nineteen unincorporated villages nestled into spots along the North Shore. It was named on June 4, 1639, when David deVries, a Dutchman, was the first to drop anchor. He described, "A commodious haven on the northern shores of Long Island. We found fine oysters there, from which the Dutch call it Oyster Bay." By random luck, the Italian explorer Giovanni de Verrazzano first sailed by in 1524, but didn't stop for lunch or it might have been called the Town of Ostrica Baia. In 1600, Richard Latting and his son Josiah, bought some land from the Matinecocks tribe and sold marsh reeds for thatched roof houses, ultimately creating the incorporated village of Lattingtown.

Long Island was first claimed by the Dutch as part of their province of New Netherland. In 1639 they purchased the soon-to-be-a-town land from the Matinecocks. In 1648, Robert Williams of Hempstead bought another large parcel of land in the area which is represented today by Hicksville and adjacent parts of Jericho, Plainview, Syosset, and Woodbury. Five years later, the chief sold the land in the northern portion of Oyster Bay, extending from Long Island Sound to a point near Hicksville, to New Englanders Samuel Mayo, Peter Wright, and William Leverich. Several other colonists joined in this First Purchase and settlement began.

As time went on, owing to the relief provided in summer by the gentle breezes off the Sound, the area began to accumulate the wealthy in splendid incorporated-village enclaves with massive hidden estates and private police forces, including one village, Centre Island, which is connected by a two-lane causeway into Oyster Bay, one that can be secured. Tiny hamlets, like Syosset and many others, grew up around those villages, at first providing the hired help for the farms and estates, then opening shops and businesses for all the new arrivals from the city in the great migration after World War II. This migration was fueled by the GI bill which allowed millions of vets to go to school and a VA home loan program that let millions more buy homes instead of renting apartments. These programs led to Levittown, the name of four large suburban developments created by William Levitt & Sons for returning WW II veterans and their new families. These planned communities offered attractive alternatives to cramped city apartments. The Veterans Administration and Federal Housing Administration (FHA) guaranteed that qualified veterans could receive housing for a fraction of rental costs. Production was modeled on an assembly line where thousands of simple houses were produced easily and quickly, allowing rapid recovery of costs. These houses came standard with a white picket fence, green grass, and great appliances. Sales of the original Levittown began in March 1947, and 1,400 homes were purchased within the first three hours.

By the time my people arrived a few miles farther east and 403 years later, in 1956, the potato fields had just been sold and sectioned off by developers and more new neighborhoods were springing up. Travel to and from New York City was provided by Route 25, Jericho Turnpike, a road that wound through all of the small and unremarkable villages along the way, or the four-lane, Northern State Parkway servicing northern Long Island since Interstate 495 (the Long Island Expressway or LIE) was still some years away. As the area developed, the hub of the village remained; a long row of small shops comprising: a chemist, several ethnic delicatessens, dry cleaner, several small clothing shops, and a few taprooms where a thirsty man could watch a baseball game in peace, and in the center of town, the train station.

Joining the exodus from the daily travails of life in the big city, my parents took a shot at the American dream of owning a home and some land. Dad was a wine salesman for Ernest and Julio Gallo in their Taylor Wines division. Taylor had champagne vineyards in upstate New York, but also distributed E&J's low-cost "fortified" wines like Twister and Ripple. These wines proved very popular with the *lower socioeconomic milieu*, a term research companies used to describe poor folks. Table wine has an alcohol content that typically falls between 8 and 14%, while *fortified* wine can have an alcohol content of anything ranging between 17 - 22%. His route was Long Island out to

Montauk Point and both ghettos, Harlem in Manhattan and the South Bronx, but the stuff sold itself, all he really needed to do was keep up with the orders.

The South Bronx was originally called the Manor of Morrisania, the private domain of the powerful and aristocratic Morris family, which included Lewis Morris, a signer of the Declaration of Independence, and Governor Morris, penman of the United States Constitution. As the Morrises developed their landholdings, an influx of German and Irish immigrants were populating the area. By 1930 the Bronx was considered the "Jewish Borough," as 364,000 (or 57.1%) of the total population was Jewish. In the late 1940s social workers identified the Bronx's first pocket of poverty in Port Morris, the southernmost section. After World War II, white flight accelerated while a migration of ethnic and racial minorities continued. The South Bronx went from two-thirds non-Hispanic white in 1950 to two-thirds black or Puerto Rican in 1960 and urban decay began in the South Bronx. This process was accelerated by landlord abandonment, economic changes, and the construction of the Cross Bronx Expressway that disrupted neighborhoods and eliminated political opposition. Arson was rampant and so the South Bronx burned. Today it is slowly being re-gentrified and becoming a hip area to live in.

With no daycare available, I spent school holidays in my father's car, riding the length of the Island on the Northern State, watching the odometer in his 1960 White Ford Falcon four-door sedan tick off the tenths of each mile and sending us further into the wilds of untamed and undeveloped Suffolk County, then with a population of 660,000. Our journey took us through small fishing villages where generations of early settlers had made a life from the land and water. As the area population grew, more liquor stores opened to meet the demands of newcomers. These new stores improved the choices of beverages available to compliment local cuisine, which was mainly smoked eel being flogged at herring stands that appeared every few miles. Called *Gerookte Paling* by the Dutch, these eels are long, fat, meaty, and one of them can feed two people. These were available from the Visboer (fish monger) or at any of the local herring shacks that dotted the landscape along that lonely and only road. I've often wondered if *Twister*, that,"Ring a ding-ding" lemon-scented fortified wine whose price was *nice at ninety-nine cents twice* paired well with the paling, but I never had the chance to find out.

Other days, our ride took us into an alternate universe where I saw burned out buildings in a landscape that looked like footage I'd seen on *The 20th Century,* a CBS TV half-hour documentary series, hosted by Walter Cronkite, that showed the destruction of Berlin and Dresden during WW II. When we were in the South Bronx, my father admonished me to remain in the car with the doors locked, as he went inside a store to make his sales call. He had no such qualms about Harlem, but the harsh urban reality of the South Bronx was that anything could happen and being a white boy didn't come with any guarantee of being a "protected species." I saw guys shooting up heroin out in the open, so I took his advice and kept the doors locked and stayed low. A couple of times, I watched some poor bastard shoot up, then instantly slump down, usually in a hallway, and I knew right there I didn't want to wind up like that.

I realized those guys I watched shooting up didn't have a job, so I determined to always have one, because I didn't want to become a dope fiend. As soon as I turned twelve years old and to make some money, it was delivering newspapers for me. I delivered fifty papers on to porches every evening after school, then early mornings on Saturday and Sunday. Syosset enjoyed a full four-season climate, with hot and humid summers, too-short autumns, and severe winters that warmed into a muddy and windy spring. It was a tough buck to earn, as we could not toss the papers onto the driveway. If it was raining I had to wrap them in plastic and put them in the holder next to the front door. Collections also offered me insight into the lives of suburban folks in 1965. I learned who tipped well at Christmas and who never had fifty cents when Friday collections came around. I also had a few bored moms who came to the door holding a glass of wine, while wearing a Peignoir night gown at three in the afternoon, who invited me in for hot chocolate and a bit of a chat.

+++

Joe's Boy

It was 1966, the "Year of Bar Mitzvahs," that religious initiation ceremony for Jewish boys who have turned thirteen and are regarded as ready to observe religious precepts and eligible to take part in public worship. This initiation involved reading at length, in Hebrew, from the Torah, the scroll containing the law of God as revealed to Moses and recorded in the first five books of the Hebrew scriptures, known as the Pentateuch.

To learn Hebrew, all of my buddies had to attend Orthodox Yeshiva (religious school) on Wednesdays for one hour under the watchful eye of old Rabbi Abe Kippleman, who we were pretty sure knew Moses back in the old days. White haired and stoop shouldered, he could still keep up with a bunch of bored and antsy twelve year olds. Despite diminished eyesight, there wasn't anything wrong with his hearing and he was quick to cuff a lackadaisical student in the back of his head. If we were rowdy he'd denounce us as "vilda chaya!" or wild animals. I attended most classes with my friends, and was a pretty good student because I didn't want him smacking me. I already had two hours of evil East German Catholic nuns wielding brass-edged rulers at Catholic school on Saturdays for that, thanks very much. He always called me "*Hey You, Joe's Boy!*" because I wasn't an adult. If another kid was especially off the mark when questioned, Abe would ask me for the correct answer, which I usually had because of my fear, which elicited his response, "So, even this goy shegetz (rascal) knows more than you. Das es ein schande (shame)!" None of those Jewish kids ever caught a break from Rabbi Abe. Syosset had a lot of Jewish families, so many in fact that there were three synagogues, Orthodox, Conservative, and Reformed, which my friends called Hebrew Lite.

My Hebrew friends had parents who believed in the importance of education in an uncertain world and made school the main priority for their children. Throughout history, Jews were put to flight during *blood libel.* These were organized, ethnic massacre *pogroms,* where peasants would blame Jews for any missing children, alleging the Jews took them to sacrifice in blood rituals. The wholesale slaughter would begin, and the Jews would flee, abandoning their lands and realizing education and skilled trades were transportable.

My parents took the more provincial approach, believing children should be informed early that life would contain lots of hard work and they might as well get on with it. This had been their experience, and, despite all their best efforts, they were almost always dead broke or in some state of grave pecuniary concern.

My mom was a waitress at Rudy's Delicatessen Restaurant in the Plainview Shopping Center a half mile away. When I turned thirteen, I got phony working papers and was installed in an entry level position as a dishwasher in the back of the kitchen. The deli in front did a brisk takeaway trade in giant sandwiches, frankfurters, and potato knishes, plus had seating for thirty diners. The kitchen in the back was staffed by an international crew consisting of Mexicans, Puerto Ricans, one Hungarian (Steve) and one Pole (Lazlo C. Lazlo), two refugees who'd escaped Communist rule. Steve deserted the Hungarian army, telling me, "It sucked very badly." Lazlo dreamed of becoming a truck driver. He learned English by watching the same movie five times on his one day off each week. I saw him once at the Hicksville fifty-cent cheap theater, watching "The Green Berets," and repeating every word of dialogue. He saved his money, learned English and got a job driving. I was stuffed in the kitchen because it gave me time to hide if a labor inspector ever came around. When I turned fourteen and got my working papers, I became a busboy and would languish there for another year, which is an eternity when you've only been alive fourteen years and can't remember all that much of the first four.

Prior to joining the ranks of child laborers, there were those few short carefree years where I enjoyed the maximum amount of free time outside. My mother insisted we leave her alone so she could relax between shifts, and, if we were home, she banished us outside until five. On September 12, 1960, Hurricane Donna struck Long Island and wreaked havoc. Schools closed, and, tired of us all being cooped up, my mother sent us outside to play as soon as CBS news announced the eye of the storm passing overhead. She knew we'd be fine, the weatherman said the winds would calm for a bit before picking back up with an even greater intensity. Sadly, when those winds picked back up, she'd forgotten about us while watching *Password* and doing the ironing We spent the next hour screaming and shouting while huddling against the leeward side of the house, hoping not to get blown away. She finally let us back inside when she came into the kitchen for a beer and heard our caterwauling.

My life in those days was about filling those hours between being grossed out by eels or engrossed by junkies shooting up. It also meant I'd be meeting and learning about all the new kids on the block, and in the neighborhood, as more families moved in. My world consisted of nothing more than my immediate neighborhood, Birchwood Park, a cluster of two hundred homes crammed into an area just under one half mile square. Bordering Northern State Parkway at exit 36, and later the LIE at exit 43, it was also directly under the approach for both JFK and LaGuardia airports. Every three minutes a 707 would come screaming overhead before splitting to its assigned airfield. Conversations took a pause while they passed.

My immediate concerns tended to focus on my own street, Avon Court, with five family homes. One family, our across-the-street neighbors, was a dentist, his wife and three stair-step kids: eight year old daughter, six year old son and four year old little sister Marie, who had teeth like a monkey. I learned this when I showed her a toy Esso oil tanker (pre-Exxon Valdez) I'd been given by another neighbor, Pucki, who owned the Esso station in town. Without a bit of warning or foreshadowing, she latched on to my bicep and bit until she left a dental impression, while ripping that boat out of my hands, promptly smashing it on the sidewalk, suggesting she had some unresolved anger issues. I got even a few years later when I threw a wayward metal dart that managed to hit her throat, just missing the jugular. Ever cautious, I added her behavioral profile to my newly established "crazy people behavior" internal file.

To our left lived Bert and Betty and their three sons, Danny, Jeff, and Allen. When I was six, I saw Danny get killed while riding his bicycle in the street by a car that ran a stop-sign. That trauma made me forever a stickler for safety. Bert was a used car salesman who loved to play opera on Sunday mornings while he had coffee in his back yard, and Betty was a lunch lady at the junior high school. She'd fled Germany as a young girl when Hitler came into power. On the other side of our house were Pucki, Helen and their two kids, Paulie and Jennifer. Directly across the street lived the O'Toole's. He was a retired telephone company executive and, with his wife, shared a home with their unmarried adult son, a high school principal somewhere. He was famous for driving all the way out west to see the Seattle World's Fair in 1962, which was pretty brave considering what a long drive that was. He was very lucky that another confirmed bachelor, a guy he'd known for many years, was able to go with him.

In 1958 I began my public education at Robins Lane Elementary School. It'd only been built the year before but was a singularly uninspired edifice, as if the winning design had been submitted by the US Post Office. By necessity, educating children is a repetitive business as teachers mold young impressionable little minds, and because of that most of my days passed (absent a stunning third grade portrayal as Mr. Clean, in a play with the same name) with nothing memorable occurring, until I entered the fourth grade under the instruction, care and guidance of Mrs. Weinstock. A newly minted teacher, she'd been drawn to this new school by a promise of nearby affordable housing, as well as peace and quiet when compared to the City. Interstate 495, the LIE, was built starting in 1957 and I'd spent that next summer watching as it crawled east at a half mile a day, bringing civilization and fulfillment of mid-20th century suburban Manifest Destiny.

One small part of that destiny was being friends with Stuart.

My neighbor, Stuart, was a mentally ill kid, born to make the wrong kind of headlines. He's long dead and I don't say that to disparage his memory, rather, upon reflection, it was amazing he didn't do more harm to persons and property.

In myriad ways, Stuart was screwed by life, none of them his fault. He'd been abandoned at birth and at that time nobody knew or understood how the effects of alcohol or certain abused prescription medication ravaged a fetus, just as nobody knew or understood the psychological effects of maternal abandonment on a child. Nobody knew how long he'd been in the unwanted baby bin, but at some point life brought him into the warm and tender embrace of his parents, Phil and Jeannie.

Not recognizing Stuart's peculiarities as something that would soon command all their attention, they adopted another child, Ricky, whose jet black hair, dark eyes and vaguely simian visage provided a stunning contrast to the sandy blond-haired, blue-eyed Aryan, Stuart. Regardless of any outward manifestations, time bore out that Ricky was much more normal than Stuart, in what passed for normal in the very early 1960s. For some reason people persist in viewing that decade through a hazy, golden lens, when the reality was that some bored and lonely housewives abused alcohol and prescription drugs, as well as some of the older neighbor boys, who didn't mind.

Stuart lived down the next block, on Berkley Lane. He'd "been adopted," something he'd say all the time. His dad, Phil, who was a successful senior vice president for a national car agency, owned a forty-foot cabin cruiser and liked to sail around Oyster Bay on summer weekends. All he wanted out of life was to sail that boat, drink beer and enjoy his free time. As an admittedly poor kid, I was really happy to be invited to go out with them for a day on the water. Breakfast at the Celebrity Diner on Route 25, Jericho Turnpike, was included, the first time I'd ever enjoyed such a treat. I was amazed at the small packets of different jams as we only had a jar of Concord grape at home. Stuart didn't have a lot of other kids who'd play with him so those incentives worked really well. His mom, Jeannie, was the original bored housewife. She was quite pale with dark black hair, usually in loopy curls, like Betty Boop, a cartoon character from the Thirties who wore curls like that. She always wore dark sunglasses, always kept a glass in her hand, and when she spoke her speech was slightly slurred most days, even early in the morning. She took pills regularly throughout the day and had pill bottles all over the kitchen. This wasn't unusual, I'd seen that plenty of times before, on my paper route, during Friday night collections. I'd be in the kitchen, drinking my hot chocolate and waiting to get paid. I'd see all number of dark brown pill bottles from Whalen's Rexall Drug Store in Plainview, and listen while a wife tore up her house gathering loose change. One tipsy lady even fell down while trying to turn over the sofa cushions while looking for quarters.

I don't recall becoming aware of Stuart until the fourth grade and never saw him again in school after that one year, owing to the events soon told. During that short time he engaged in behavior that would alarm psychiatrists today, like bedwetting, fire-setting, and cruelty to animals, the behavioral trifecta for a serial murderers, but back then his behaviors went unremarked upon by anybody in any authority. He was also the most interestingly weird kid I ever knew and knowing him taught me to recognize serious mental illness, be wary of those afflicted, and to never underestimate crazy.

+++

Show And Tell

"Hey, Teach," came the dull and monotoned voice. Mrs. Weinstock automatically responded, "Yes, Stuart?" He was seated at his desk situated in the back, off to a corner, just the place where an adult might want to park a kid who was a bit creepy and always on the cusp of some bad act. It seemed better for all that he work by himself. In a time when it mattered, Stuart was the sort who looked forward to running with scissors and absolutely did not make good use of his resources. In fairness, while I had the good sense to run, only without scissors, I was not making good use of my resources, as was noted in the comments on my report card. "Glue wastage" was cited in particular, right next to "fails to apply himself" and "continues to write using left hand despite attempts to train."

Mrs. Weinstock was wary of Stuart because there was no telling what his next move could be, he was just that unpredictable. It was a "Show and Tell" day which had gotten off to a dramatic start when a girl named Reva came into class crying, complaining that her poor hands were frozen because she hadn't worn her mittens. Long Island weather could be absolutely brutal in winter. High humidity, coupled with a bitter cold, thanks to the

Arctic express, helped spawn blizzards, severe snowstorms with high winds and limited visibility. Those violent storms blowing in off the Sound could be deadly, but if the busses could roll, the kids could walk, and Reva was a walker. She was tiny, maybe sixty-five pounds, so it took much more energy for her to walk into those gusting and howling winds as she made her way to school.

Mrs. Weinstock had stepped out of the room for a moment to wrangle the stragglers and, in her absence, Stuart jumped up quick as a mongoose and said, "I'll help you, Reva!" as he ran to the just-our-size-sink with-gooseneck-faucet and cranked it on HOT, full volume. The school boiler was a model of efficiency and in seconds clouds of steam were billowing from the sink while Stuart turned towards the now openly skeptical Reva and urged, "Come on, Reva! This will fix it!"

Reva began to back away as some other kid yelled "No! It's supposed to be cold water, not hot, Stuart!" in the way those little kids who know the correct answer are wont to shout, but Stuart, convinced of the merits of his position, focused like the recently invented ruby laser and was not about to be deterred. He moved on Reva with surprising quickness, grabbed her thin wrists in his hands and began to drag her half frozen, squirming body towards the sink and a serious scalding. She was still wearing her winter wool and tweed coat with one button missing and frayed cuffs, the sure sign of a hand-me-down from an older sibling. This was no disgrace, it just showed she was just as far down the child ladder as the rest of us.

With about two feet to go before Stuart could plunge her hands into the near-boiling water, we all heard "Stuart STOP RIGHT NOW!" from Mrs. Weinstock coming towards them at the teacher quick step pace. Stuart gave it another few heart beats calculating his odds before he gave Reva up. The now free, but still semi-frozen Reva immediately began sobbing hysterically while Mrs. Weinstock shut off the hot water and turned on the cold faucet.

She took this as a "teaching moment" and reinforced in all of us the correct way to way treat frostbitten limbs should the need ever arise. She slowly inserted Reva's trembling hands into the cold water, gently massaging them until Reva said her hands were getting cold. Only then did she begin to slowly add warm water. That lesson stayed with me to this day and I've had occasion to use it.

With that crisis averted, our teacher again turned to Stuart. It was, after all, still a Tuesday "Show and Tell Day" and Stuart had history there as well. Earlier in the year, Stuart discovered Phil's stash of prophylactics in a bedroom dresser so he brought one in and opened it as part of his presentation. Mrs. Weinstock was slow off the mark, but she managed to stop the show before too much damage was done to our young psyches. She turned warily towards him, asking what he had. He said it was a surprise for the class. Now fully alerted, Mrs. Weinstock said sweetly, "Maybe I better take a look and see if this is something to share with the class." Stuart played it coyly and agreed, but insisted she close her eyes while he set up his display. She agreed and closed her eyes, something I'd have never done.

What Mrs. Weinstock could never have known was that, a few weeks earlier, Stuart had developed an intense interest in how things worked. Phil and Jeannie, delighted their son had finally taken an interest in something other than torturing Ricky at every opportunity, went out and bought him a state of the art chemistry set that included radioactive radium and poisonous liquid mercury. This in addition to some radium laced "glow in the dark model paint" and companion home dissection kit. They felt they'd done their parental duties in giving Stuart everything he ever asked for.

They had visions of Stuart pursuing an academic track, but his interest in destruction and mayhem had cranked up recently since we'd both watched a black and white original, Boris Karloff, "Frankenstein," with all its crazy science and electricity. Stuart was fascinated by Igor, the ghoul/henchman who got to do cool things like score the body parts for the doctor so he turned his attention to anatomy. Since he couldn't dissect his brother Ricky, though not for a lack of desire, he cast his eyes about and landed upon a most unfortunate tabby cat that was wandering by. Our neighborhood was full of cats, everybody had at least one, some several. This cat in question belonged to a classmate whose parents rented the farm house on the one acre remaining after the owners sold off all the rest of the surrounding farm land for development. His folks operated a "farm stand" that was replenished when Sal, the dad, would drive into the Hunt's Point Terminal Produce market in the City on Sunday night and purchase the fresh veggies and fruit for the upcoming week. I loved it when I was invited along; it was an exciting place full of brawny working stiffs hauling produce orders on hand carts and shouting out "Sal's Farm Stand! Sal's!" and we'd wave them down and transfer the loads to our truck. Not only did we get our fill of fruit, we saw a guy who looked like a werewolf with so much hair sprouting out of his wife-beater tee shirt. He also said, "Fuck" a lot.

Stuart set out to catch that cat and almost did, but the cat, using those animal instincts, correctly recognized that Stuart's aura was signaling mortal danger. Stuart had lured the wee beast with a bit of ham he'd gotten from the kitchen and when the cat got close enough Stuart tried to snatch it up with the goal of a vivisection, but the cat escaped his grip and went flying into the street where it was promptly struck and killed by David Ahl's mom, who lived two doors down, as she was coming back from grocery shopping at the A&P in Plainview. Her 1960 gold Pontiac Safari station wagon came screeching and rocking to a stop right after the impact, which sent the unsecured brown paper bags in the back flying. We heard the crunch as the car bumper hit the cat in the head, an instantly fatal blow. The poor woman got out of the car and began crying when she saw the cat who now looked vaguely like a strawberry and butterscotch sundae some petulant child had thrown on the ground. Stuart approached Mrs. Ahl and smiled, saying, "I can get rid of it for you!" and, just like that, Mrs. Ahl's immediate problem was solved and she left to go home, have a drink, and forget about that episode.

Stuart eagerly scoped up the remains of tabby and brought them into the garage and on to Phil's seldom used work bench, then fetched his dissection kit and an old thirty-two ounce clear glass Mason jar. Working with a fair amount of determination given he'd never dissected anything, let alone a cat, he got pretty much all the organs and any other cool items off of the carcass and into the jar. When he finished his pieces and parts, he filled that jar with formaldehyde to preserve them. He screwed on the lid while admiring his handiwork, turning the jar slowly and examining each item with great intensity, concentration and clinical detachment. He was pleased that both eyeballs had migrated to the walls of the jar with one golden iris perfectly visible. We'd seen a giant eye monster that looked like that a few weeks earlier on *Chiller Theater*, our Saturday night black & white horror show on Channel 11 WPIX. Then he wrapped the entire thing in aluminum foil and was ready for Show and Tell.

On that frigid and fateful morning, most of the kids were finally settled after the Reva show, but as soon as some kids nearby realized Stuart was having a pre-show, one by one the awareness began to build and soon there were sly tugs on sweaters and quiet pointing.

Mrs. Weinstock moved towards the back of the room, away from the clustered desks and closer to Stuart's, ready to minimize the exposure. She leaned against the outside wall with Stuart facing her. This let her see the presentation while keeping an eye on the rest of the class. Stuart reached down by his desk, pulled out and opened his imitation leather briefcase, the kind required by the school. This was part of a subtle training program preparing us for the rigors of a commuter's life. With this same thought they regularly exposed us to mass transit and taught us how to use the subway. They also trained us to form up and stand in line for all activities. Sliding our plastic slotted trays along the counter as we asked for food from the hair-netted lunch ladies prepared us for prison or the military.

From that pseudo leather case produced, with some flourish, the now aluminum foil wrapped jar in which he'd stashed the remains of Michael's cat. He held it up and deftly pulled away the wrap from the center and found an eye. He pulled away more foil to provide an unobstructed view of it. He had about half the jar visible when he turned it so the lifeless orb faced her, up close and within arms length, then said, "OK, Teach" in that same monotoned voice devoid of emotion.

Mrs. Weinstock opened her eyes and came eyeball to floating eyeball, and some other pieces of unrecognizable cat guts. She let out a shriek worthy of the Bride of Frankenstein when she meets her intended. Shrinking backwards while raising her hands to clap her mouth in horror, those hands knocked that Mason jar right out of his hands and back towards the center of the classroom. It arced, traveling just a few feet before shattering at the feet of Reva, who was still paying attention to her own hands. Hearing the glass shattering, Riva looked left and backwards. She saw the cat guts and eyeballs come flowing along the mottled blue and white linoleum tiles right towards her. She screamed, jumped up and down and vomited on the cat guts, adding a component that made other kids scream, and one kid, David, seeing Reva's vomit, followed suit. Bedlam ensued.

While Mrs. Weinstock was trying to restore order that could not be restored, children screamed and cried out how bad it stunk while others added sympathetic dry heaves. In moments, the teacher next door burst in, asking if everything was OK. She got us all moving outside quickly, sans coats, for unscheduled recess and airing out.

Mr. O'Hagen, our perpetually florid-faced custodian, with his shock of flyaway white hair and forest green Sears brand work shirt and pants was summoned. He shuffled up the center hallway, pushing his gray fifty-five gallon garbage pail on wheels with the myriad tools of the custodial trade attached. He'd come to clean up the mess with his janitor stuff that included some kind of absorbent material that smelled like Bazooka bubble gum. He'd spread it all over, we knew, because we'd all witnessed puking before. However, this time, as he reached to get the puke absorbing stuff, the sight he beheld, or perhaps the whisky he steadily drank, caused him to add his own contribution to the mix. O'Hagen did stalwartly finish the task, and after a good airing out, we were steered reluctantly back into the classroom, but we never saw Stuart again in that class.

Word got back that the school psychologist believed there were alternative routes for Stuart. He was gone and nothing more was ever said. He was just gone, as if he'd never existed. Of course, his expulsion didn't mean I couldn't still hang out with him in the neighborhood after school was out. The pickings were slim since a lot of other kids went away for the summers and we just weren't among them.

The summer of 1965 was record-breaking hot and humid. The local news informed us it was going to be another "long hot summer." This was not referring to the weather, but, the race riots that were setting inner cities ablaze with increasing frequency. Rochester, Harlem and Philadelphia all experienced civil unrest and riots in 1964 after the Civil Rights Act was signed.

We were warned that THE NEGROES, who said they simply wanted an equal shot at a better life, were probably going to rampage and burn down more of their neighborhoods. While being sworn in as governor of Alabama in January 1963, George Wallace said, "Segregation now, segregation tomorrow, segregation forever." We were always seeing on TV loads of Federal troops and national guardsmen walking black students into schools. We had no idea what it all meant, not having any black folks in our quiet hamlet. This urban unrest would lead to a lot more social changes. Replacing the term "negro" with "black" did not occur in the media until WABC's Roger Grimsby announced it one evening in 1968, citing the NAACP.

None of this really mattered much to my twelve-year old self because I'd been invited to go out on the "Stu-Rick, " Phil's forty-foot dream boat, for a day on the water with the family, even Jeannie. We watched as she slid onto the front bench seat of the large and brand new Chevy Impala Phil enjoyed as one of the job's perks. She was careful not to spill a drop from the glass she'd just filled from a plastic gallon Igloo water jug she always had. We loaded up and made our way down to the marina in Oyster Bay. Phil was also rich enough to own a small rubber raft he used to get to the boat, board it, and fire it up, then bring it alongside the pier to pick up the rest of us. Jeannie brought aboard the food we'd packed, and her personal cooler, remaining there while the rest of us went to get additional fishing tackle and bait from the marine supply shop.

We came back and, as we learned from watching WW II movies, began to "make all preparations to get underway" then cast off for a pleasant cruise. Phil left no wake as he departed the marina but after a bit we were in open waters and the speed climbed. Once Phil reached his desired location we'd usually troll for a while, but today Phil put the gear into neutral, killed the engine and left the key in the ignition. He went forward, set the sea anchor, and headed below to make himself a drink. He told Stuart to grab a swim mask, fins, snorkel, and a paint scraper, then jump overboard to inspect and scrape any barnacles from the hull. Jeannie had earlier developed a splitting headache and gone below to rest.

Stuart donned his gear, then stepped on to the small diver's platform on the stern. He dangled his feet in the water and spit in his mask like Mike Nelson did on a popular show, *Sea Hunt.* Mike's typical adventures were finding a downed satellite or sunken treasure, so cleaning barnacles was great training for any young lad who wanted to be diver like Mike. Once ready, Stuart spun around backwards, dropped over, in, and was gone. He resurfaced, looked back at the boat, and waved at me while I sat seated on the white couch at the stern, serenely taking it all in.

Stuart swam back towards the gently rocking boat, took some air and vanished below the waterline, a trail of bubbles leading beneath the hull. A moment later I heard the sound of him scraping along the keel a few feet below, near the stern but on the starboard side. Phil dropped down two steps into the cabin and quick as a flash Ricky came out of nowhere, and jumping up to the operator console, turned the ignition key while engaging the starter.

Hearing the whine of that starter, I knew Ricky was trying to fire up the boat and shove it into drive, hoping those spinning propellers would chop up the evil brother who tortured and abused him at every opportunity, in the tradition of older brothers since Cain and Abel. I anticipated cavitation bubbling up in the water as I heard the engine catch and Ricky slamming it into gear. After a brief lag, the propellers began to turn.

Phil exploded out of the cabin and flew up those two steps, in one motion knocking Ricky out of the way while grabbing the ignition key and turning the engine off. Peering over the stern I figured I might see some blood and stuff if Stuart had been near those blades when the ignition switch was hit. I couldn't miss the sound of Ricky screaming as Phil laid into him with a serious beating. It was not more than a few seconds when Stuart popped his head above the water, pulled back his mask and asked what was going on.

The behavior between brothers was not to let up, at least not for any of the time that I hung around with Stuart. Ultimately, he was transferred into a more suitable location with a full time professional staff and no doubt some heavy medication.

+++

The Strange Demise Of Jerry Mahoney

It was that 1965 Long Island summer, between fourth and fifth grade. Everyday was incredibly hot and humid. That excessive moisture in the air made sweat pop out on parts of your body that don't usually sweat. In this case I suffered damp forearms, but at least that thick atmosphere masked those constant sounds generated by all the traffic on the LIE and passing aircraft, muffling the noise and making it less irritating. I was further tortured by ground so fertile you could see the grass growing. What made it worse was my father insisted on using a push style reel lawn mower, which was impossible for my twelve-year old self to operate, so he bought the cheapest Briggs & Stratton lawn mower Sears sold and set me to the task. He insisted the clippings be swept up owing to the crappy grass catcher bag that clogged routinely on the heavy wet grass, so it took twice as long to gather the clippings as it did to mow. That started off as one of those rotten summer days. I'd started sweating the minute I left the house; and, as the temperature soared, even the shade would provide no relief. My mother wouldn't let us stay in the house. We did not have air conditioning, and we generated body heat, so it was "out with the lot of you!" Exiled, we wandered about the neighborhood, looking for something to do and somebody to do it with.

On this particular day, I found myself hanging out at Stuart's house. His father was at work and his mother was out and not likely to come home before evening. Phil & Jeannie tried to compensate for their constant absences by purchasing gifts to show how much they really loved their kids. In one particularly expensive gesture Phil bought Ricky a "Jerry Mahoney" ventriloquist's dummy, complete with working jaw, rolling eyes, and swivel head.

Jerry was part of an act by a local TV entertainer, Paul Winchell, a wonderful ventriloquist. He was also a brilliant inventor, holding over thirty patents and is credited as developing and patenting an artificial heart in 1963. From this came the Jarvik-7 artificial heart that went into one grateful Barney Clark of Durban, South Africa, in the first operation of its kind. Meanwhile, Jerry's other sidekick, Knucklehead Smith, was not nearly as flamboyant as Jerry and served as the straight man for the often snarky Jerry.

Ricky loved Jerry and took him pretty much everywhere. He would stick his hand up Jerry's back where he could pull the handle to make the jaw open and close, while trying to sound like Jerry and not move his mouth at the same time. Of course he sounded nothing like Jerry, unless Jerry had decided to become a mouth breather who sounded exactly like Ricky. Regardless, the two were inseparable.

Stuart really, really hated Ricky. During that winter we were playing in the sump across the street from their house. There, loads of water runoff pipes led into a pit. If it was dry you could crawl in those pipes undetected for as long as you liked. One long pipe led into the pit at the lowest level and at the top of the pit, level with the street, was an access shaft, a vertical pipe with a metal steps made of rebar that would allow you to climb up or down. We spent many afternoons exploring those pipes.

The hour was late and the sun was low in the sky. It'd grown colder and was time to for getting on home. Using the frozen water on the sump floor, we'd been playing ice hockey without skates, and using branches to shoot the frozen bird we used instead of a puck. It was fun, but it was time to go. The sides of the sump were covered with snow and weeds so we entered the long pipe, low-crawled our way to the ladder and climbed up and out.

Ricky was still wandering about in the pit when Stuart called down to him to come out because we had to get home. When Ricky went into the pipe, Stuart gathered up some old newspaper he found, plus some leaves and a bunch of pine needles, pulled out a Zippo lighter, and started making a fire. It was actually taking off pretty well when his bother popped out of the horizontal pipe and onto the ladder, climbing up to us. Stuart waited until Ricky was about halfway up when he started dropping flaming pieces of detritus down on top of his brother. Naturally the kid was looking up while he climbed and saw those burning materials raining down at him. He screamed for his brother to stop but that worked to encourage Stuart who scooped up as much burning material as he could, then and tossed it all down on his now-hysterical brother. Ricky survived the assault but couldn't tell his mother because Stuart promised to kill him if he did and nobody ever wanted to test Stuart's resolve about anything.

Thus, it was on this very hot and humid day, sometime before noon, that we were sitting in a discarded refrigerator box we'd found, pondering questions like, "Isn't it weird that Dog is God spelled backwards?" and why couldn't you drop a cherry Life Saver into water and flavor the water?

Finally growing bored of our random thoughts, Stuart went inside and I trailed after him. It was cooler in the downstairs lounge. Their house was split level and five steps below this lounge was a finished half-basement, paneled in knotty pine and boasting a fully stocked bar complete with beer signs, a place for entertaining neighbors and friends and where we once decided to make a "mixed" drink, so we mixed a bunch of liquors together and drank it. Vomiting a few minutes later put me off liquor for several years. The lounge was the place though because they actually owned a color television in a large, heavy Mediterranean style console that also had an AM radio and record player. It was complimented by a large, heavy dark wood couch and single seat overstuffed chair also done in the Med style so popular then. The cushions had all been shrink-wrapped in a very thick clear plastic so nothing would ever detract from their singular beauty. The plastic also made for an uncomfortable seat, but assuring they'd always remain showroom-new.

While still casting about for something to do, Ricky came bounding down the stairs with Jerry, both equally interested in something to fill the empty hours of a boring summer day.

Stuart looked at Ricky and said, "Hey, Rick, wanna see something pretty cool?" Of course Ricky was ready for anything, so he nodded his assent in a perfunctory manner. Stuart disappeared upstairs and returned in only a few minutes and with some flourish produced a no-kidding, honest to goodness, genuine set of Smith & Wesson police handcuffs! These weren't the cheap-ass "Chinese finger handcuffs" that got tighter if you struggled; no, these were the real deal, something I'd never seen in my life except on TV.

Ricky was likewise impressed and his obsidian eyes shone as he excitedly reached out, saying, "Let me see! Let me see!" Stuart said, "OK, but first I want to show you that they are real." Ricky agreed and Stuart directed him to sit in the overstuffed chair while Jerry took a seat on the stairs. Once he was seated, Stuart directed Ricky to bend forward and put his hands down by the front left leg of the chair, and Ricky did. Stuart then quickly cuffed Ricky's left hand and worked the other cuff around and behind the massive chair leg. Finding that scrawny little wrist, he snapped the ratchet into the bracelet, the multiple teeth clicking as they tightened.

Once fastened, Stuart said, "OK, try to escape." Ricky struggled gamely but, after a few moments of furious agitation, he remained bound just as tightly as before. "I can't get out!" he whined while Stuart just looked at him and said, in his flat unemotional voice, "OK, wait a minute."

He walked over to the stairs and picked up Jerry, who remained mute. Ricky immediately sensed things would not turn out well and began to squeal, "What are you doing with Jerry? What are you doing with Jerry?" Stuart ignored the question and opened the sliding glass door that led to the bricked patio and backyard. Stuart took Jerry to one of the white, wrought iron, chairs, heavy and indestructible. Stuart tenderly placed Jerry on a seat, taking care to cross the dummy's legs, giving an appearance of being at ease. Stuart walked back inside where Ricky continued to scream for answers and some relief.

Walking over to a wall closet, Stuart pulled out a twelve-gauge double barrel side by side shotgun I didn't know they owned. When I was five and watching the LIE being built, I saw a crazy old lady living in a tumbledown shack try to stop construction from coming through her living room. She pulled a shotgun on the work crews until the cops finally came and took her away. I'd never seen a shotgun up close before and was simply in awe.

He also pulled down a box of 00 (double-ought) buckshot shells and smiled grimly at Ricky who was beginning to play "connect the dots."

Stuart left Ricky howling for help and went back outside to the table. He set the shotgun and ammo down, checked the angle of the chair so there was a clear space behind it, walked back to the table, picked up the shotgun and put two shells in the chambers, then snapped it shut. He lifted the shotgun up while pressing it tightly into his shoulder like he learned on TV and touched off one round. At his firing distance of three feet it was simply impossible to miss the target Jerry presented. The eight pellets had little opportunity to separate during the short flight, thus transferred a considerable amount of kinetic energy into Jerry's cheeks, nose and the near orbit of his right eye, hurling fragments of wood and plastic into the air and away on the breeze. Another round and the ear and most of the cranium was gone with nothing much left to recover and grieve for. This carnage seemed to go on for a considerable time, and with each shot, with every violation of Jerry, Ricky's pleas got a little softer and his weeping more mournful. Stuart emptied that box into Jerry. I slid out because I knew it wasn't going to turn out well when his parents got home.

That was the last time I saw Stuart.

He went off to an extended-stay place for crazy kids, finally written off by his parents, most likely over the destruction of the doll and imprisoning his brother which finally topped off the litany of abuses from years gone by. His departure marked the sad recognition that Stuart was just a bad seed and nothing was ever going to change that. All through my remaining years in that neighborhood, not a word was said about him until finally, in 1975, while working at the Vietnamese Relocation Project in northern Florida, I called my mother just to see what was going on. Matter of factly she told me: Stuart was dead.

I was shocked by this news. He was my age, twenty-one, and he was dead! Naturally I asked about the circumstances. Mom told me that Stuart had had a bad time of it. After getting out of the juvenile facility/mental hospital, he lived rough, out on the streets, and became a heroin addict. He wandered about our little hamlet, where he was arrested for burglary, and some other petty crimes, until age nineteen when he came back to live with his folks after shaking his heroin habit and was beginning to straighten out his life. He'd started out as a yardman mowing lawns, and, over time had developed into a budding tree surgeon. Stuart had done a lot of work around the neighborhood, and it was Mr. Schlacks, the plumber living next door, who hired him on the job that killed him.

Schlacks had a lot of trees in his backyard that had been neglected since he'd bought the house fifteen years earlier. He hired Stuart to clean things up. Stuart went over and set his ladder up against the fence where their property lines met, near the telephone pole with the power and utility lines. Using a twenty-four inch chainsaw to cut away the branches of the tree, he maneuvered to trim one branch which, although undercut, did not fully detach from the tree. When he cut it from above, and met less resistance than he'd anticipated, the saw sailed through the wood and momentum carried the chain saw down, striking an energized power line. The explosion knocked Stuart off the ladder and his head struck a concrete bird bath, instantly knocking the life out of him.

As she told me the circumstances, my mind flashed back to that summer's day so many years earlier, and, for just a minute, I wondered if those little pieces of Jerry that'd been blown away were borne on the humidity-laden breezes to the trees in Schlacks' yard where they'd waited ever so patiently for their revenge.

+++

Losing My Religion

Like my parents, grandparents, and all the others in my Euro-centric familial past, I was born a Catholic because that's just what our people were. There are degrees of Catholicism: ultra-traditionalists who want it all in Latin and a return to the 1500s; charismatic Catholics, created in 1992 in Pittsburg, who are more into the Holy Spirt and talking in tongues; and finally the dreaded liberal Catholics who want women priests. Our family were none of those.

We were "rote" Catholics, descended from peasants. I knew nothing about any liturgies, or philosophies, or even any of the relevant symbols of the Holy Roman Catholic Church. All I knew was we showed up each week for the Sunday noon service at St. Edward the Confessor church because that's when my father performed duties as an usher, finding people seats and passing the collection basket. For me, it was the price of admission to a candy store on the way home, where I could spend some of my hard-earned quarters purchasing the latest *Superman* or *Green Lantern* comic books.

From my seat, in the middle of an overcrowded row, in the middle of a giant section, surrounded by people who were always coughing or sneezing, Dad's "duties" looked like a way to get out of having to actually sit through a church service. Ushers were always walking around and keeping a general eye out for fainting old ladies. If they weren't on the prowl, they were out in the hallways talking, or outside catching a smoke, while the rest of us five hundred or so miserable souls shared too close a proximity in a large room with most of the windows shut because of the noise from jets screaming overhead on their way to LaGuardia or JFK. This resulted in us all breathing in some very stale air, which explained the people fainting during services, especially in winter when the windows stayed closed and people were bundled up.

The noon service was a high Mass, the service rendered meaningless by being conducted entirely in Latin, except for the sermon, which was delivered in English. With that behind him, the priest would remind us of the bishop's upcoming overseas-aid charity drive, or that the roof was needing repairs, so we had to reach deep for our second offering of the service. I had to donate my own money from my paper route so I didn't much care why they were bumming more money, and I didn't care about the roof, and I knew charity began at home, so I gave them my quarter on the first pass, and did a fake drop on the second go-round of the begging bowl.

My mother didn't attend church often, she being responsible for creating the nice Sunday afternoon dinner. This weekly treat always comprised some exotic dish, like lamb or a roast, accompanied by roasted seasoned white potatoes, vegetables, and brown gravy. The Sunday feast was always served on the good china and placed on a white linen table cloth in the dining room. We even used the wedding-gift silver cutlery. This justified my Mom making my sisters polish it every Saturday.

What I didn't know until 1969 was she'd been divorced before marrying my father. By church canon law, that meant she and my father were excommunicated from the Catholic church. As dismissed believers, they could attend and ponder their transgressions; they just couldn't ever take the sacraments again, unless one of them died, or they divorced.

It was 1967 and I'd spent six weeks that summer with my buddy, Brant and his family, in their twenty-four foot Holiday Rambler travel trailer, making our way to upstate New York and camping at many wonderful parks along the way. Our trip included two weeks at Long Point State Park, outside of Watertown. This park was absolute slice of kid heaven. Plenty of woods during the day, a lake to swim in, and a nightly educational movie shown under the blanket of stars that was our own Milky Way galaxy.

Before we got there, however, there was a two-day period where I was made to pay the price of admission to this dream holiday, while also being the genesis of my later dilemma.

Brant's folks were really nice people. His dad worked in the city as a comic strip editor, and his mom was a suburban housewife and homemaker, originally from South Carolina. She loved the Pennsylvania Dutch period and its heavy German influences. Her home was a wonderful display of these simple and utilitarian pieces. Her undiagnosed Obsessive Compulsive Disorder drew her towards the straight lines, simple turnings, and tapered legs made from walnut, oak, and pine. She'd happily break out the Murphy's Oil and polish that wood, using that time to admire its beauty. But as beautiful as all that wood was, it made for really uncomfortable furniture. Nobody would choose to sit in those chairs if anything else, like the floor, was available To be fair, the uncomfortable design did have the unappreciated benefit of never having to be sealed in two-mm-thick hard plastic to protect it.

Brant's family were Jehovah's Witnesses. This meant nothing to me; I'd never heard of their religion. Other than my Jewish friends, everything I knew about all those other Christian religions was what I read on the owner's labels when passing outdoor marquee church signs. Lutheran, Episcopalian, Methodist, Calvinist, none of it meant anything much to me. I had friends who were neither Catholic nor Jewish, and they didn't know much about their own religions either, so it just never came up.

Through our travels, I learned the Watch Tower Society was started in Brooklyn, New York, by Alexander Hugh Macmillan, a man who believed the world would end in 1914 with the Devil being released upon the Earth and Armageddon and Judgment Day coming shortly thereafter. WWI certainly seemed to fill that bill, but Witness chronologists later rechecked those original calculations, then newly predicting that the world would in fact end in 1942. In 1943, they performed some minor adjustments to the JW celestial chronometer, finally and forever calling 1969 the year it all ended. We still had some time, so we were enjoying ourselves while waiting for the rapture or whatever it was that made up Armageddon.

They told me only the twelve tribes of 12,000 will get into heaven so the place maxes out at 144,000. I thought this all very interesting because I had learned there were over two million JW adherents around the world and the competition for those seats must be fearsome. Once Judgment Day ended, it was off to the burning lake or someplace equally bad for everybody else. While they were teaching the horrific penalty, I wondered if eternal damnation would be as bad all those concentration camps I'd seen watching Walter Cronkite's, "*20th Century*" on TV, and did those doomed people have to go to new hell after dying in the old one in Germany? It didn't make any more sense than anything else I'd ever heard.

We traveled with another family, a mom and dad plus their two teenage daughters, and we always had camp sites next to each other. They formed a study group at the local Kingdom Hall every Wednesday night where they'd all take a shot at reading and discussing religious stuff. Boring as it was, it was still better than all the scripting and rigidity of Sunday mass. During the day, after we finished chores like pumping and hauling water, we were free to occupy our time as we wished, which was swimming and exploring the forests. Brant had started smoking so he'd bring along cigarettes and we'd smoke one and later take care to stand in the smoke from the campfire to mask the odor. Our evenings were spent sitting around that campfire toasting marshmallows while Brant's mom told ghost stories. She was from South Carolina and all of her stories revolved around ghosts or escapees from insane asylums who victimized bad little children who didn't mind their adults or heed their warnings.

Before we'd get to fully enjoy ourselves however, there was the little matter of attending the weekend Jehovah Witness District Convention being held somewhere around Syracuse. The selected campgrounds were spartan and terribly flat. Each morning we'd get up, putter about, and have breakfast until it was time at nine to go the convention, which was being held in a stadium of some kind. I had no idea of exactly which kind because, thanks to the overflow crowd of true believers all trying for one of the 144,000 astral seats available, we found ourselves outside in a large circus tent in the parking lot. We had seats in the front row there and listened to a disembodied voice preach to us through a nearby large gray outdoor speaker with the volume turned up.

For this first session, Brant's parents took seats furthest along the edge of the tent which afforded Brant and me some shade as the sun made an arc across the heavens. The trade off was that I was seated next to a true believing older black lady, one with ample bosom. She smelled like lavender, a scent I associated with all my old Italian aunts, but then realized it was just old ladies generally who liked smelling like the flowers I had always associated with funerals. She wore a large church hat and a billowy flowered print dress and waved an oversized, professionally made paddle fan which she used pretty much all through the service, given it was over ninety degrees and muggy. Betraying her earlier Baptist roots, she'd shout out "Amen!" periodically. The preachers droned on for what seemed like hours, until a break at noon set people free to get lunch, but then, to my dismay, again to return for the two final afternoon sessions.

Lunch was at a stainless-steel diner on the side of the highway. We liked it because they had a pinball baseball game machine. Three games for a quarter. You waited for a shiny steel ball-bearing to be spit out from underneath a rubber flap covering the pitchers mound. A button controlled the bat. Provided you didn't miss the pitch entirely, you tried to hit some targets at the back of the machine, each one indicating a play, like a single or double. Every once in a while, you hit a home run and watched the lighted base bags glow and go dark as the imaginary runner rounded the bases. All this helped keep idle hands distracted while lunch was being cooked. I was as happy as I ever could be. I liked eating in a diner because normally, at thirteen, you can't make many of your own food choices. When somebody says you can order what you like, to me, a cheeseburger was always a fine choice because we never got that on the menu at home. The diner chef usually gets some input as well, and would set lettuce, pickles, tomato and onion slices on the side to add as you wished. In that particular single-wide stainless steel roadside diner near the campground, it was "chef's choice" and all hamburgers came with fried onions on top, which I was happy to enjoy along with the pickle relish.

Brant and I had finished lunch and returned to the tent for the afternoon session, taking up our same seats as before. Two hours later, I could no longer make any sense of what the speaker was saying. I was day dreaming, just trying to keep my eyes open, when I felt a pressure beginning to build in my lower abdomen. My lunch was being digested and during that process the requisite gas was building up. In what seemed like mere seconds, I recognized pressure building, gas cramps beginning, and I knew it was not going to get better.

Farting comes easily enough to children and most times the important thing comes down to laying the blame elsewhere once the odor was detected. After the initial "Ewwwww!" and revulsion, the hunt was on for the manufacturer with lines like, "Whoever smelt it dealt it!" or, "Whoever denied it supplied it!" These accusations were hurled about until finally the odor dissipated and we moved on to something else, because very few people would happily admit to being the one who did "pass the gas." This was especially true when around adults and certainly if you were around religious adults who weren't your parents or family, so here I am knowing full well that I could only keep it inside for a limited amount of time before I couldn't.

The speaker was getting louder and more excited about something; an announcement came, then organ music began to play and people started singing. The loudspeaker was blaring the joyful noise of the tent's jam-packed faithful adherents, and that's when the gas finally passed. Any trumpeting to herald this completely natural gastric event was drowned out as the crowd of celebrants praised and offered adulation as required. I myself felt relieved but, looking to my left, saw Brant's delicate nose twitching as the scent's trail came into range. He knitted his eyebrows and shot me a questioning look. Running out of options, and since speaking was impermissible, I cocked my right eyebrow and gave a slight nod towards the now heavily sweating lady next to me, her fan going back and forth like a metronome on speed. That was all it took, blame laid upon some unsuspecting soul who hadn't dealt it and never smelt it, thanks to that fan. Given the nature of the rapture and celebration, I figured God would forgive me, but I'd clearly lost any shot at one of those reserved seats.

The rest of the vacation was wonderful as we camped at a succession of wilderness campgrounds on our voyage in Brant's parent's brand new 1967 Ford Country Squire Station Wagon, pulling a 24-foot Holiday Rambler trailer. We entered Canada through Buffalo and followed the St Lawrence Seaway to visit a succession of Canadian cities. We drove into Toronto and later into Ottawa, and eventually into French-speaking Montreal, where we laughed ourselves silly at the stop signs that said, "Arrête" instead of "Stop," like normal stops signs. We finally entered Nova Scotia so Brant's dad could visit Minas Basin, in the Bay of Fundy, where the guide books assured him the height of the tide can reach an incredible 16 meters (53ft).

We arrived shortly after eight in the morning and got to see those rapidly rising tides while set up camp. We spent the rest of the day doing chores and messing about. It was the height of summer and still light at nine that night when the tide finished fully receding. With this never-to-be-repeated odyssey winding down, I was bummed as we turned south down the coast of New England, before finally returning to Syosset just two days before school was set to begin.

It was always a bit of a let down to return home and slip back into the familial rotation and pecking order. My two older sisters always seemed to enjoy bossing me around and generally making my life difficult, and I wasn't a big fan of school, which was about to start, plus there were the chores.

Saturday came on that last free weekend, and I'd just finished mowing the lawn my father had neglected for the several weeks I was gone. Coming outside while it was still cool, I saw dew running down individual blades of grass and knew I was screwed. I fired up that mower at eight and finally finished mowing all four thousand square feet of grass around four. To deal with that verdant jungle, I raised the lawnmower to its highest point, mowed, lowered the wheels a notch, mowed, down another notch to mow some more until I finally got to the normal setting. That took until noon and, after lunch, I spent the next four hours raking those damp green clumps into piles. My father believed work gloves were for sissies, and a useless extravagance. I think he just never thought about it because his hands never turned dark green from handling that chopped up mixture of protein and other organic matter leaking the grasses' juices, including chlorophyll.

Meanwhile, I was experiencing some pretty severe epidermal discoloration. Ignoring this staining for the time being, I knew I was in for some serious scrubbing later. I continued loading those moist piles onto a wheel barrow which I hauled to a newly created compost pile by the rear of the house. I was tired and beat and looking forward to a cold drink as I walked by my father who was watering the lawn with a hose, a lawn that needed absolutely no encouragement. He looked up at me and asked if I was done. When I told him I was, he said, "Good, now go take a shower because you need to go to confession."

Confession! Aargh! Started in 1551, the Council of Trent declared a belief that Confession, aka Penance or Reconciliation, was one of the seven sacraments of the Church instituted by Christ. It was really just an intelligence gathering network whereby priests would hear about all the happenings in their community and could then report that information to the local supervisor, the Bishop, who would then brief the regional supervisor, the Cardinal, a politician who would then put it to the benefit of the Church and even the King, if convenient and profitable. The two biggest selling points were these : it was all absolutely confidential, your identity and sins would never be revealed by a priest under the penalty of being defrocked and excommunicated, and with a sincere heart, ALL sins would be forgiven, and the Kingdom of Heaven was yours.

For me, it meant figuring out what I was going to say. I never told the priest the things I actually did, usually falling on old standards like not taking out the garbage when asked, fighting with my sisters, and not doing my homework on time. I never talked about any of the good stuff like smoking, cursing, and drinking, and certainly not about jerking off, because he'd think that was messed up and judge me, plus he'd have something over me because I wasn't convinced he didn't talk to those Brooklyn nuns at Our Lady of Mercy about stuff he heard from kids. He might not name the penitent outright or their offense, but a well-placed "You might want to keep an eye on that one" would be enough of a flag. I'd just missed church for the last six weeks and that was a really big deal, not one I was eager to confess to.

We drove the two miles down South Oyster Bay Road and I felt my chest tighten as we crossed Jericho Turnpike and the street went from four lanes to two and became Jackson Avenue to mark the change. We came around a small curve at the Lutheran Church and shortly thereafter pulled up to the front entrance of the aptly named "St. Edward the Confessor" Catholic church with its large circular stained glass window, and inside through double doors, bypassing the stairs leading to the loft, and on into the chapel. Wooden pews led to the altar, while the interior was lit by sunlight filtered through stained glass windows along the walls. Each panel told a part of the story of St. Edward kicking heathen ass, somewhere that involved him sailing, until he died in 1066. These handcrafted storybook panels were proudly donated by folks hoping to get on the right side of the pearly gates. The altar was elevated, made of cool white Italian marble, and housed the Tabernacle where the Body of Christ lived inside the holy communion wafers when not needed. His being in-residence was marked by a lit candle in a red glass holder, suspended from the vaulted ceiling on a gold chain. The candle was positioned just slightly above his only door. I always supposed this would make it easier for visitors to see if he was in, if any came calling and needing him.

All in all, it was an ambitious effort for our small hamlet and reflected well upon the good citizens whose generous pockets supplied the cost. The attached rectory provided housing for six priests overseen by a Monsignor, the pastor for the entire parish. Along the back wall and under the choir loft were two different confessional booths. My protocol was to check the lines standing along the wall under the Stations of the Cross wooden panels and compare its length with the line of sinners standing under the sailing St. Eddy and the Confessors stained glass-panels. Both were equally attractive. The glass-panels offered me a chance to read what was essentially a medieval comic book; while stations told the sad, wood-carved, illustrated story of Jesus getting his ass kicked by really mean guys who made him wear thorns and carry a cross while being whipped. These illustrated infomercials were meant to inspire me to pray and, reflect on his sacrifice for me. That was really nice, but I usually just picked the shortest line.

The priest sat in the center of the confessional booth. Sinners would pull back a heavy-looking purple crushed velvet curtain on either side to walk in. Kneeling down hit a switch inside the padded kneeler that turned on a red light over the doorway. This let all the other filthy sinners know the booth was occupied, and to just keep contemplating the error of their sinful ways. Kneeling sinners were in the "on-deck circle" and had to be ready to step right up and confess as soon as the other eternally lost-soul finished. That could be a while, depending on the list of offenses that person on the other side of the booth had brought to share. Those still-sullied, but always faithful, folks were left stewing in their personal guilt-juices, waiting for the priest to slide open his small screened wooden door. True believers spent that time in reflection about what truly miserable and pathetic creatures they were. I had my story down pat and used it each week, so I usually just daydreamed. Separated by that thin bamboo screen, a priest could hear you; but couldn't see you, or know who you were, theoretically.

Having booths on either side of the main aisle meant two priests were usually available to hear confessions. Not really buying into the whole anonymity thing, I felt it prudent to try to "spread the wealth" when picking my personal St. Eddy's confessor, hoping whoever it was wouldn't remember my voice, or those same tired lies I told the time before. I checked the little printed name cards over the priest's door on the Stations of The Cross side and saw it was the Monsignor, Father Henry. This was not good. He had a significant speech impediment and sounded remarkably like the cartoon character Elmer Fudd. When he said, "Hello" it came out "Hewwoe" and "remember" as "wemembuh." With thinning white hair and ruddy cheeks, he looked a bit like Elmer as well. Father Henry was the senior priest in our church and knew my father from Dad's service as an usher. Father Henry already suspected me of being a heretic after he came to visit our fourth grade catechism class one Saturday morning two years earlier and, in an avuncular way, asked if any of us had any questions for him.

Our class used an indoctrination book, the Baltimore catechism, to teach the beliefs of the Catholic faithful which included lines like "Who made you?" and "Why did God make you?" These questions provided all the information good Catholics needed to know because the correct answer to pretty much any of those questions was "God." This instruction was improved upon by the Sisters of Mercy, an order, despite their name, consisting of some very cruel East German refugee nuns. These tireless brides of Christ operated out of Brooklyn. Like the good spiritual wives and educators they were, those nuns administered the girls' preparatory school, a nearby orphanage for boys, the Saturday Catholic schools at St. Edwards and Our Lady of Mercy, in Plainview, the next village over. These celibate, fundamentalist, Catholics were crazy in love with their etherial husband, having run the risk of getting shot while escaping to the West. One thing was absolutely certain: they hated Communists. Active supporters of the war in Vietnam, they knew killing commies for Christ was the right thing to do. They told us we should consider it an honor to fight, and maybe even die, fighting commies, because dying for Jesus (who himself was against commies) meant automatic admission into heaven.

I was a fan of Superman comics and had always wondered how going to the bathroom worked with that one-piece indestructible suit of his, or if he even needed to go. Since the padre called for any questions concerning Jesus, a concept I never really got a grip on, concerned the whole, "Was he human, or the actual Son of God?" I saw Jesus like a visitor from the heavens, which is outer space, which made him like Superman, late of Krypton, in outer space, so where's the harm? Regardless of my philosophical conundrum, I went ahead and raised my hand. Mine was the only hand. Father Henry looked at me and said, "Yes? Hewwoe, Joe's boy, what is your question?" Like Rabbi Abe, he didn't know my name, only my father's.

All eyes were on me as I asked, "Does Jesus go to the bathroom? I never see Superman going to the bathroom either, so does Jesus have to go?"

My question hung up there in the air as every other kid turned towards Father Henry. There was no giggling. I'd asked a question kids thought about, but never dared verbalize.

Father Henry stood up and said, "Well that's a vewy interwesting question, Joe's boy," adding, "but why don't you all wisten to your teacher now?" He moved to the door, black cassock hiding his feet as he called, "Goodbye, childwin."

Now, standing in the knave, contemplating my choice of confessionals, I knew I couldn't pick Father Henry, so I crossed the center aisle and saw a handwritten name tag identifying the occupant as a visiting Jesuit priest from the Army Chaplain's Corps. This was great because there was no way this guy could know who I was, so no predisposition or other judgment. Also, he was in the Army, which meant he'd been to Vietnam and probably heard hundreds of guys talking about killing VC and having sex with prostitutes and smoking weed, so missing a few weeks of Mass because there weren't any Catholic churches around, because we were in the wilderness of another country, shouldn't be such a big deal. My offenses were nothing, and, at most, all I'd have to say was a good "Act of Contrition" and he'd hand me a few "Our Fathers" and "Hail Marys" to recite as penance. The best part was, Father Henry had a couple of old ladies in line prepping for the final and, my guy had no line.

I confidently strode over and entered the small booth, kneeling and hearing the click as the "occupied" light came on, and almost instantly the small wooden panel shot back. Through a woven bamboo privacy shield, I could just make out the black cassock and purple stole laying across his chest and lap and denoting the healing power of confession. He had rosary beads in his hands and was thumbing through them. I was still composing myself when he stopped praying and said, "Well? You got something to tell God?" As I made the sign of the cross, I felt his piety. This guy really thought he was a direct line to God, so I started reciting the rote opening. "Bless me Father, for I have sinned," I felt my comfort level began to drop.

Picking up the pace to begin overwhelming his capacity to track my story, I pressed on. "It's been six weeks since my last confession," as I hustled straight into my list of regrets. "I got into a fight with my sister, and I didn't take out the garbage when my mother asked me to, and I lost a library book, and, I said some bad words….." I figured that was plenty, so I stopped and waited. I was uncomfortable because I knew I had to get through this evaluation and penalty phase without getting grilled. I just wanted to get out of there and back home and eat dinner before my mother's deep-fried tuna-and-rice patties, with mushroom sauce, got cold and that sauce congealed.

Our silence went on a few beats too long as he drew in some breath, and sighing, said, "Okay on the rest of that, but let's go back to why you missed taking the sacraments for six weeks?"

I was screwed. He didn't say, "How come you missed Church?" No, he was much more specific, I'd missed "the sacraments."

"Well, yes, Father, I couldn't go to church because we were camping in the woods, up around Watertown and even in Canada!" I was hoping he'd understand the scant population in the great white north so, naturally, not many churches around.

He took a sharper, probing, inquisitional tone, one I knew from listening to my teachers when they were grilling me about some dubious event or another. This was not over by a long shot. "So you're telling me your parents wouldn't make an effort to find a church where you…" but I cut him off. "No, father, I wasn't with my parents. I was with my friend Brant and his parents."

"And they didn't go to Church?" to which I replied that they weren't Catholics. I thought he just wanted to make sure I spent an hour talking to God so I offered "I did go to Church with them!" He asked what the denomination was. I imagined I'd have been okay if I lied and said Episcopalian, they being some kind of former Catholics, but I knew nothing about any other religions, I barely knew anything about Catholicism. My ignorance prompted me to tell the truth, so I confessed that my traveling companions (Brant, his mom and dad, the other couple, and their two cute teenage daughters) were all Jehovah's Witnesses. That's when time appeared to stop. He took in a sharp rush of air and, realizing I was in a jam, I offered, "But I only had Catholic thoughts while I was there. I said the mass and everything…." He wasn't having any of it and he exploded on me saying, "What kind of Catholic do you think you are? Who the hell are you to go to any other church except our church! You should be ashamed!" He was so angry and so loud, I just wanted to run out, but once you're in that box you cannot leave until the priest gives you a blessing and tells you to "Go out and sin no more," which was always like saying, "See you next week!"

I closed my eyes while he was shouting and, once he stopped to catch his breath, asked, "Can I be forgiven? I'll say an Act of Contrition!" There passed but a moment before I heard those words, "You are NOT forgiven. Now get out of here!"

Not forgiven? Holy crap! I was not in a state of grace. I was a dirty sinner and if a truck ran me over I was going straight to hell, no questions asked, no excuses taken. I felt shaky as I walked outside and into the late afternoon sunlight. I saw my father sitting inside the white Ford Falcon. He was leaning back in the seat, listening to the news on the radio while holding an unfiltered Pall Mall cigarette between his fingers. I saw the blue smoke drifting up, leaving some to coat the window with a blue haze, the remainder flowing on out and into the mid-summer evening. I knew these were his last happy moments on this planet because I was an unforgiven sinner.

I started crying.

I was unforgiven. I'd never heard of anybody not being forgiven. All the nuns and everybody else said that if you went into the confessional and confessed your sins, and gave a good act of contrition, then your sins would be forgiven. That was just the deal I'd had hammered into me by those nuns. It just was so wrong to learn that hanging out with my friend Brant, because he wasn't a Catholic, was an unforgivable sin. This made me really glad I never talked about going to a synagogue thirteen times with my Jewish friends when they had their bar or bat mitzvahs.

My father heard me crying as I walked up to the car and opened the door. I was blubbering because the enormity of what just happened was hitting me. My father shook me and said, "Calm down, tell me what the hell just happened in there." I told him word for word as he got madder and madder. He straightened up, tossed the butt into the street, and told me to follow him. As we walked back up to the entrance, he said, "He said he wouldn't forgive you, right?" I was still choked up and could only nod as we walked inside.

Father Henry's flock had cycled through, old ladies never having anything salacious to report, so he stepped out of the confessional as it was just turning six and another day of listening to the problems of others was complete. We came in as he walked past the altar after genuflecting, heading back into the vestments room where all of the clerical garments were kept. We made the obligatory stop at the altar as well, even though it seemed a now useless gesture since I was unforgiven. We found Henry on tiptoes, just finishing placing his black, three-peaked biretta hat on a shelf above him. He relaxed and immediately pulled a cigarette out of a pack and lit it. He was taking that first puff and turned, surprised to see us in the doorway. He waved us in, exhaled and said, “Hewwoe Joe and Joe’s boy. How awe you?” My father laid into him. “It’s about your goddamn priest, Henry! He won't forgive my kid!” If I was shocked at being unforgiven, I was stunned at hearing my father take the name of the Lord in vain and blaspheme in God’s own house, plus he dropped the “Father” honorific. He was just that mad.

Father Henry looked confused and my father said it again. “Your goddamn priest refused to forgive my kid!”

The cleric’s brow crinkled as he listened to this nonsense as if saying, “What the hell? Not forgiven?” He looked at me with a skeptical eye and said, “What did you do?” So much for the sanctity of the confessional, as I told him about Brant and the Jehovah Witness connection, and was glad I hadn’t mentioned attending the district convention. He listened and about the time I finished, the Army priest came walking in, taking his stole from around his neck and kissing it as he folded it neatly. He saw me, my father, and Father Henry, who asked, “Did you weally wefuse to forgive this child?”

The priest said he had and took the opportunity to share with all concerned just exactly what kind of rotten Catholic I was and how I needed to learn how to be a good Catholic. My father interrupted his ecclesiastical tirade by saying in a low voice, “You better forgive my goddamn kid.” I’d never heard menace in his voice before.

The priest, realizing he didn’t have much choice told me to drop to my knees and make a very sincere Act of Contrition, which I was happy to do. He then gave me two hundred Our Fathers and two hundred Hail Mary’s to recite as my prayer punishment. I went out into the Chapel to begin my penance. I thought it unfair and excessive, so I said one Our Father “times fifty” and the same for the Hail Marys — I did have to pay some penalty, after all. I waited a suitable amount of time and walked out to the car. My father was leaning against it and as I walked up he put his hands on my shoulders saying, “Listen kid, don’t let those guys scare you. They don’t know everything.”

I took him at his word.

+++

Keeping Kosher

In the summer of 1967, while Buffalo, New York, Newark, New Jersey, Minneapolis-St. Paul, Minnesota, and 12th St, specifically, in Detroit, Michigan, were all having riots, I applied for a job at the East Nassau Hebrew Congregation, because in addition to having an orthodox Temple and a Hebrew school, there was also a huge catering facility for weddings and bar/bat mitzvahs. Some of the Jewish neighbors objected to this crass commercialization of this house of worship. The protests mainly came from members of the Midway Jewish Center, a progressive conservative synagogue. As a sole source fund raiser, they had cash Bingo in their community hall on Wednesday night, the Catholics at St. Mary's had Monday, and St. Edward's had Tuesday. East Nassau could have had Bingo on Thursday, but the rabbi considered Bingo déclassé, plus there wasn't enough money in it. The Reform Jews had no Bingo, but they made do because the congregants forked over regular donations so they wouldn't feel guilty as they all went to the track to watch the dogs and ponies or to the Garden to see basketball and fights. The Rabbi responded to those neighborhood protests by putting up the Hebrew version of the Ten Commandments and writing in English at the bottom "*Love thy neighbor.*"

The interview was just a formality owing to Rabbi Appleman's "hearts and minds" policy which was hire any neighborhood kids who wanted to work. I'd already shown my work ethic when first offered five bucks to come over each Friday after sunset to turn on all the lights, because Orthodox Jews were not permitted to flip a switch, it being considered work. I was later paid ten dollars for being the required tenth man on Friday nights when the minion (prayer group) said a Kaddish for the dead. I put on a yarmulke and prayer shawl, stood to the rear, and rocked back and forth like all the old guys did. I was the first kid and longest lasting employee they ever had. I took every lesson offered, paid attention, and East Nassau opened my eyes to another world. The weekend service staff were all Poles from Bellmore, a forgettable town on the South shore. During the food courses, and behind curtains on a break, the ladies taught all eight of us young busboys how to polka. The janitorial staff was two black guys, the first I had ever met. The kitchen staff were all secular Jews. I was the utility goy (non-Jew) who could work anywhere, anytime.

Growing up in a largely Jewish neighborhood where menorahs outnumbered Christmas trees by a huge margin meant our schools also closed on Jewish high holy days. I knew that some, but not all of my friends, "Kept kosher" and only ate food prepared in accordance with kashrut, the Jewish dietary laws. I'd worked at the deli where they specialized in kosher food, but also sold brisket and other non kosher cuts of meat for the less observant members of the tribe and all the goyim who ate there regularly. I learned those nuances when I went to work in that Orthodox kitchen.

My first surprise was that they had two kitchens, one at ground level and one in the basement, each only preparing certain foods, also keeping completely separate sets of dishes and utensils—one set for dairy, one for meat. Foods that are neither meat nor dairy, and not containing any meat or dairy derivatives, and have not been cooked or mixed with any meat or dairy foods, are called pareve. Eggs, fish, fruit, vegetables, grains, and juices in their unprocessed state are pareve, as are pasta, soft drinks, coffee and tea. It was Rabbi Abe Kippleman, that dean of students for the Yeshiva school upstairs, who, in his spare time, served as the Mashgiach, a rabbi who supervises the enforcement of "kashrut" and keeps the kitchen kosher.

Rabbi Kippleman was from Budapest, Hungary, where his family had been bakers specializing in *Kiffles*, traditional Hungarian cookies made from cream cheese dough and filled with various flavors of pastry filling. Delicate and rich, they made a beautiful addition to any holiday cookie platter.

In the spring of 1944, the Hungarian gendarmerie swept up Abe, his family and 440,000 other Jews. Most were deported to Auschwitz-Birkenau, where; upon arrival and after selection, SS murderers, aided by Lithuanian and Latvian volunteers, immediately killed the majority of these condemned Hungarians in gas chambers. Out of his entire extended family, Abe alone survived and came to America as a refugee.

Just like upstairs in Hebrew school, nothing got past Rabbi Abe. When the kosher meat guy showed up, Abe was out there, checking each case as it came in, faithful to the Ashkenazi eastern European tradition of only permitting consumption of meats from the forequarter of a cow and he made sure there weren't any roasts made from other prohibited cuts. Likewise he inspected all the fruit that came in because while fruits and vegetables are permitted, bugs cannot be eaten. There were rules for everything, including methods of properly cleaning (or koshering) utensils, which included immersion in boiling water or heating the offending cutlery with a blowtorch. The method used depended upon the type of utensil and how it has been used. His diligent application of those rules came into sharp focus one Sunday morning when I was working the annual "Buy a Tree in Israel" breakfast, which funded the creation of the Yatir Forest, named after the remains of the Israelite biblical town Yatir, in the Negev region. Begun in 1965 and planted in a region of low rainfall which made it unsuitable for reforestation, the Yatir Forest grew to be one of Israel's largest and most beautiful forests.

When the food service ended, it was now coffee, liquor, and cigars as the tree sale got underway. This big social event offered a charitable religious deduction while providing a chance to play people against one another to see who would be biggest donor. Each tree was fifteen dollars and would be graced with the donors name attached on a tag. I even bought one because the Rabbi nailed me while I was pouring coffee at a table by saying, "Look! There's Joe's boy and even he will buy a tree for Israel!" With a whole bunch of adults clapping for me it was impossible to refuse and I learned the Rabbi was a master of squeezing out a charitable buck from anyone.

Benny, the grill man, had to come in early that day since there were many events on the weekend schedule, two afternoon affairs and three evening weddings. He alone prepared and cooked all the meats to be served at all the events so on weekends he owned the downstairs kitchen. I thought he was pretty cool because he showed me the scars of three bullet wounds in his right leg where he'd gotten shot while in the First Marine Division during the seventeen-day winter battle and breakout retreat from the Chosin Reservoir in Korea. Benny was hungry so he decided to make some breakfast for himself. He got some eggs, mushrooms, onions, parsley and cheese from the walk in, added some left over steak, and threw it into an omelet. The process of mixing those items instantly transformed his breakfast into inedible non-kosher treyf. He was happily eating it at the stainless-steel food prep bench when Rabbi Abe came through as part of some never ending-loop inspection of every square inch of property. He smelled the offense long before he determined the source. Once he saw Benny eating that inedible treyf, he let out a scream, followed by a long string of Yiddish expletives, as he ran over and snatched the plate off the table, pausing only long enough to pluck the knife and fork from a startled Benny — the old man continued running those offensive materials outside, and into the dumpster, as if they were infectious. Visibly upset, he came back inside, looked around, saw the contaminated coffee cup, saucer, and spoon, and they too were instantly given an equally unceremonious heave-ho in the name of koshering.

As his breathing slowly returned to normal, the old teacher continued to look around the kitchen, wondering if he'd nipped this disaster in the bud. Looking at me through narrowed eyes, he said, "Hey, you! Joe's Boy! Did you wash anything?" I told him I had, pointing to the skillet and spatula which were now air drying, as required by New York State health laws. After satisfying himself that they hadn't contaminated any other cookware, he tossed them out, along with the green plastic holder that secured them during the washing and drying process, all the while yelling at Benny to wash his "filthy" hands. Benny complied and, for a full twenty-seconds, vigorously scrubbed away every last potentially non-kosher and soul-damning molecule. When finished, he held up his red and raw hands for inspection. The old man took those hands, all the while praying, and held them over the sink as he poured water from a glass, first twice over the right hand and then twice over the left hand, taking care not to let the unwashed hands touch the water used for the washing. Rabbi Abe then dried them with a towel, which he also threw away.

Properly chastised, Benny went back downstairs to his meats. Never missing the opportunity to instruct, the Rabbi leaned in close to look at me, his light blue eyes now shining behind his small round spectacles. In his teacher voice he said, "You see? This is what happens! You were in class and you know these things. You should never have let this happen! Fershtay?" I did understand and of course he was right. In those words, and with that look, he taught me that while it was important to respect elders, it was more important to respect the law and to stand for it. When I saw something I knew to be wrong, I had an obligation to stop it and try to correct it.

+++

"Steve, He Hit Me!"

It was the second week in June 1968. I'd finished ninth grade and, not being a math whiz, I had some open days while waiting for summer school to begin, a habit I picked up in the eighth grade. I was a victim of "new math," a brief, dramatic change in the way mathematics was taught in American grade schools during the 1960s which quickly became highly discredited. These questionable teaching practices were a knee-jerk reaction introduced in the US shortly after Sputnik, the first satellite, was put into earth orbit by our global nemesis, the Union of Soviet Socialist Republics (USSR). This feat ignited a crisis and fears that the US didn't have enough engineers to counter this Soviet menace. "New math" was created and promulgated in order to boost science education and mathematical skill in the US population and meet that technological threat from Soviet engineers, seemingly all highly skilled mathematicians.

I was certainly no impediment to Soviet global domination having once scored just four pity-points, out of one hundred, on a new math test, only because I spelled my name correctly. Now my boss Steve asked me to come in early, starting at nine the next Monday morning to begin training as a food preparation worker. I'd be working under the watchful eye of Mario, the chef *garde manger*, or pantry chef, who was charged with creating the decorative elements of buffet presentation like ice carvings and edible fruit centerpieces, as well as salads, hors d'oeuvres, appetizers, canapés, pâtés and terrines and other foods that could be refrigerated for storage until needed.

On Monday morning I went into the main kitchen and Steve directed me downstairs to Benny's kitchen, which it turned out was only his during the weekend, because during the week it was Mario's domain. This was the place where he would summon up all his artistic skills to create ice swans and replicate multiple edible offerings for the upcoming weekend trade. He had a list of the requirements for each reception kept on a schedule written on a paper cake doily. Each piece, when completed, had its own doily with the party name written on it to avoid any confusion because the building had room for three large receptions at the same time, and weekends were always hectic.

Mario was maybe five foot ten and slightly built. He wore his thinning red hair tousled, so while not covering his bald spot, it provided enough cover to make it less noticeable. With his thin pointy nose and thin lips, he talked in an animated way that I'd never heard before, almost sounding breathless. I introduced myself and he asked a series of questions to gauge my kitchen abilities. Once satisfied with my admittedly thin resume, he began the process of teaching me the various steps and techniques in preparing edible display pieces. I learned how to cut watermelons to preserve the exterior for later use and also make fruit kebabs. We worked at a six-foot long stainless steel work table, a duplicate of Benny's breakfast fiasco site. The nature of our work led to conversation. Mario asked me all about my life, my friends, and experiences I had. He was especially pleased when I told him I'd been to Montreal, Canada, on a camping trip with my friend Brant and his family. He stopped what he was doing and looked up and away, as if recalling a memory from years gone by saying, "Oh, I can remember going to Canada as a young man, there were so many gay people. We would all camp in the woods and drink all night and have a wonderful time. Did you notice that as well?" I really didn't understand the question, but I did recall a lot of movies where jolly French guys in berets carrying accordions and wearing black and white striped shirts would pull their girlfriend's long hair and drag them off to the casbah, whatever and wherever that was, so all I could do was mumble and shrug my shoulders.

The next day I was shown how to prepare other foods and work with jello molds. At about eleven, Mario told me, "That's enough for now, let's get breakfast." When I explained that I didn't have any money, he laughed it off and insisted that I come as his guest. We went to the Howard Johnson's restaurant in Plainview and sat at the counter, I still being amazed that there were people who apparently went out for breakfast routinely. This is not to say I'd never been to the HoJo's. I once went there with two friends, Steve and Brian, to "*All you can eat!*" chicken night. Brian ate sixteen pieces of chicken. The manager remarked that was all the chicken Brian would ever eat there; telling Brian to leave and never come back.

While I was enjoying this decadent indulgence, Mario regaled me with tales of how he and his friends would go skinny dipping in the lake at night and then crawl into sleeping bags together to warm back up. Back at work Mario continued to ask questions about my friends and what we did, with an excessive interest in camping and, wondering if we ever went skinny dipping, questions that seemed a bit odd coming from an old guy. Something in the way he asked those questions, with little tremors in his reedy voice, set off some alarm inside me, but I paid it no heed because he had been really quite kind and if he asked odd questions, what was that to me?

Around this same time Robbie, one of the two janitors, took to wandering through the kitchen as he moved between the different rooms vacuuming and wiping things down. He would stop occasionally and ask how I was doing, usually when Mario was upstairs in the other kitchen. It was just small talk because everything was fine and I thought no more about it. I liked Robbie, he was somewhere in his early forties and one of those adults who knew how to talk to kids to make them feel like he was listening like you were an adult. Apparently he came through one too many times for Mario's taste because later that afternoon when he came through, Mario called him up short and told him that his "constant interruptions" were interfering with his work and he wasn't to come through the kitchen anymore. I felt bad, like my talking to Robbie had gotten him into trouble.

The next day we began work like always and Mario was asking if I was good in school. I told him I wasn't a very good student and he responded by telling me that I could always drop out and take up a profession. He said I was coming along nicely and had the makings of a *garde manger*, but the usual route was to become the protege of a chef. I didn't understand so he explained that I would be a personal student of his. I would travel with him as he went from job to job. He would let me live with him in his apartment and I'd receive an excellent salary. It sounded like a great deal, out of the house and on my own, with plenty of cash and living in New York City, but I knew I'd have to ask my parents about something like that and I let the matter drop. As the day wore on, I noticed that wherever I was working along that prep table, Mario was standing right along side me, his left forearm constantly brushing against my right forearm. This was making it difficult for me to reposition the fruit I was working on, so I'd shift a few inches away and continue working, only to realize a few minutes later that he'd sidled up next to me again.

At midmorning, I was chopping piles of onions as a condiment for the black caviar station and began tearing up. I started rubbing my eyes, but Mario quickly set down his paring knife and directed me to the sink. He turned on the cold water and instructed me to cup my hands and let the cold water irrigate my eyes to stop the tearing. I did as he told me and in a few moments the burning had ceased and I could see again. Mario took a handkerchief and began dabbing at the corners of my wet eyes, looking into them saying, "You have very beautiful eyelashes, did you know that?" and I said, "Yeah, my mother says the exact same thing." After a moment, he let go of my face and I went back to the prep table. I began taking clear plastic wrap from the long industrial roll to wrap the various platters and display pieces for storage in the walk-in cooler where the temperature was always 36°F. Two six-foot tall slotted racks on wheels held the tightly wrapped fruit trays. We always started at the bottom by squatting down, aligning the tray on the holders, then sliding it in. Depending on the tray's weight, it could take some effort to slide it completely on to the rack. I filled the first rack and pushed it to the rear of the cooler, bringing the other empty one forward. Back outside, I grabbed a heavy tray with several intricate pieces, then went back inside the cooler, leaving the door open. Kneeling down by the lowest slot, I was lining up the tray, which meant I had to lean forward with my butt pointing backwards as I pushed the tray on the rack. What I didn't notice was that Mario had quickly come in behind me and quietly dropped to his knees. I felt his hands on my shoulders as he was drawing himself close, just as I pushed my own butt backwards and heaved that tray into the rack.

I instantly realized *exactly* what was going on, and that was Mario trying to "dry-hump" me. I also knew exactly why he was doing it, and there was no way on God's green earth I was about to get rubbed on by some old queen. In one more instant, I drove my elbow backwards, smack into Mario's crotch, which caused him to screech in pain to accompany me letting loose the loudest, foulest, and longest, string of invectives ever uttered in the business end of a house of the Lord. I jumped up, inadvertently elbowing Mario's thin nose in the process, and tore out of the cooler just as Robbie, running, came into the kitchen, holding a broken mop handle at the ready, yelling, "Did he touch you?"

Robbie had recognized Mario as a pedophile, but couldn't say anything because Robbie was a black man in 1968, on Long Island. Robbie was a man without the power to correct, or comment, on a white man, especially one with talent. I learned right there those who acted like Robbie were protecters and I admired, and was grateful for his readiness to help me. I was pretty sure he'd have beaten Mario senseless with that broomstick if I'd told him what had happened, and I knew right there I wanted to be like him, one of the good guys. When I told him he had come in time, Mario hadn't molested me, he looked relieved and led me to the stairs telling me, "You'd best go on now." I was still mad as hell and fairly ran up those stairs. I reached the kitchen, where Steve was at the table cutting up something, while Trey and Kenny, the two upstairs kitchen guys were standing by the stove talking. I burst into the kitchen yelling at the top of my lungs, "Sonofabitchingfaggotmotherfuckerwhotriedtostickhisdickinmyasscocksuckermotherfucker…" and I tore off my white apron, tossing it on the table while yelling at Steve, "and you KNEW he was a cocksuckingmotherfuckingfaggotsonofabitch and sent me there to work with him!" Steve looked up over his glasses, in shock and disbelief, a filtered cigarette dangling from his lips and said, "What are you talking about?" I yelled again and finished by saying, "I'm going home and you're paying me for the full day!" I was making my way to the exit, just as Mario was coming up the stairs with his head tilted back and a white cloth napkin showing a red stain pressed to his nose. When he saw me coming toward him, he backed up towards the exit, whining in a his reedy but now stuffed nasal voice, "Steve! HE hit me and I'm going home!", then stomped off. I rushed forward yelling "And I'll do it again…" but was cut off by Trey who grabbed my arms and stopped me. The completely mystified Steve called after Mario, but he was already in his blue 1966 Dodge Polaris convertible and screeching out of the parking lot.

Trey relaxed his grip and I stepped away, moving to the exit. I passed Robbie coming up the stairs and gave him a sincere, "Thank you" then headed out the door.

It was six months later that Steve told me Mario died of a heart attack in his bed after having sex with his sixteen-year old protege.

I'd learned how to spot a homosexual chicken hawk.

+++

The Purple Heart

Between 1968-69 the Vietnam war was at its maximum intensity: 549,500 American servicemen were serving in-country during some of the nastiest fighting of a very nasty guerrilla war. Over fifty-thousand of them were grunts consigned to be in the field at any given moment, the other ninety percent were in non-combat support jobs that only required the ability to read and write well, a skill the average grunt lacked. Every week on average, 320 fine young Americans were dying for a total of 16,592 dead youth in 1968 alone. Vietnam was sucking up bodies at a rapidly increasing rate.

It was during that summer, right before my sophomore year and I was hanging out with my buddy Brant at the WT Grant's Department store in the Plainview shopping plaza, just a ten minute bike ride away from my house. His dad's vacation didn't start until the middle of July, so we were escaping the heat by sitting at the lunch counter where it was all the iced tea you could drink for a quarter. It was a pretty good deal because Grant's, unlike our houses, was air-conditioned. Some days we'd shake our stomachs and laugh at the sounds of the iced tea sloshing around, which is what passed for entertaining ourselves, until the weekday when Ed came marching home. He was one of the guys from our neighborhood, now barely nineteen years old, and a nice enough, but slightly dopey, guy who never gave any of the younger kids a bad time. He lived in another part of the neighborhood and his older brother had dated my older sister, so I knew him enough to talk with.

Barely getting his diploma from the NY State board of Regents, even after repeating his sophomore year, he certainly hadn't earned the 3.5 cumulative GPA now required to get into any New York State public college or university. Thanks to the war, those institutions of higher learning were over-enrolled with hundreds of thousands of young men who knew that sitting in a college classroom beat the hell out of walking around some rice paddy, waiting to get shot at. Lacking a college deferment or some excluding malady like bone spurs, it only took the draft board a week or so after graduation to snatch Ed up and spit him out ninety days later into the chaos that was Vietnam.

He strolled up, resplendent in his green US Army Class A uniform displaying a combat infantryman's badge, Vietnam campaign medal, National Defense service medal, and a Purple Heart. We were very impressed because Ed was a "blooded" combat vet and a genuine war hero to us because we both knew exactly what a Purple Heart was awarded for: being wounded or killed in any action against an enemy of the United States. We'd grown up watching WWII movies and TV shows like "*Combat.*" We always saw guys get shot, jump on grenades, and be gravely wounded by machine-gun fire, but they were tough guys who, after getting patched up by the medic, went right back into the fight. Ed, while sporting much shorter hair than when last we saw him, seemed outwardly none the worse for wear, so we wanted to hear the whole story.

Ed ordered an ice tea, loosened his black army tie, then leaned against the yellow formica luncheonette countertop. He started regaling us with his tale and it emerged he'd been somewhere in the Quảng Trị Province in May, just a month earlier. His air mobile unit was choppered to what turned out to be a hot Landing Zone (LZ). During the ensuing firefight Ed was ordered to help load injured soldiers onto the MedEvac "Dust-off" helicopter that would swoop in under enemy fire to retrieve the injured and deliver them to medical attention.

He was unemotional as he spoke, just telling us what happened like you'd tell somebody about your visit to a laundromat. "It was bad. Those choppers didn't even set their skids down, they just slowed and came to a low hover a couple of feet off the ground, so we jumped off and fanned out, while they booked up and went didi." We nodded at him, because we understood the cool Vietnam slang describing the helos clearing the LZ. He picked up his story, "There was all this noise from those birds and the wind was pushing the grass flat and then there were bullets flying everywhere and I could see green tracers from the VC that were coming from behind the tree line. Right then a guy near me got zapped, so my platoon sergeant yelled for me to get him on board a dust-off when it came in." He shook his head slightly as he recalled the moment. "It was just crazy, there were fucking tracers going everywhere and I saw our red tracers going to meet their green ones. A guy popped purple smoke and right then this dust off bird comes floating on down into it. The smoke was swirling everywhere, so I picked that guy up on my shoulders, carried him over to the hatch, and dumped him in. I was still standing on the skids when the pilot started lifting off. I just didn't want to let go and I didn't want to be there and I thought I'd climb back in and get the hell out of there."

He stopped and took a drink of his iced tea before continuing. "I threw myself forward and tried to grab something so I could pull myself in and the last thing I saw was the boot bottom from the crew chief who kicked me out of that helicopter which was just a couple of feet off the ground and, while falling, I got shot in the ass and now I'm back here just waiting for my discharge."

He looked awfully proud of himself, just grinning from ear to ear. It was Brant who leaned forward and said softly "I'm not sure I'd tell that story again."

+++

CHAPTER TWO

Those Formative Years

Underage Drinker

The train station was a humble building, a waiting room really, its hard benches painted with cherry red enamel. They always looked welcoming as was fitting this place, the very center of our hamlet, the place Syosset sprang from. Open during the day so tickets on the Long Island Rail Road (LIRR) could be purchased, the train station demonstrated that Syosset was in fact becoming a new type community: a commuter town. Every weekday morning, hundreds of stalwart commuters, many of them battle-hardened veterans of World War II or the Korean War, would be driven there in a station wagon by a wife in bathrobe and hair curlers, with maybe a few kids in the "way-back."

The precise "show" time was determined by which train the commuter had a regular seat on, because those trains ran just several minutes apart. There were informal seating arrangements on those daily trains; travelers sat in familiar groups to play cards, read the paper, or catch up on some work. Smoking and non-smoking cars and an evening bar car were choices on every outbound LIRR train. These morning men would kiss their wives goodbye and gird themselves for the long trek into Manhattan. After queueing on the platform, these fiscal warriors loaded themselves in orderly fashion on the next arriving train; while chugging out, the next wave was leaving the warmth and comfort of their Ford Country Squire wagons, then taking their place on that platform in whatever weather presented itself.

Stoically they waited those few minutes to board the iron conveyer that would speed them into the bowels of the city for another day of work, hoping to earn enough to pay off the American dream. Every trip included a disembarkation in Jamaica, Queens, to change trains for the city. Nobody ever explained why trains changed in Jamaica; that was the thing, back then you didn't ask why they couldn't align the tracks, you just followed the crowd to the next train. During the summer, hot and humid in the late afternoon, the platforms in Jamaica looked like a never ending retreat from Dunkirk as worn out, exhausted, and now wrinkled men in crumpled suits and loosened ties made for the bar car.

As the area grew, so did the need for certain essential services, the most crucial being fire and ambulance. Such a small village could never afford professional full-time fire protection, so the reasonable solution to this societal need was the Syosset Volunteer Fire Department. Created in 1915, over the years it had grown, from one small building in the center of the hamlet near the train station, to two firehouses, the newest one being just one quarter mile from my house and only two miles to the main station.

One of the perks of being a volunteer fireman was driving with a flashing or rotating blue light to alert people that you were responding to the siren's call for help. This privilege was granted by the New York State Legislature with the express understanding that volunteers would drive responsibly and soberly. Unfortunately, this wasn't always the case because, truth in fact, drunk driving in those days was not unusual. Despite a driver's education program that included loads of gory black & white photos of real people who'd gone through windshields while coming home drunk from the prom or office Christmas party, nothing deterred us until the Mothers Against Drunk Driving got MADD in 1980. Before then, traffic accidents were legendary, enforcement was sporadic and mostly ineffective since fines were negligible. It's just the way it was.

The place where most of our volunteers did their drinking was at Kyle & Moran's **Syosset** Inn, "*The Place Where All Good Fellows Meet,*" named as if somebody in nearby Hicksville might try to claim a few good folks of their own. Syosset only had a couple of bars, and none served food unless you counted those horrible little sandwiches wrapped in clear plastic that were heated in a sort of easy-bake oven. One Italian restaurant offered a bar but they were scrupulous when it came to checking ID. NY licenses at the time had no photo and draft cards were recognized as ID, which didn't do much for the bars' attempts to curtail underage drinking. Some guy I knew found a draft card on the bar floor and made some good copies. Five of us became "Gary Walker," which worked fine until one night a bouncer who actually read the names nailed us as we all tried to walk in together. He kicked us out and wisely kept the IDs. Lesson learned: when you are sixteen years old and choosing drinking options, you want to go someplace that doesn't ask too many questions.Tipping well was another behavior which helped our cause. The conventional wisdom, we found, was to follow the crowd to the one place that didn't check IDs.

In my case it was Moran's, a tap room of no particular renown which was painted with high gloss paint, providing easy-to-wash down walls and lacking in any decorative or period charm save the stone fireplace with mounted moose head. The plaque beneath it was inscribed "Moose shot by President Franklin D. Roosevelt" and a date. This was some wag's silly dig to the more robust and ambulatory Roosevelt, Teddy, of Sagamore Hill fame, who'd lived only a few miles away, because FDR was in a wheel chair, after all, and no hunter. It was there for the tourists, as was Billy Joel, the singer, who showed up on occasion to hustle drinks off the relative fame of his band "The Hassles," who played at a joint called "My House" in nearby Plainview.

The bar was shaped like a **J** with the top of it at the service opening.That made it easy for the bartender, Jimmy, a tubby, florid-faced Irishman with thinning black hair, an equally thin mustache and a propensity to sweat even in winter, to get out from behind the bar to either break up a fight, wake up a drunk, swab the toilet, or get more ice. There was no table service offered unless you counted getting one of the regular girls to get you a beer and bring it back. Two rectangular windows on either side of the front door wore dark green curtains that were always fastened back. In the evening, anybody pulling up was lit by the harsh red neon glow of the Schaefer Beer sign. Walking in and looking to the left, a patron saw two wooden phone booths in the corner that provided a clear look out the window if you were the nervous sort. Phone calls cost a dime but, knowing how to slap the coin return button just right, you could make a call for a nickel.

As your gaze moved right, you saw three timeworn, dark-brown, stained wooden tables bearing scars from cigarettes and pen knives, and well-garnished with gum wads stuck underneath. There were six straight-backed wooden chairs at each table and a few additional chairs set against the exterior fireplace wall. A short hallway led to the bathrooms and a small back room with three four-top tables for the guys hoping to get a hand job from their drunken date. Cheap dark linoleum tile floors led back up to the bar and into Jimmy's unsmiling Irish eyes, because he was an innkeeper with a slow burning fuse til it hit his explosive temper.

This was a drinking man's bar; it only served domestic beer and "*no fucking spritzers*," just shots of liquor with water or coke. If the TV was on, it was only a Yankees, Knicks, or Rangers game because there were no other teams in Jimmy's universe. The only book in the bar was the World Almanac and Book of Facts because it was the only recognized authority for settling wagers. Bar bets were encouraged and welshing, or not paying off on a lost bet, was frowned upon.

Sometimes pathos walked into the bar, like when we learned sad old Mr. Metz, a former Nassau County cop had shot and killed his wife after coming home that day to find her in bed with another guy. Screwing around seemed to be pretty rampant then, as now, but catching a spouse "in flagrante delicto," as was the case with the late Mrs. Metz, was considered a justifiable homicide committed in the heat of passion. Mr. Metz was acquitted at trial and pensioned off, but he was now a broken old guy who plopped onto the stool when the doors opened at eleven and left when they closed again at two in the morning. He mostly talked to himself which was OK, unless one of the other solo talkers came in, because then things got confusing.

Among all the solo talkers, one of the greats was my next door neighbor.

+++

Ruthie Don't Love You No More

My immediate neighborhood consisted of the five houses that made up Avon Court, a small part of the two-hundred home Birchwood Park subdivision. Paulie was the only son of the couple next door. His dad, Pucki, ran the Texaco station two miles away, next to the fire department. In addition to providing oil and lubrication services, he was also the local bookie and took action out of his station. Pucki was a stout fellow, his skin permanently tanned from a combination of working outside in harsh weather and his Polish origins, his peasant parents having come over in the early part of the century. He drove an old Willys Jeep with a snowplow. This made him really cool, because when it snowed, he'd park his jeep in his garage, fire it up in the morning and come busting out spewing snow everywhere. As a bonus, this cleaned his driveway in about a minute. Meanwhile, I shoveled the heavy, wet, Long Island Sound-generated snow from our narrow one-car driveway plus the sidewalks, my father more concerned with being sued if somebody ever slipped than he was about giving me a heart attack.

Pucki's wife, Helen, was a red-faced woman with spider veins in her nose which were attributed to sun exposure, drinking, and smoking as she enjoyed all three, especially vodka. Hair curlers were a common adornment, and she, along with her daughter, even wore bright pink curlers to my sister's wedding. I could see them from the altar although they were kind enough to sit in the back. The curlers were not meant to be rude, but necessary because their hair had to be perfect for the reception afterwards. During the week, Helen worked at the toothpaste plant in nearby Hicksville, injecting toothpaste into tubes and crimping the ends. She once patiently explained to me how they put plastic bits in the "Stripe" brand tubes to keep the different color pastes separated until mixing properly when the tube was squeezed. She and Pucki had a daughter, but the star of most shows had to be Paulie, the mildly-addled oldest child.

Paulie had a bit of a walleye; that made him inhibited and anxious. He ran hot and cold; it just sort of depended on where he was in the cycle when you met him. All this led to confusion on the best way to interact with him on a social basis.

In 1968 rural Long Island, all we knew was that Paulie was a bit touched and it was best not to anger him which also meant trying to figure out which eye to look at when talking to him.

There were different versions of exactly what scrambled Paulie's brains but it came down to one of three possibilities depending on who you were talking to:

- Dropped on his head as a child, forever rendering him about half-goofy.

- Flew off the jeep and whacked his head when Pucki braked too fast, forever rendering him about half-goofy.

- Took a shot to the head from a 2 x 4 he'd shoved behind a rear tire trying to help Pucki get the jeep unstuck from the mud, which instead flew out when Pucki hit the gas and clocked Paulie, forever rendering him about half-goofy.

All three sounded right and made sense, but most likely Paulie just happened to have been born with a lower IQ. Hard working and enthusiastic, Paulie was lacking common sense and situational awareness. In any event, this tall, slender, yet powerful, hulking kind of man-boy, was able to land and keep a job as a trash collector for the Town of Oyster Bay. His employers graciously allowed him the freedom to respond to emergency calls with the Syosset Volunteer Fire Department (SVFD) while on duty. Armed with a rotating blue light, while being about half-goofy, the formula for moments that would make him a local legend were complete.

There is no denying Paulie was anything but an enthusiastic volunteer. When we heard the siren warble, it was not uncommon for us to look out our living room bay window to see Paulie leaping into his 1968 Silverstone-blue Chevrolet Impala convertible, with complimentary blue interior. Turning on that spinning blue light he'd go screeching out of the neighborhood with oily smoke trailing from the exhaust, as he raced to help his neighbors in their time of need. He understood speed really well, but sometimes didn't get braking, as evidenced when he came flying into the fire station station's parking lot on Saturday and failed to apply the brakes in time. His Impala popped over the curb to the library lawn where he turned the wheel sharply to get off the grass while hitting the gas, which caused the car to spin in a circle. Another kind volunteer donated the replacement sod and Paulie laid it in the next Sunday.

Over the years Paulie studied his craft, making every call out, even the ones at four A.M. and eventually he rose from probationary fireman to nozzle man, to driver/engineer. As engineer, he was responsible for keeping the water pressure up at the nozzle. Excelling at that task, eventually Paulie was promoted to lieutenant and given operational command of one of the fire trucks.

Truth told, he wasn't really "command" material because, as an engineer, he had a hard time remembering the formula for computing water pressure by factoring pressure lost due to the length of the hose plus any elevation. As a driver he'd hit too many inanimate objects and so the decision was made to promote him, if only to reduce maintenance and insurance costs. That decision came down right after Paulie served as the rear driver on a hook and ladder truck while upstate at Ft. Drum for a fire-fighting competition. One evening, while driving drunk through nearby Watertown, he steered the ladder into the Watertown Fountain, damaging it and injuring some visitors who were taking tourist photos at the landmark while tossing in coins for the luck that would bring.

The department was asked to go home and not come back for a while.

In his play "Henry VI," Shakespeare wrote, "*Uneasy lies the head that wears the crown,*" and for Lieutenant Paulie this was true. The burdens of command meant more time away from his home and his new bride, the charming Ruthie, which was actually good for him, as some days it seemed like Ruthie's main goal in life was to make something out of Paulie if she had to kill him trying.

Ruthie was the eldest daughter of Frank and Barbara. Frank's parents, like Pucki's, had emigrated from Poland shortly after WW I. They assimilated quickly, learning English and moving into the American working class. His father was a chauffeur and his mother a cook at Oheka Castle, the 109,000 square foot country home of financier Otto Hermann Kahn. Frank's parents were devout Catholics and, following the teachings of the Holy Roman Church, they were proud to have produced six children, the first-born being Frank. From childhood he was imbued with a strong sense of cultural identity, learning Polish as a first language and taking great pride in educating all within earshot of Poland's numerous historical successes and various important persons. He was forever extolling Copernicus, the Polish astronomer, who died four hundred years earlier, while the original English settlers on Long Island, the Lattings, were still selling reeds and eels.

Frank was living the American dream, owning his own business as a mechanic and operating a garage along Jericho Turnpike. In his free time he was passionately devoted to the SVFD and was one of three Battalion Chiefs, the on-scene commander for any fires. Frank had known Paulie since he'd first signed on as a "probie" and had recognized him as no bright spark, but brought him along because Frank was a guy who always tried to take the long view. When he decided the time was right, he offered up his daughter, Ruthie, as a potential wife.

His eldest, Ruthie, was considerably past her "best buy date." The phone didn't often ring for her, but she was her mother's daughter and Frank, always a pragmatist, didn't relish the idea of growing old with both his wife's and his spinster daughter's twin personalities in the same house. He thought it better if his daughter was nearby in case he needed something, or maybe, if the wife was lonely, there would be somebody, who wasn't him, to talk to her. Yes, he believed it'd be so much better if she were handy and convenient, but not in residence. In his mind, Paulie would be the perfect son-in-law so, after many drinks one night,

Frank put forth his offer and outlined the dowry: a huge three-day, full blown, old country Polish wedding, her hope chest containing a full set of china and linens, plus a serious down payment on a house just a few blocks away.

Despite her father's careful consideration of personalities, drama became a constant component in the lives of Paulie and Ruthie because people in New York are loud; a product of living with a couple of million other people, never ending traffic jams, and Boeing 707s screaming overhead every few minutes. Ruthie was never afraid to hold back her thoughts with Paulie, hectoring him pretty much anytime he wasn't working because somehow he was always getting into some kind of trouble. These episodes usually arose over some stunt or another and when he screwed up his habit was to hide from her. Usually he went to the Inn to drink, settle his nerves, chat with other villagers and think about the road of his life going forward. In truth, he was scared of his powerfully built wife and bewildered at the misfortune that routinely found its way into his life.

A few years later, the much beloved Frank dropped dead of a heart attack and his wake was well attended by every volunteer in dress blue uniform. A grief stricken, but irreligious Paulie nipped out during the Rosary being led by Father Henry and headed to the Inn where he was consoled by Jimmy and all its current patrons, who bought him many drinks. Now thoroughly fortified and effecting a mildly lurching gait, Paulie got into his car and wove his way back down the four blocks to Beney's Funeral Home. He entered, wobbled through the foyer, making his way into the large viewing parlor which was overflowing with mourners and flowers. He approached Frank in his coffin, drew himself up into a position of attention and rendered as fine a salute as any man has ever thrown, quickly releasing it as if launching a prayer to God above. Whether it was grief or liquor will never be known, but Paulie went off balance, staggered forward and fell onto the coffin, set upon a pair of saw horses, which is usually all the stability a coffin required, its burden usually immobile. But on this evening, Paulie's impact pushed that coffin forward to drop down head first as the front sawhorse toppled and Frank began a post-mortem backwards somersault. Paulie was now falling with the coffin as the other horse gave way, the casket slamming to the floor. Ruthie, and several other men and women, screamed in shock and horror and it took the funeral director's best efforts to settle the place back down. In fairness, since only the upper half was open, Frank did remain in the box.

This was Paulie. He came to us one night, as he did many nights, after a falling out with his bride over something he couldn't even recall doing. He'd simply appear, lonely, befuddled and just a bit more intoxicated than might have been good for him. On this occasion, I was sitting at the bar with Maggio on my left and two open stools to my right, into the bend of the **J.** On the third stool, Mr. Metz occupied his reserved seat. That night's ball game was the Yankees playing somebody under the lights in the Bronx.

Jimmy did not like Phil Rizzuto, who was then the voice of the New York Yankees on WPIX, Channel 11. Jimmy preferred Red Barber and since Yankee management never consulted him about Red's replacement in 1966, he expressed his displeasure by putting on WADO, 1280 AM, which had recently begun broadcasting completely in Spanish. The announcers were all Puerto Ricans who spoke so rapidly you could enjoy watching the game and chatting with friends knowing that if something big was underway the excited announcer would be screaming like crazy into the microphone:

> "El lanzador se ve a la primera base, luego de vuelta a la placa,
> que mira por encima del hombro, una vez más,
> y termina aquí viene la….
> **MARIA SANTA MADRE DE DIOS que es HOME RUN! HOME RUN!"**

And of course, then we'd all stop, look up to see the replay, and order another round before going back to whatever we were doing to pass the time.

Paulie stood in the doorway, looking about to see who would be his best bet to talk with. He took a fast pass on Mr. Metz who was clearly engaged in a very animated conversation with some disincorporated friend. Near the fireplace, by himself at a table for six with plenty of room for the five friends he never had, sat

Sammy, a twenty-seven year old mechanic who worked on cars across the street at the Shell station. Marginally brighter than Paulie, he leveled that playing field by taking a shot and a beer with great regularity. Sammy was never a great conversationalist and most of his chats eventually ended with "How the fuck should I know? Now shut the fuck up and leave me alone!"
It was actually no surprise when Paulie joined us at the bar, sitting just one stool from me and Maggio with old Mr. Metz on his right. He nodded hello to us, pulled out his wallet and slipped a five on the counter. That told us he was in for the long haul, since a draft Schaefer beer was a quarter, a pitcher was a buck and a quarter and, if you wanted a shot, it was seventy-five cents. Jimmy started pouring whatever bottom shelf whisky he regularly poured into empty bottles of better brands like the one he was currently pouring into Paulie's glass. Paulie tipped his glass to begin drowning his sorrows while he settled in to the evening rhythm at the bar, while the Puerto Rican announcers kept us informed of the play.

It was somewhere in the bottom of the seventh inning, just after the stretch and the announcers were hawking beer. "Tiempo para una cerveza Schaefer y una séptima entrada!" (Time for a seventh inning Schaefer beer stretch!) I'd just gotten another drink when Paulie began to openly wail and lament, "Ruthie don't love me no more." The first time it was spoken softly and I didn't catch the words, only that he was talking and, given all the single conversations happening in that bar at any one moment, this was not something to draw my immediate attention. All the while, his big sad puss stared glumly down at the bar in the direction of his beer glass. His left eye was cocked and seemed to be looking at me, but I think he was actually looking in his beer, which didn't seem to matter because his thoughts, like that other eye, were somewhere else.

"Ruthie don't love me no more."

I heard it that time and looked over at him. He was still talking, but now possibly to the ashtray. He said it again and again, two more times. Okay, it's one thing to accept and commiserate over life's pains and disappointments in this setting. That's why bars were invented, because self-medicating in the company of strangers has always provided a way to smooth over life's rough little moments; most humans are empathic to the hurt of other human beings. Well, that might have been true somewhere, but he was in a bar in rural Syosset at a time when the hillbillies of Long Island found great sport in breaking the balls of anybody else who might walk in. It was considered particularly good sport to take on a local as circumstance dictated.

Ball breaking is an art form. Too harsh and you're a jerk. Too soft and people start bagging on you and shouting their disapproval, "Eyyy! Whoa! What the Fuck? What kinda fuckin' shit was that?" If you were too harsh somebody might clip you in the back of the head saying, "Eyyy! Whoa! Whattaya fuckin' stunad? The guy's Mom just died!" Whack. You also had to factor in the anticipated response to the ball breaking. Paulie might have been a little "stunad," but he was also pretty strong from tossing trash cans all day, plus he had a low frustration point. I couldn't really read him, nobody could. This was a guy who also got very upset at invisible things we couldn't see, so the trick was to come up with something that would work, but would not be traceable back to you.

Maggio and I talked *sotto voce* and came up with the plan. I would get into one of the tandem phone booths against the wall, close the door, and pretend to make a call. After a little bit, I'd dial the phone in the next booth. Maggio would follow bar protocol and wait for several rings before answering. This delay let people who were expecting calls get up and take it, or signal with the "throat-cut" hand gesture that they weren't in the bar if it might be for them. It was risky business asking this group to do that because somebody breaking balls would tell a wife her husband was in fact sitting right at the bar watching TV and talking to some girl.

Now, with our the plan set, I stood up and said to Maggio, "I gotta make a phone call." I went into the booth, closed the door and pretended to make my call. After a minute I slipped the nickel and called the booth next to me. Maggio waited the prescribed time, walked nonchalantly to the booth, picked up the phone and, being one of those New Yorkers who do not pronounce the letter H, he said, "Yellow?" I whispered into the phone "Paulie." Maggio, told me to hold on, held the phone up and, as scripted, yelled "Yo! Paulie! Phone!" Maggio put the receiver across the top of the phone and casually walked back to his stool, while I continued my phantom discussion.

Paulie picked up the other phone. "Hello?"

"Ruthie don't love you no more."

As I severed the connection with my finger while continuing to pantomime my call, Paulie reacted with rage. He popped out of the booth, turned to look into my booth where I continued to talk to no-one until I saw him glaring at me. I shot him the finger and turned back to my imaginary partner on the other end.

Confused and angry, Paulie stomped back to his seat and drank a few more eight-ounce beers while he mulled the situation. After twenty minutes or so, Maggio got up and went to the bathroom. He returned and walked by us, announcing he had to call his girlfriend. He went into the same phone booth Paulie had used, closed the door and began his call. As I ordered another round for myself and Maggio, the phone rang. This time Mr. Metz thought it was his dead wife calling, so he got unsteadily off his stool and lurched towards the ringing phone.

He went in, picked up the receiver and said, " 'ello?" His eyes crinkled as he listened to the new voice inside his skull. After a few moments of bobbing his head up and down, he smiled to no one in particular and said, "Whoa-kay" then went back to his stool. I was watching in the mirror on the wall behind Jimmy, who was staring absently at the TV, smoking a cigarette. Mr. Metz took a sip of his watered-down whisky and then, as if the memory had just come to him unbidden, turned to Paulie. Leaning on the bar while sliding around on his stool, he began tapping a pale, shriveled digit on Paulie's shoulder to gain his attention. Paulie turned to him as Mr. Metz said with great sadness, "Ruthie don't love you no more." His bony fingers tenderly patted Paulie's shoulder. He leaned forward to stare at Paulie for a long moment, those rheumy blue eyes brimming with tears. Then the moment passed and Mr. Metz returned his gaze, and attention, back to the pale amber liquid in his glass and some deep sorrow known only to himself.

Paulie jumped up and scoped the crowd. Maggio was still on the phone and Sammy was still in his chair contemplating "lifting a cheek" which was his thing and could explain why he was so often lonely. He was famous at the gas station for lifting a cheek to pass gas while he held his Zippo lighter, spinning the spark wheel to ignite the methane. This worked well until the day he wore a set of much larger work pants. According to the ambulance guys who took Sammy to the hospital, he passed enough gas to put some real volume into those pants. A slight tear he hadn't been aware of leaked enough that the subsequent spark from that wheel ignited the vapor trail which raced back inside his pants, instantly burning off all the hair in his nether regions and lightly toasting his junk.

Maggio hung up and walked back to his stool. He looked at Paulie, then looked at me and said, "What's up?" and I said, "Ruthie don't love him no more."

Sadly, I used my telephone voice.

I was less intoxicated and thus quicker. After I avoided the place for a week, Paulie had forgotten all about it.

+++

The Big Dinner

It was the annual Fire Department Ball, a formal affair where all of the volunteers and their wives or girlfriends attended a large dinner at one of the many fine catering halls in the area. Such a gala affair cried out for tuxedos or dress uniforms for the firemen and formal dresses for all the ladies. Long Island folk loved any catered affair — weddings, baptisms, bar mitzvahs, fraternal organizations, it just didn't matter. Since Paulie was one of the officers, he and Ruthie were assigned seats on the dais where they'd face the assembled company at the many ten-seat tables scattered around the ballroom and dance floor. Since Paulie was a perpetually junior lieutenant, their seats were at one far end with him as the anchor and Ruthie on his right and towards the center. Two large candelabras on either end of the dais lent an elegant air to the proceedings.

These dinners, given at cost by management, were complimented by the free and flowing alcohol which was made possible by the generous support and donations from the drive-through beer-barn and multiple liquor stores. The volunteers would always help the merchant produce a suitable donation by asking directly, "What if this place burned and nobody came?"

As the collective volunteers got drunker and drunker, they began toasting their annual heroics, and also departed members, grateful that none of them died in the line of duty, but from heart attacks. This went on for a few hours until the dinner was finished and the dancing portion of the evening began. A song Ruthie really liked was being played by the band so she slapped Paulie on the shoulder and said, "I wanna dance, Paulie!" (She pronounced it "Paw-lee.") She had to hit him to get his attention as he was almost deaf in his right ear, the result of twenty years working the left side of that garbage truck, banging cans without ear protection. Her words were an order, not a request. Paulie, the ever faithful husband, immediately rose and turned to pull the chair to allow Ruthie to stand up.

From that moment on the evening was doomed.

During the course of the meal and most likely after returning from a visit to the toilet, Paulie sat back down and tucked his napkin back into his cummerbund, as was his habit. Sadly for him, he didn't actually pick up his napkin, that had fallen on the floor. Instead he tucked in a corner of the tablecloth, so as he stood up and turned right and backwards to pull out Ruthie's chair, he began inadvertently wrapping the tablecloth tighter around his waist. As the plates, cutlery, ashtrays, and candelabra began inching towards the table edge, Ruthie, in a panic, further spun things up by furiously slapping Paulie on the head, which certainly didn't help him, while shouting "Wait! Stop! Go away! Aaaaaaah!" All of this only served to further confound Paulie, given he was easily confused on his best day. He was now understanding that his Ruthie wanted him to back off, which made him turn away from her to leave and avoid being yelled at anymore, which only served to pull her plate, left-overs included, onto her lap, while coffee cups and water glasses were clattering to the floor. Others joined in the general screaming and commotion as plates and silverware collided, fanning the confusion. Paulie lurched backwards towards the wall as the candelabra joined the crockery on the floor, the speed of the fall happily extinguishing the candles, thus avoiding more potential unpleasantness.[1]

+++

That Fat Fireman

Despite all his trials and difficulties, Paulie maintained his outstanding response rate, the likes of which were difficult to find, especially during the day, when most folks worked in the city.

It was understood that a community must rally to support their volunteers and, in addition to free food and liquor for department dinners and barbecues, there was the inevitable incidental loss at the scene of any fire. If there was a jewelry store fire, a nice ladies watch might have been lost in the fire, only to appear later on a wife's wrist. The prevailing thought was "They got insurance, right?" That was just the price of being a wealthy merchant living in our rural hamlet in those halcyon days.

---

[1] Paulie was not unlike Hassan the carpet merchant. In 15th century Baghdad, Hassan was the most famous of all carpet merchants. He was so famous that he was invited one day to show his greatest carpets to the King. On the appointed day, he gathered his finest pieces and with his assistant's went to the palace where he amazed the court with the beauty of his workmanship. He was preparing to roll out his prized carpet, one made from silk smuggled all the way from China and had been years in the making. As he bent over to pick up the carpet and unfurl it in all its glory, a most unfortunate gastric event befell him and he passed an incredibly loud fart in the quiet of the King's reception hall. Mortified, he left all the carpets and fled Baghdad. He traveled for many years throughout the region, but as an old man whose time was drawing near, he wanted to make his way home to his beloved Baghdad, to see it once more before he died. He made the long journey and could see the lights of Baghdad in the near distance as he walked into an oasis town and stopped at a small hotel where he would spend this last night on the road as a wanderer. He greeted the proprietor with the traditional Arabic greeting, "What news?" and the hotelier regaled him with tales of big city life, palace intrigue and scandals. After one particularly ribald incident that left him in tears, Hassan asked "When did that happen?" The owner looked thoughtfully and said, "I think it was about five years after Hassan the rug merchant farted in the King's Hall."

One evening a big fire broke out at a men's clothing store on Jericho Turnpike; Paulie's engine was first on scene. He directed a two-man crew run a hose to attack the fire. His other guys put a ladder against the wall and were cutting vent holes in the roof as second engine arrived, along with a Battalion Chief.

An attack crew has a lot of latitude regarding how to respond on their entry. In some cases, a stream is required to send that water further to a single known point. If the fire is more fully involved, the choice would be a fog setting. The nozzle man would then wave it around the room to reduce heat from the fire equation while creating thick steam to further blanket and extinguish the fire. Of course, a fire hose puts out a tremendous volume of water and the engineers try to maintain a target flow of 250 gallons per minute in a standard 2.5 inch diameter hose to create and maintain a pressure of at least 100 psi when through a fog nozzle. That's a lot of water in an enclosed space and that means a fair amount of water damage will occur. Naturally, Paulie wanted to begin salvage to protect the interests of the merchant, recovering as many undamaged goods as possible and moving those goods outside.

As the attack on the flames produced the desired results and as Paulie's fireman's jacket could hold no more merchandise, he waddled outside to pop by the idling engine to put the materials in a storage compartment for safekeeping, grab a quick cigarette, and locate the Battalion Chief. He'd report in and get further instructions for overhaul and additional salvage. With the fire knocked down, and no particular hurry to report, Paulie lit that smoke as he moved outside and into the harsh white glare of the spotlights and headlights of the engines. He blinked and moved towards his idling engine then turned, looking back at the continuing firefighting efforts, just to take in the scene. He failed to notice the owner of the store arriving after being called by the police.

The owner was a short, potbellied, Jewish guy with fringe male-pattern baldness and thick black-framed glasses that might have made him look like an erudite monk but for the long unlit cigar he was gnawing on. Very upset, the owner wandered up to where Paulie was now standing, still looking back towards the store and smoking. The business owner startled Paulie, asking questions that Paulie had no idea of how to respond to. A sense of panic came over him, so he pointed the guy towards the Battalion Chief, hoping for an opportunity to get that wadded clothing into the truck compartment. The owner walked over the Chief saying, "That fat fireman sent me over, what's going on?" The Chief looked up briefly, whistled and yelled to Paulie to join them. When Paulie turned, the salvaged clothing, curiously all in Paulie's exact size, dropped from inside his fireman's turnout coat and into one big pile at his feet.

The owner was righteously indignant, but since there was the matter of insurance and the Battalion Chief did have one report suggesting there were some indications from the burn patterns of an accelerant being used, it was agreed that perhaps it best that the matter just be forgotten. The only caveat was Paulie accept demotion, return to being a regular firefighter, and only work a hose as nozzle man to keep his hands busy, focused, and more closely supervised in the future.

+++

Time To Leave

There comes that moment in your life when the realization that it's time to leave home slaps you in the face. For some people, it comes when they graduate college, or later, when their parents sell the house out from under them, as happened to my older sister, who had lived at home in a private room with half bath and her own phone, while working full-time as a legal secretary. She had no intentions of ever moving out until my father sold the house and moved to Florida in 1978. For me, it came in early November 1971.

Still seventeen years old, I was at the Wetson's hamburger stand where I'd been employed for over a year. It had been great during my last year of high school to have a "work study" job to go off to after only a few hours at school, since higher education had never been pushed at my house. My parents couldn't afford college tuition, so they encouraged simple, honest work at the prevailing minimum wage of $1.65 an hour. That summer was a blur of booze-fueled fun and never ending days of suntanning, waterskiing, evening parties at the town beach on the ocean, the last summer before adulthood began. It was the summer when singers Carol King and Carly Simon dominated AM radio but, as autumn started closing in, I saw friends and acquaintances go off to college. I'd taken some road trips in October to party with guys who'd gotten into the State Universities at New Paltz and Binghamton. The weekend ended, they went back to school, and I went back to my burgers. Now it was early November, I was six months out of high school, still sweating behind the grill and seeing the same tired faces of my co-workers. This tragic tableau included two older guys, Irv, a forty-five year old former department store floor manager whose department store had gone bust, and Wally, a fifty-five year old truck driver with a suspended license who needed a job where he could walk to work. They were not poster boys for job security.

Each day offered few diversions, like the day I was making a milk shake and looking out the window while the cup slowly filled. A lady was sitting in her car eating her lunch and I noticed flames popping up from the floor on the passenger side, the result of a cigarette falling out of the ashtray. I yelled, "That lady's car is on fire!" and Ray, the owner and a proud US Navy veteran, had learned about shipboard firefighting and, before anybody else could react, he grabbed a fire extinguisher, jumped the counter, pulled the pin, pointed the nozzle through the open window, and let it rip. This put out the fire in an instant, but resulted in a screaming lady with CO2 in her face. I also didn't notice my milkshake cup overflowing. Ray showed me the value of always thinking ahead of how to react to an emergency, but those moments were few and far between.

On the weekends, I was off to Moran's to waste the evening drinking. I'd tried attending night school at the local Ag and Tech two-year college over in Farmingdale after somebody advised me to sign up for the hardest course I could think of so I'd devote my full energies to conquer it. I spent fifty bucks signing up for Euclidian geometry. I went twice, realized the wild haired professor was a Martian or a close facsimile, because he sure wasn't speaking English, so I just started going to Moran's on Tuesdays and Thursdays instead. My lesson about unsolicited advice being worth what you pay for it was completed.

It was raining that Monday in November, a steady Long Island drizzle that promised to last all of the day and into the evening, the leaden overcast skies making it seem much later than it was. I looked at my watch and was surprised to see it was only ten. We were opening for lunch, because in 1971 you either ate breakfast at home, in a coffee shop, cafe, or diner, and a hamburger was not breakfast.

"Ding-Dong," the befuddled "go-fer" for the salesmen at the Ford dealership next door, came over for his daily challenge: giving us the salesmen's coffee order and keeping the change straight. His solution was to put each salesman's change in a different pocket. The only flaw was the hard time he had remembering which pocket held which salesman's change by the time he got back to the showroom. In that moment I suffered the terrible realization that I was becoming just another neighborhood character, no different from poor old Ding-Dong or Sammy or even Paulie. I was on the glide slope to join right in and become one of those guys who simply never move on. I'd stay there, graduating to some other entry level jobs until finally getting a job in a liquor store where I would work and wait until I became the murdered victim of a robbery gone bad.

I couldn't have that. I looked out at Jericho Turnpike, that four-lane concrete ribbon that ran 105 miles from east midtown Manhattan in New York City to the Cross Sound Ferry terminal at Orient Point on the end of Long Island's North Fork, and I knew it was time to leave.

When my shift finally ended, I was restless, bored and concerned about my future. I got in my faded autumn gold 1963 Chevy Bel-Air four-door sedan, with straight six cylinder engine and a trunk big enough to store Jimmy Hoffa. I fired it up, pulled out of the parking lot and turned left, taking me east on Jericho Turnpike. I could go a short distance and then turn right on to South Oyster Bay Road and be at my house in three minutes or so, but today wasn't that day. I continued down the turnpike for about eight miles and soon found myself in the small village of Huntington, just across the Suffolk County line. Huntington had a great Irish bar, small and narrow which made it intimate, a place where you could talk to people and, of course, it was closed. However, the US Armed Forces recruiting station a few doors down was open and on a whim I went inside.

The first guy I met was a Marine Staff Sergeant, tall and trim in his uniform. I was taken aback by the size of his massive biceps and intense shade of red used to provide background color for his forest green chevrons, which were currently wrapped around my neck in a firm, but not dangerous, embrace, as he proclaimed, "Damn, son! I knew you looked like the kind of guy the Corps is looking for on any given day! Give us just a few months and we will make you into the man your Momma always hoped you'd become." I'd grown up watching *Gomer Pyle, USMC,* and the one thing I remember was Sergeant Carter screaming at Gomer all the time, so I thanked him very much, but proceeded down the hallway. I didn't stop at the Navy office, as the thought of sailing for long periods of time with only other men didn't sit well, given my experience with Mario.

I came to the Army recruiter's door, opened it, looked inside and saw an Army Staff Sergeant resplendent in his Class A's sitting behind his desk. He stood, came around, shook my hand, and immediately asked, "How would you like to fly helicopters?" Helicopters? The thought had never ever even crossed my mind, given my spectacles had some fairly thick lenses. I mentioned that to him and he said cheerily "Oh, don't worry about that, we're waiving that requirement because we need more pilots." I asked about the training school and he said, "After basic you'll go to warrant officer school, then pilot training at Ft. Rucker in Alabama and then after a..." his words were muffled and then I heard "probably get an assignment to Germany."

I said, "I'm sorry, I missed a part there, after finishing pilot school, where would I go?"

He drew back the muscles on his right cheek and pursed his lips, making a slight sucking sound, that sound you make when you don't know quite how to say something, so you suck in air which signals to the other person that you have something you need to say that will not be good. He mulled his choice of words, finally answering, "A tour in Vietnam." I didn't know where he'd been the last few years, but the one thing I saw nightly, when watching news and videos of the war, were an awful lot of images of burning Huey helicopters and the still-strapped in pilots. Over 7,000 Hueys were used in Vietnam, and twenty-eight percent, some 2,500, were lost during that war. I thanked him for his time and went to the office at the end of the hall.

The Air Force guy was likewise a Staff Sergeant. He was on the phone with his feet up on his desk. He waved me over and motioned for me to sit down. I looked around his office and saw a lot of plaques and awards, plus posters of airplanes, including the USAF Thunderbirds precision acrobatics team. I was still considering all the attention-getters when he finished the call, swung his feet off the desk, sat up in his chair and reached across the table to shake my hand. He introduced himself by his first name only, no mention of rank. He asked if I wanted some coffee and told me to help myself. I poured a cup and sat back down. He asked what brought me to him and I told him I thought I needed to make a change and just didn't know which way to go to get out of my town and on with my life.

He pressed his lips together, gave a few bobs of his head, then set his elbows on the US Government issued 365-day desktop appointment calendar and notepad, with fingers interlaced. He looked at me over the top of his clasped hands and, as he started to speak, extended his index fingers to point at me. He leaned forward, saying, "Let me ask you three questions and answer yes or no, OK?" I agreed and he said, "Do you like good coffee?" I did! "Do you like sleeping between clean sheets each night?" I did! "Do you like air conditioning?" Hell, yes, I did! He took a sip of his coffee, shrugged his shoulders while jutting his chin towards to hallway.

"Those guys can't give you that, we will"

My recruiter then explained how aircraft are, by necessity, tethered to the concrete runway and buildings for maintenance. He also shared that aircraft are expensive, and so are the pilots. He opined how this made it sensible to spend money on quality of life items, "So mechanics don't get pissed off because the chow sucks, and throw a bolt into an engine." This made sense to me, and then he trotted out the pay charts. I'd go in as a no-stripe airman basic "slick sleeve" with less then four months experience, earning $288 a month. This worked out to $1.80 an hour if I worked a standard forty-hour week, which was a step up from the $1.65 an hour I was currently making flipping burgers. The job also came with thirty days paid vacation each and every year. Once I graduated basic training, I'd get my first stripe and a $47 monthly pay raise. Being seventeen for ten more days, I knew that my parents would have to give permission for me to join, but I figured they would; it was just having to tell them so abruptly. Like the Spanish explorers burning their ships on a beach in the new world, there was no going back; we started the paperwork and I left the recruiter to go home and give my folks the big news.

I drove around Cold Spring Harbor, once a whaling town and important place during the Revolutionary War. From 1850 through the 1860s, it also just happened to be the only US Port of Entry. I thought about all that history and all those other young guys throughout Island history who were once seventeen like me and taking that same giant step. Just like me, they'd start with hardly a clue about the enormity of the instant transition from child to adult about to be undertaken. All along that drive, I really never gave any intelligent thought to my immediate future, only idly wondering what was going to happen.

Two days later, I was ready to tell my parents about my decision. It was on a Wednesday afternoon, on a cold, but clear and bright autumn day. I walked into the kitchen and found my mom working over the stove, getting dinner ready because she had the evening off from Rudy's. Stalling the moment as long as I could, I got a beer out of the refrigerator, sat at the chrome-edged yellow Formica kitchen table. I looked out the window at the now slanting shadows climbing slowly up the western wall of Paulie's house, thinking about how to start a conversation I hadn't a clue how to begin.

A small GE clock radio sat on top of the refrigerator, forever set to WABC at 770 on the AM dial. That radio came on when my mother woke up in the early morning and went off when she went to bed late at night. She kept the volume loud enough to hear, but not enough to discourage conversation. I sat there sipping my beer and looking outside, noting the moisture beginning to form around the edges of each of the nine small panes of glass that made up the kitchen window. Two of the columns were three pane casement windows that opened by turning a crank handle, but were now closed and latched. While that blocked any breeze, the glass provided little insulation value. The humidity generated from the water boiling for the spaghetti hit the glass, condensed and got thick enough to form a drop that ran downwards. This forced my mother to put a dishtowel on the window ledge to keep the white enamel painted wood from warping. At night this occlusion provided surprising privacy from anybody looking in.

As I pondered my future, DJ Dan Ingram, who ruled the airways by playing the weekly Top 40, put on a song just released by Carly Simon. It was called *Anticipation* and I listened while she sang to me.

We can never know about the days to come
But we think about them anyway,
And I wonder if I'm really with you now
Or just chasin' after some finer day?

Anticipation, anticipation
Is makin' me late
Is keepin' me waitin'…

And tomorrow we might not be together
I'm no prophet and I don't know nature's ways
So I'll try and see into your eyes right now
And stay right here 'cause these are the good old days.[2]

And from those words she sang, I knew I had to leave and I knew that I'd best remember this particular day because, once I announced my plans, everything would change in terms of my relationship with my family. My mother was about to learn that her only son, the child she bore and raised, was leaving home,

---

[2] Written by Carly E. Simon • Copyright © Universal Music Publishing Group, BMG Rights Management US, LLC

joining the US Air Force during a shooting war, and that child was never to return.

The news came on and it was always worth a listen because it had been crazy the last few years. In September 1971, Attica prison riots in upstate New York resulted in the death of ten hostages and twenty-nine inmates. The Bayway refinery in Linden, New Jersey, blew up on Dec 5, 1970, resulting in multiple injuries but no fatalities. Windows were shattered and the explosion was felt more than thirty miles away, in Jackson Heights, Queens, where we were having dinner with my Aunt Lizzie, who thought it was the Communists attacking. A Greenwich Village townhouse blew up March 6, 1970, caused by the premature detonation of a bomb being assembled by members of the Weather Underground, an American domestic terrorist group. That blast reduced the four-story townhouse to a burning, rubble-strewn ruin, killing the two bomb makers instantly. There were also the "Stonewall riots" in June 1969, when a series of spontaneous riots and violent demonstrations erupted in the gay community. Those disorders were in response to an early morning police raid at the Stonewall Inn, a gay nightclub in Greenwich Village.

On top of all this mayhem, there was the continuing and never-ending Vietnam mess, race riots, wildly changing music urging revolution, and blaxploitation films. This genre came into vogue in 1970 and produced massive hits like *Superfly,* where a black hero pimp battles other drug dealers, crooked cops, and the Italian Mafia, for control of the drug trade in Harlem.

It might seem everything was falling apart, but tonight, since there were no immediate reports of any murders, horrific highway traffic accidents or major structural fires to grab her attention, I turned to my mother and said, "Hey, just wanted to let you know I've decided to join the Air Force and I'm going to leave for basic training right after New Years."

My mother stood stock still at the stove as she digested my words. She lowered the gas flame to keep the water hot, took three steps over to the cabinet above the oven where they kept the hard liquor and pulled down the bottle of four-year-old Schenley Rye whisky. She opened another cabinet, pulled out a shot glass, set it on the counter, filled the glass, put the bottle down, picked up the glass, and tossed it back. She went to the refrigerator, pulled out a Schafer beer in a brown glass "shortie" bottle, popped the top using the bottle opener I'd left sitting on the table and took a big swig. She then walked over to her chair near the window, sat down, lit an unfiltered Pall Mall cigarette, took a deep drag and looked at me for a long moment. She shrugged her shoulders and exhaling smoke while talking said, "Okay, If this is what you want to do, but you do need our permission and what if I say No?"

+++

Little Old Ladies

It was a fair question. I saw the love, concern, and fear in her brown eyes. I loved my mother and never wanted to make her sad. Consequently she took liberal advantage of this and spent some considerable time shaping me as a young man by routinely heaping a fair amount of guilt on me to reinforce and maintain that good son attitude. However, things had changed in the spring just past. I'd gotten my driver's license a year earlier and was experiencing the intense joy at having the mobility, independence and freedom that comes with being a fully licensed driver. On afternoons when I was in school, I'd get out at five minutes to three, be in the car and out of the lot by three. Because I was a good son, I would happily drive the 3.7 miles from school to Rudy's to pick up my mother, who claimed to have been a licensed driver in the late forties, until she let her license lapse. She never needed to renew it because there was no way we could ever afford a second car, so now I could save her walking that half mile back to the house.

Likewise I'd happily drive her back to work each evening and pick her up as well. It was a fifteen minute drive from the school to Plainview when traffic was good and I made the lights. I tried to get there before three-fifteen when she got off shift and came outside, because I didn't want her to wait in the cold. I'd pull up front and double park until she came out. If I was ever late by more than five minutes (which happened, but rarely), I'd pull up to find her looking tired and worn from the day and I'd know I was a bad son for being late. That might have continued, but for that one fine and sunny day in spring when I'd decided to try a new route from school to the shopping center to see if I could improve my time and even save a few minutes. This was my village after all and I was supposed to learn where to go by driving around and noting the time and route. I was also expected to learn routes to both airports and getting into and around Manhattan, just in case I ever needed to pick up Grandma.

My new route brought me to the rear entrance of the shopping center and past the car wash. Every day sixteen black guys in yellow rain suits would spend eight hours with a soapy brush in their hands as they side-slipped along with the car that had been hooked to a chain. Each man expertly ran his brush along the exterior. After a rinse, the drying crew would wipe down the exterior and vacuum the cabin if desired. They were there when it was 95 degrees or 34 degrees, only closing if it rained or snowed, which it did, a lot.

I cut between the two sections of low buildings, emerging just a few doors down from Rudy's. I looked over at the clock on the nearby Chase Manhattan bank, standing alone in the center of the parking lot, saw it was 3:25, and I was ten minutes late. I looked left and saw my mother standing on the leeward side of the building façade. She was blocked from the occasionally gusty winds while enjoying a bit of a sun bath after a day indoors. I could see her lips were pursed and knew she was whistling. I made the left turn and pulled up a moment later. Her eyes were closed and she still hadn't seen me so I tapped my horn. She looked in my direction and in an instant her shoulders drooped, her lips drew thin and a frown formed making her look forlorn. Despite what I'd just seen, I still felt like a bad son for discovering she was a fraud. She came over and got in the car and I apologized for being late, which made it all better. I still loved her, but never bought the "poor little old lady" gag from her, or anybody else, after that.

So there I was, knowing these really were the good old days and I'd enjoyed them, but I was leaving. I heard her question and told her, "I understand that, Mom, but I can sign the papers myself in a few days." She shrugged her shoulders and sighed.

She took another pull on her beer as did I. She shook her head and said, "If that's what you want to do, go ahead. I can't blame you. There isn't really anything for you here." She wasn't kidding. The unemployment rate was rising as was inflation and things were hard all over. The draft might have emptied the ghettos, but hadn't killed all those draftees, so now those veterans were returning to old jobs while others were needing work.

My parents signed the papers; my father relieved that I wouldn't be using any more resources; my mother sad because her only son and driver was enlisting in the service of the nation during a war. I took all the tests to see if I qualified for enlistment and what jobs I was eligible for. It turned out I had almost no mechanical aptitude and would never be permitted to hold a wrench. I suffered an equally unimpressive score on electrical, but enjoyed very high marks in the administrative and general categories. My recruiter told me my scores were "top of the charts" and I was eligible for any job not involving tools or electricity. He mentioned I could even be an air traffic controller, which certainly involved working steady hours in an air-conditioned building, but I heard none of it. I knew what I wanted to be and I told him. "Can I be a cop?"

He shook his head and smiled saying, "Are you sure you don't want to shoot for something a little higher?" I thought being a cop was pretty good, and my sister Donna was dating one, so I heard all the stories. The job seemed straight forward: drive around and wait until there was a problem, then go see about the problem. Of course, my decision might also have been a repudiation of the admonishment my guidance counselor, Mr. Seaman, gave me during my sophomore year, when he encouraged me to sign up for plenty of metalworking and fabrication shop classes, "So you can get a job making license plates in prison."

And that was that.

+++

Getting There Is Half The Fun

Few things are more dehumanizing than the bureaucratic medical machine processing thousands of men each day, solely for the purpose of seeing if they are fit enough to fight and die. During the Vietnam war, somewhere close to thirty percent of the guys fighting and seven percent of those dying were from the greater New York City area. The draft emptied ghettos in both the South Bronx and Harlem, as well all of the hundreds of hamlets, villages, and towns on Long Island and upstate. The machine vacuumed up all those unfortunate peasants not clever enough to get a university educational deferment that would spare them from selection, or if they were in school, fail to maintain a 2.0 GPA. This amounted to an academic eugenics program that created a huge bow wave of college graduates.

There were 58,220 combat deaths in Vietnam and 4,121 of them came from New York. Syosset High School had about 500 people in each graduating class and had already lost two people, Army private Mitchell Sandman, 20, at Quang Ngai Province, shot dead five months after arriving in country and Marine PFC Gregg Lavery, 18, a former track star who died in Quang Tri Province, just forty-eight days after stepping off the plane. Everybody in town knew, or knew of those young men.

Jimmy, a guy who worked at Gene's Esso gas station where we hung out, was one of those guys who got snatched up. To get into any school in the State University of New York (SUNY) system after 1969, you had to have at least a 3.5 GPA and score high on your SATs, the Scholastic Aptitude Test. A perfect score was 1600 and the average was 1000. I think I scored 500 combined, but learned not to take an important test while hung over.

In 1968, Jimmy was accepted into SUNY at Stony Brook, but in his second year forgot why he came to college and his semester GPA slipped to a 1.8. The school sent copies of his semester grades to him, his parents, and the draft board. He was gone within two weeks and on his way to Vietnam. Back in a little over a year, he was never quite right after that. Loud noises, like when Al the mechanic popped a tire on a rim, or July fireworks, sent Jimmy diving under the cash register. He wasn't an exception; there were lots of other guys, older brothers of my friends who also came back with physical and psychological wounds. They became some of the new crazy regulars down at Moran's.

I was one of the few volunteers that month and was told to report to Ft. Hamilton in the Bay Ridge area of Brooklyn. The original New York induction center was located at 39 Whitehall in Manhattan. It was an eight-story building with a portion designated as a barber shop used to shave the heads of individuals entering the military. After a bomb blast inside the building in October 1969, the "Whitehall Examining and Entrance Station" moved to the more secured Fort Hamilton Army Post and into a warehouse. Two years later and they hadn't spent a lot of money on the facility. I was instructed to show up at seven and told it would take two days to complete the physical. I drove myself in and, after getting a pass and parking the car, I walked up to the large MEPS building, the Military Entrance Processing Station, a huge machine that evaluates fitness for military service.

In 1971, the military would take in almost 700,000 people. Rejection was hard to accomplish. On the steps leading up to the entry doors, a hippie freak wearing a tie-dyed shirt, Ho Chi Minh sandals made from old tires, and sporting a blown out white guy Afro, was saying, "Hey man" a lot and making a big production out of taking a tab of what he claimed was LSD. "Hey man, they can't take me if I'm high," he said to no one in particular. He walked inside while again making his pronouncement in front of concerned witnesses and was promptly escorted to a residential holding facility, where he could remain until the effects of the drug wore off. Uncle Sam absolutely needed bodies and could deal with him.

I walked in and a soldier directed me to the hatcheck booth. It was manned by a one-armed veteran of World War II. He smiled cheerily and said, "Give me all your clothes except your underwear and socks." I gave him my shoes, then took off my pants and handed them to him. With surprising dexterity, he put the hanger in his mouth, folded my pants along the crease, and added them to the hanger. He then took my shirt and jacket, deftly putting them on the same hanger. He hung the clothes up, handed me a chit and directed me down the hallway.

I turned the corner and found myself in another hallway at the end of long line inching towards a sign that said, "Station 1." I soon found out there were about twenty stations where they checked your vitals, took fluid samples, checked hearing and vision, including color vision, and generally evaluated your fitness. The line only moved as fast as the one technician conducting that particular part of the examination took. I spent the first morning getting through four stations. Everybody looked pretty much the same, a bunch of guys in white underpants, white T-shirts and white socks. We were separated only by skin tone and hair length, except for one guy. There is always one guy who stands out in any large event and at the Ft. Hamilton MEPS station on that cold November morning, this guy was the stand out.

Homosexuality was an absolute bar to military service in 1971 because homosexuals were then considered to be mentally ill. This meant that an awful lot of formerly loud and proud heterosexual guys were willing to attempt switching their official sexual orientation to avoid getting their butts shot off like poor Ed. The challenge for the US Army was to determine if the inductee claiming to be a homosexual was in fact a homosexual and not just willing to pass himself off as one. This required an examination by an Army psychiatrist, of which there was only one, the rest of his kind treating the massive numbers of drug addicted and psychologically wounded troops coming back from that meat grinder in South East Asia.

I was standing in line for the hearing test, and had been for about an hour and now it was 11:30, and time for lunch. Turned out it was lunch time for the medical technicians and, when they were ready to go, they'd simply tell the next specimen to wait until he got back, never offering an estimation as to exactly when that would be. As the machine shut down, some of the fluorescent lights were turned off and we were handed bag lunches to eat in the hallway, all of us reduced to just leaning against the walls, chewing our bologna sandwiches on white bread. Some random Army person periodically came striding through, looking neither left nor right, but projecting an air of urgency and importance. I think it was mainly to discourage anybody trying to leave.

From somewhere behind me, I became aware of a high lilting voice, all breathy tones with rapidly changing pitch and a pronounced lisp, and I knew, thanks to Mario, exactly what to listen and look for. I confess at the time I had a rather considerable dislike of homosexuals. This guy was about twenty, had dyed blond hair with black roots, wearing a tight fitting lavender sleeveless undershirt and sporting red and white polka dotted boxers. To complete the ensemble, he wore green, black and gray calf length argyle socks, and was cradling a trembling teacup poodle. He was slowly moving along the opposite wall excitedly saying, "I need to speak to the psychiatrist! I need to speak to the psychiatrist!" sounding about as stereotypically gay as I thought possible. Just as he was slowly drifting past me, having survived being met with blank stares and more than a few sniggers, a harried, burly, equally stereotypical United States Army Master Sergeant, a top non-commissioned officer and no-doubt genuine tough guy, turned the corner and strode down our hallway, leaning forward from the waist as if he had a full head of steam and was eager to get somewhere.

The gay draftee threw a slender right arm into the air and began a delicate wave while saying, "Yoo-hoo! Excuse me, Admiral!" which made that Master Sergeant stop dead in his tracks, most likely taking offense at being mistaken for a sailor. He eyeballed the candidate with unconcealed disgust. "Its MASTER SERGEANT, fruitcake, you got that?" The trembling fellow shrank back as much from terror as from the breath coming from a guy with a cigar stub set in his mouth. "Yes, Master Sergeant, I need to see the psychiatrist!" The NCO looked at him and said, "You can see him when he gets back." Not to be put off, the fellow spoke to the broad back of the now departing soldier and called after him, "Do you know when that will be?" The reply came back, "In two weeks, Cupcake, he's on leave!" and with that he was gone. The lights came back on full and the stations began to move. Another Army guy came along and ushered the now very distraught fellow away to some other location, while I shuffled along to get my hearing test.

Along the way I heard varied and sundry experts share their foolproof plan for gaming the system, most of which centered on taking some kind of drug in front of the doctors. One fellow showed me two slivers of lye soap and said he was going to put them under his arms and that would raise his blood pressure and they wouldn't take him. I asked if it was painful and he said he didn't know but heard it was okay, with maybe some slight burning. All of the moaners and schemers were guys who'd been called up to report and I could understand because they knew where they were going, but that was their problem. I was going into the Air Force where I'd have great coffee, clean sheets every night, and air conditioning.

Those final stations the next day became more degrading. The mass genitalia/hernia check was somewhat mortifying, but it was the final station, the hemorrhoid exam that remains the clearest. Twenty-five of us walked into a large room and were told to take a quarter turn to the left, drop our shorts and spread our cheeks while keeping eyes straight ahead. I was somewhere towards the rear of the group. The examining physician started at the back of the line, accompanied by a technician with individual charts who would record the observation into the newly created medical record. He walked past me with no comment and continued down the line for another five or six butts when he stopped and said, "Hmmm?" which meant he was going in for a closer examination. Out of the corner of my right eye, I could see a medical technician and another doctor walk over and bend down by the inspecting physician who had snapped on an exam light and was waving it around. This hadn't taken but a few seconds and we were all waiting to see what was up. The doctor said, "Hmmmm" again, then asked, "Son, what's that in your ass?" The specimen, an absolute hippie freak with long blonde hair and a "Make Love Not War" tattoo on his forearm, reached behind with his right hand, stuck a finger between his butt checks (we were all looking now) pulled it out, stood up, stuck that brown-coated digit in his mouth and started sucking. This produced a quick display of revulsion as assembled viewers were taken aback. After a moment he withdrew that clean finger and proclaimed, "Peanut butter, sir!" The Doc just laughed and said, "Nice try, son, but you ain't crazy. Enjoy your time overseas."

I finished the process and was accepted for enlistment and a promise that I'd attend the police academy technical school. I just had to wait a little over a month for my January report date. It was the day after Thanksgiving when my recruiter called me with the news that my report date had been moved up and I'd be going earlier than forecast. I spent the next few days saying goodbye to all my family, friends, and co-workers. I also got a fresh, close haircut. My sister's boyfriend had been in the USAF before becoming a cop and he said the drill instructors look for the hippies and would be extra hard on them. He also told me to only bring a toothbrush and the clothes on my back because it'd all be taken away when we got there. I followed this advice and he was right.

The night before I left, my mom came into my room and talked with me. She looked around the room and touched on all of the memories attached to each item. The table lamp we bought, the GE alarm clock radio and so on, each time saying, "And I remember when we got you this…" When we got down to shoes, I kissed her good night and told her I'd be back on leave right after basic and school. She made me promise to write often and I did. She even told me I could call collect.

I woke up at four-thirty and dressed, got my father up, and was ready to go. My younger sister asked me to wake her up before I left so she could say goodbye. I went over to the bed she shared with my older sister and gently woke her up saying, "Hey, I'm leaving now. This is goodbye." She wiped the sleep from her eleven-year-old eyes and said groggily, "Goodbye! Can I have your room?"

I drove my car to Ft. Hamilton, stopped at the gate, said goodbye to my father, and walked inside. We were identified, accounted for, gave the first of three urine samples, and then two hundred of us were sworn in en-masse. We were given another sack lunch and spent the remainder of the afternoon raking leaves. At four o'clock, all seven of us brand new USAF airmen were directed onto a green Army bus for the twenty mile ride to Kennedy Airport. Whether by design or accident, the driver took us down Ft. Hamilton Parkway and on to Route 27 and we were given a scenic tour of Brooklyn as we made our way to JFK, and for the second time I'd be riding on a plane.

I was leaving everything I knew, leaving my world. I looked out at the neighborhoods flashing by: Prospect Gardens, Flatbush, Ozone Park, until then really just familiar names I'd heard on the news. It was an unremarkable scene, just block after block of small businesses in small neighborhoods. Only the names and restaurant cuisine changing from Italian, to Greek, or Jewish and always a Chinese restaurant and laundry, like they were a mandatory matched set of *must have* businesses in some city planner play book. Still, they were familiar to me, as was the New York culture, so deeply engrained, so familiar and I was leaving it, just like my grandparents left theirs in Italy in search of something better. I was entering the diaspora and didn't even know it. When we came to Brownsville, a name familiar because of riots, it reminded me that I was now heading into a completely alien environment and I needed to pay attention.

I'd took my oath of enlistment on December 7, 1971, the 30th Anniversary of the sneak attack on Pearl Harbor, and just like that, I was gone.

+++

CHAPTER THREE

Off We Go, Into The Wild Blue Yonder

For the second time in my life, I was on an airplane, this time flying off to join the United States Air Force. My very short haircut was already paying dividends. I must have looked more responsible than the rest of my companions, because an Army transportation guy came over to where we were raking leaves and handed me a large brown envelope, saying, "You're in charge of making sure nobody gets lost between here and San Antonio. Give this to the guy who meets your bus."

Almost all of my group were young, single guys under twenty-one, except for the one married guy. He started complaining about missing his wife before the wheels even left the runway, an unhappy trend he kept up throughout basic. The services generally discouraged married people from joining because the demands of the military are trying on a marriage and the divorce rate is so very high. There was also the attendant fuss, drama, and general bother, of having to move an unhappy young widow out of base housing. Thanks to Vietnam humming along, everybody was welcome to join.

We made it to San Antonio in a few hours and, sure enough, as soon as we came down the boarding stairs a sign read, "USAF RECRUITS THIS WAY" and an arrow led us into a large hall. We were rudely greeted by an Air Force Drill instructor, with a dark blue "Smokey the Bear" campaign hat firmly atop his head. He saw us and immediately yelled, "Fall in with this group!" I saw the yellow footprints on the floor and took my place standing there. I stepped forward and handed him our packet. He took it saying, "Get your ass back in line."

The next thirty-six training days went by with non-stop yelling, a large ration of stress, and more than a bit of melancholy because our training would continue through Christmas and New Years. Despite seasonal sadness, I was getting a great education about people, while living within a microcosm, a community encapsulating, in miniature, the characteristic qualities and features of less affluent America. Black, white, none wealthy, all had a high school education, and some had a bit of college.

My fellow trainees were Northerners, Southerners, West Coasters, Texans, everybody from anywhere. We were eighty young men from radically different American backgrounds sharing a two-story dormitory. It was a learning laboratory because, coming from my tiny piece of America, I'd never met, much less lived with, people from anywhere outside of that burg I came from.

The USAF taught me how to do my own laundry, figure out a budget, clean and shoot a rifle, and even sew, because adding your new stripe was a requirement to graduate. I also marched in my first and last military parade when we marched around a parade field to demonstrate our mastery of close order drill.

We packed up and left one cold morning in early February 1972. By afternoon some of us were on the bus driving across Lackland and arriving at the Security Police Law Enforcement technical school where for the next several weeks I would learn how to be a policeman.

Upon arrival, and to prepare us for what lay ahead, we were shown a series of short training movies. These civilian B&W productions were from the fifties. A Chicago PD film demonstrated proper handcuffing techniques so a prisoner could not slip them off or climb any object you locked the wrists around. My favorite part was at the end when it showed a cop's fist curled around the inside the cuffs. This effectively made them a set of brass knuckles and, punching the other fist, the narrator saying, "And if you ever come across a guy who needs more persuasion…"

However, before I would begin to become a guardian of the good order and discipline, there was a ten-day training break while we waited for other students to join up once they completed their basic training. Being on a break didn't mean sleeping in and catching up on all the TV we'd missed over the last few weeks, rather, it meant that we had jobs that started at 7:30 in the morning and ended at 4:30 that afternoon and included a one-hour lunch break. This was so very much easier than waking up at O'dark thirty. That was when the lights snapped on and the cranky dormitory fire watch guard who'd lost two hours of sleep would yell at all of us "sleeping beauties" to get up.

I arrived and met our dorm chief, Danny, from rural Tennessee. He had the two stripes of an Airman First Class, awarded to him for his prior service in the US Army. Drafted in January of 1969, he was literate and had nice handwriting, so he did his entire two years at a base in Maryland. He got out and went home but couldn't find work, so he came back in for the clean sheets and coffee. Since he was the only A1C in our dorm, he was the Chief, which was a big thing because he handled the assignment of the work details during the week. I shared my room with two Texans, a black guy named LaMont, from over east in Beaumont, and a white guy, Tom, from Wichita Falls up north near Oklahoma, which just made me wonder how bad unemployment in Texas must be.

Tom was lean and had a remarkably weather-worn face for a young man. He wore USAF-issued black bakelite-framed glasses. Referred to as BCGs or "Birth Control Glasses," they are so ugly you'd never get laid wearing them. They gave him no pause for concern since they were the first new pair he'd owned in a while. We'd both come through basic together and became friends because he'd never met a Yankee and I'd never met a Texan. Taking charge of my education in things locally, he introduced me to Lone Star beer, jalapeño peppers, and Hank Williams music.

We got off the bus together on that cold afternoon and spent the next two days listening to the finance guy, education guy, dental guy, and chaplain give us education, divine guidance, and inspiration. Attendance at a religious service while in training was not compulsory, but the alternative was picking up cigarette butts, so everybody went. Being a lapsed Catholic, I went into the confessional to get my sins forgiven. I told the priest what I'd done, like smoking standing next to the vent in the bathroom at night while on dorm guard, when we weren't supposed to smoke at all. He was unconcerned about this but asked, "Did you ever touch yourself in an impure manner?" as his breathing became a bit shallow and his voice began quivering. When I said, "Sorry, father, what was that?" He repeated the question and added "like when you're in the shower…." I told him I didn't know anything about that, got the prayer penalty and left thinking there was something not quite right about that guy, confirming my belief that all priests were weird. This marked the end of my willing participation in organized religion.

Our first Friday as free men came upon us and we were told "Don't care where you go, just be back by Monday morning at zero-seven-thirty."

Most guys were happy to sit in the dorm, drink beer, eat pizza from the base exchange (BX), and otherwise luxuriate in the relative autonomy and freedom of movement that comes the with the end of basic training, but not Tom. It was 350 miles north from San Antonio to Wichita Falls and Tom had a light blue 1969 Olds 442 convertible sitting up there waiting for him. He insisted I come along and see "the best part" of Texas.

We'd been paid up to date and I had a couple hundred dollars tucked into my wallet, so Saturday morning found us hungover at the San Antonio airport waiting for a Texas International airlines flight. We were impressed to learn that flying into somewhere in Mexico made it international. It also had stops in San Angelo, Midland-Odessa, Abilene, and finally Wichita Falls.

Tom was a big believer in the "hair of the dog that bit you" philosophy, that states "If you're hungover in the morning, have a drink and it will fix that hangover." Having just turned eighteen, I gave credence to his counsel. When the bartender asked what we were having, Tom immediately said, "Two red draws," beer with tomato juice, which Tom opined was a healthy breakfast. I'd never heard of this drink before, so again I followed his lead and we kept taking the cure every time our Boeing 727 jet took to the skies on the next short leg because the stewardesses (they became flight attendants in 1976) were obliging.

We finally got into Wichita Falls by late afternoon and were met by a friend of Tom's who'd brought the car to the airport. Even though it was February, the weather was now warm, the top was down, and a cooler full of ice-cold Lone Star beers was sitting in the back. I spent that evening being introduced to north Texas honkey-tonks and crazy-fun big-haired women. The next day we nursed our hangovers as we drove those 350 miles down a two-lane blacktop that was US Highway 281 south. We cruised the length of the Lone Star State as we made our way back to San Antonio under a wide open Texas sky.

+++

South Of The Border, Down Mexico Way

The training was pretty easy and having evenings and weekends off, plus a car, made the next six weeks nothing but fun as the paychecks kept coming every fifteen days. When the weekend rolled around, Tom and Danny suggested we all go to Ciudad Acuña, Mexico, and visit the nearest "Boys' Town." These walled compounds, conveniently located along the U.S.-Mexico border, operate as commercial red light districts. Tom, the Texan, assured us of a variety of other nocturnal entertainment in a sprawling community of neon signs, cantinas, dope pushers, and prostitutes.

This was exactly what we were looking for that Friday afternoon; we were in the car and gone by a quarter to five. We headed west and clocked those 160 miles in pretty good time. It was just a little after seven when we crossed the border. The Mexicans never stopped or checked you coming in, they knew why Americans came, and that was to transfer some of those Yanqui dollars into the local economy.

The streets were not paved, just hard-pan with interspaced potholes of varying depth. We found a spot to park a few blocks off the main zone. The biggest risk was somebody stealing your car, so we hired a kid to keep an eye on it. He only asked for fifty cents and Tom handed it over, but told him if he washed it he'd get two dollars.

Our security arranged, we walked the two blocks to the main street where, just like anywhere, location was everything. The best was closest to the entrance for the ease of wealthy patrons and we saw this as we passed all the brothels, freelance prostitutes, cantinas and bars. Boys' Town is protected by a substation of the municipal police complete with jail and a health clinic that performs blood tests and weekly screenings of sex workers for venereal diseases.

We made a complete loop of the zone, pausing only for a shot of tequila or a beer, and somehow failed to notice those establishments and services exhibited a typical distance decay pattern. The better establishments were closer to the exit and this was also true for the free lancers; the younger, more attractive prostitutes occupied cribs on the main street, whereas older, or less attractive women worked out of cribs in the back. These poorer quarters were conveniently located near the transvestite bars to try to catch any cross-traffic.

Having missed all that intelligence, we came to once again rely upon Tom, a Texan, to make a recommendation. Wanting to showcase entertainment south of the border, he bypassed all the pretty girls on the street or leaning out of a brothel doorway, all calling varied and sundry terms of endearment. "Hey Meestah? You want me?" and the occasional sibling offering, "Hey Meestah, you want my sister? She's a virgin!"

Instead of us taking up any of those offers, Tom directed us towards some clapping hombres, touts extolling the virtues of their establishment. Based on no further consideration except garish exterior neon lighting and loud brass and accordion so emblematic of Tejano music, we were hustled right into a cantina. Through a heavy velvet curtain we entered a large saloon, the entire room dimly lit in red light with an occasional blue bulb visible. This light made it easy enough to see to get around, but not enough to make out any particular person or item. The tables had a lit candle in a red glass holder to either add to the ambiance or burn off the odors of people in various stages of sexual arousal and rut, as well as different levels of hygienic preparation in anticipation of what the night might bring.

I learned that ten cents would buy an awful lot of English Leather, a cologne so powerful it could mask the smell of death. While in the gents, I was also amazed at the depth and breadth of prophylactic gear on offer. One brand had some sort of spiked penis ring that looked like it was clamped on to either inflict pain, or pleasure your partner, it wasn't clear and it wasn't something I was going to buy. I did take special note of the brand that glowed in the dark and imagined how that played out. In the end it was just the cologne, the USAF previously having made available to us the highest-grade government-approved "raincoats" to use as we saw fit.

The waitress came over and asked what we wanted. There wasn't really much of a choice; they had tequila and beer, Cerveza Carta Blanca to be precise, and all she really wanted to know was how many drinks we wanted. Hungry to get the evening underway, the tequila started flowing and pretty soon some girls showed up. They came around looking to see who was ready to have a good time and, one by one, they joined our little party as the drinks continued to flow.

It was long past eleven when the old man in a serape came wandering up to us, his thin white hair poking out from under his sombrero. His peasant ensemble was made more authentic by a thin white linen shirt, worn white pants held up by a belt made from rope, and open-toed sandals. I couldn't help but notice he also had a hump back. He came up and, without introduction, asked who of us was the most macho. Tom begged off because he was nuzzling the neck of a bright bottle-blonde young woman who'd become rather attracted to him, and a very drunken Danny deferred to me, so I told the old man I was his guy. He smiled and said, "Señor, I will bet you one dollar you cannot hold these two pieces of wood for five-seconds." In the dim light provided by the table candle I saw the dark shapes of two wooden handles that were on a wire, but failed to notice them running up and under the leather serape. I had no idea what he was talking about, but I handed over the dollar bill and said, "So, what now?" He said, "Please, take this one and hold it tight." I did as he instructed. He then said, "Now please, grab the other one and count to five and if you still hold, you win." Fair enough, I thought, as I put my drink down on the table and grabbed the other handle.

Well, I tried to grab the other one. I'd no sooner grabbed that wooden peg when I was shocked about senseless and I dropped them both instantly and fell back on to the padded naugahyde seat. The old man was laughing and waving his index finger at me, then turned to the left so I could see his back. He flipped up the serape and I saw the Sears Die Hard brand 12-volt battery and knew "The Forever Battery" had just kicked my ass. The wooden pegs had been painted so the groove that had been cut to allow the wire to wrap around it wasn't really visible in the dim light. My hands were damp from holding the drink and, once I touched that other peg, I closed the circuit, letting the current flow along an uninterrupted path in an instant. He won that dollar fair and square and it taught me to look at every angle before committing to a bar bet.

Midnight came and passed amidst a blur of whispered endearments, entreaties, and concentrated massaging, while discussions concerning costs ebbed and flowed. Most wanted ten dollars, but even though I was drunk, I wasn't quite there. I was a virgin and hadn't the faintest idea of how to go about closing this deal, and even if I did, I didn't think I wanted to do it there, so I declined their entreaties. Somewhere around one, Tom got up with his date and went off behind a curtain and into a red-lit open courtyard leading to a two-story dormitory building without doors or an exterior wall, just sheets on a wash line held in place by clothes pins.

Sometime later, around two, tired and drunk, we'd all had enough fun and made our way back to the parked car, stumbling into unseen potholes, alternately laughing and cursing. Along the way, we stopped at a shop selling sombreros and serapes and bought some for the ride back to San Antonio. The completely intact car was right where we left it. Our little insurance man had washed it as well, so after receiving his compliments on our fine clothing selections, we gave him two dollars and watched as he ran off into the night.

We approached the border crossing which was a couple of well-lit booths, but only one inspector on duty at that time of the morning. The top was down and we presented a pretty picture to the agent because he started laughing as soon as we drew up. Smirking and shaking his head, he asked, "You boys have a big night down there?" We told him we did and he asked if we had anything to declare and did we purchase anything? Danny was drunk and laying against the passenger door, his sombrero pulled low, and offered a muffled, "I declare I'm about as drunk as I can be!" I offered that we'd only just this morning purchased our new Mexican heritage accoutrements. He waved us through with the admonition, "Drive carefully, boys."

It was somewhere after five but before six and the dawn, when Tom said he was getting tired and couldn't drive anymore. I had fused eyes and said, "I'm seeing double back here." Danny simply said he was seeing four of everything, so when the next hotel popped into view, somewhere outside of Uvalde, we decided to get a room.

Tom and I got out of the car and rang the door bell for the manager, who showed up wearing a cream-colored nylon nightgown and floral patterned pale blue bathrobe. She leaned against the door, rubbing both the sleep and fresh cigarette smoke from her eyes as Tom explained our situation and asked about a room for a few hours sleep. She obliged us for six bucks and handed over a room key. I opened the room and let Danny stumble into a bed while Tom put up the convertible top and locked the car.

The room was spartan with only two double beds of advanced age and sagging in the middle, a sink permanently stained by motor oil, the original toilet, and an aluminum shell shower. The door had louvered jalousie windows that wouldn't close all the way as we found out a few hours later when a dust storm blew through heralding a Blue Norther. This fast-moving cold front causes temperatures to drop quickly and dramatically. Under a dark blue-black sky with strong winds, the air temperature began to drop rapidly and the cold spurred us onward.

We got back to Lackland around sunset, the weather winter-like again, and we were still recovering from the terrible abuses we'd visited upon our bodies the night before, so it was off to shower and bed because the next day was Sunday and we could sleep in and recover.

I woke up around nine, not because I was refreshed but rather, because I heard Tom screaming from somewhere down the hallway. I walked to the communal bathrooms, poked my head in and saw Tom's pale butt peeking out through one of the gray stall doors. I asked what was the matter and he said, "My piss is burning and my balls are swelling! I think I got the goddamn clap from that whore in Mexico! She told me she'd just been tested, too!" This meant a mandatory trip for him to the clinic and, after confirmation, an antibiotics injection as well as an oral dose of azithromycin to take care of any chlamydia infection. A mark was entered into the official medical record, not for punishment, but for mandatory re-education on safe sex practices.

Upset and still slightly hungover, we lingered in the hallway as the gravitas of the situation became clear. Finally, Tom looked at me and, with his eyes, pointed mine towards the half ajar door opening into the room where Frank, an Arcadian guy from the northern woods of Maine, lay in deep slumber. This was the end result of a night of excessive ingestion of alcohol, right there in the barracks. He'd foolishly gotten into a drinking contest with Hatteras, this guy from New Mexico. Frank drank two six-packs but lost when Hatteras shotgunned fourteen beers. His secret was to punch a hole at the bottom of the can with an opener and wrap his lips around it, then popping the top so the beer exploded down his gullet.

Arcadians are genetically predisposed to be hairy people and Frank was a shave-twice-a-day kind of guy. In basic, he was required to do just that to keep his appearance military. Frank responded to his new-found freedom by growing back his mustache, one denied him during the previous seven weeks. In the few days since we'd graduated, like some kind of human ChiaPet, Frank grew a beauty: thick, black, and shiny, those bristles reminding me of a new paint brush.

It seemed worth it to try to influence the positive outcome of Tom's upcoming STD test, so we grabbed a Bic disposable razor and some shaving cream. Minutes later, a rudely awakened Frank protested the intrusion and violation. Tom had offered up half of Frank's new mustache as a sacrifice, an effort that proved to be futile. Frank was made despondent by the desecration of his lip. Trimming the remaining half closer to see if he could salvage anything, the result looked like an off-centered Hitler mustache, and nobody wanted that. By the next weekend he was fine.

I learned that anybody will lie to you about anything if the money is right.

+++

Remember Him?

To receive our first assignment after graduation, we were brought into a large auditorium where a personnel guy yelled out the last four digits of a social security number and, when the owner raised his hand, he would be told the assignment. I heard my number and found out I was going to the Third Security Police Squadron at Clark Air Base, Philippines. I was unaware that this was the world capital of sin, debauchery, and sexual depravity, opting instead to trade for a slot with the First Security Police Squadron at MacDill Air Force Base in Tampa, Florida, so I could be near a girl I'd known in high school and had a crush on. It was a bad move for both of us because I never dated or even saw her, and the guy I swapped with got shot in the back by a communist guerrilla while in a movie theater in Angeles City. He survived but was paralyzed.

After graduation, while we were packing out, our training instructors relaxed and spent time just talking with us. The subject of leave came up and one offered, "Everybody takes two weeks leave after school, just to go home and show off, but you'll find with the next visit you'll be looking at your watch, and that will be the last time you go home on leave."

Orders in hand, I took two weeks of leave to go home and see the folks and impress the crowd at Moran's. Everybody coming out of basic has an idea of what they think their homecoming ought to entail. My idle thoughts included a band playing in the park near the train station.

I was quickly disabused of this notion when I stepped off the mid-morning eastbound train and onto the platform. Spring was still a few days away so of course the rain was coming down and being whipped about by gusts of wind. The train pulled out and I was greeted by an empty platform and scant vehicle traffic, with nary a band in sight. Resigned that one wasn't ever going to appear, I slung my duffel bag across my shoulder and headed to the cab stand to go home. It was good to see my parents and they were happy to see I'd not only survived, but had an assignment to Florida, because they planned on moving there when they retired in just a few years.

I went to Moran's on Friday and saw all my old friends from school, enjoyed some drinks and caught up. All the while I had been away, I'd thought about all the good times I'd had with those guys. My buddy Maggio had written to keep me appraised of all the happenings back home. We'd spent the last four years growing up, drinking, smoking, and engaging in other bad teenage behaviors, but now, it seemed as though, in just a few months, things had changed. I began to sense that I no longer belonged there when somebody showed me a picture from a road trip to Pennsylvania. I realized a lot of the conversations were beginning with "Remember when?" and I didn't. In a very short time I'd missed some big events. Realizing I wasn't going to be a part of any future "remember when?" stories helped me understand I was transitioning and becoming, "Remember Mike, that guy who went into the Air Force? Wonder whatever happened to him?"

I was now ready to get on down the highway.

+++

First Assignment - 1st Security Police Squadron

Song of the South

It was March of 1972 when I arrived at MacDill, along with ten guys from my tech school. I'd road-tripped down with Sherman, a friend from the training academy. He was a black guy, the same age I was, but a bit shorter. Whatever he lacked in height, he made up for by having the largest and most developed biceps I'd ever seen on a person, thanks to his having worked tossing bags at the airport.

I flew into DC and met Sherman and another airman, Melvin, a friend of his who'd also been assigned duty at MacDill and was along for the ride to share costs. We took off in his sky blue 1966 Mercury Monterey with power rear window.

We discovered Melvin was a whiner when he started complaining about everything from the moment we hit the Virginia State line. We were both grateful that he fell asleep when we got on I-85 out of Richmond and drove towards the next way point in Raleigh, North Carolina.

Large chunks of the interstate had yet to be built and as the dawn broke we were hurtling down a two-lane state highway driving into North Carolina with me at the wheel. As we rolled past some fields, I stared at a billboard with a picture of a hooded and robed KKK knight holding a fiery cross in his left hand while sitting on a likewise hooded and robed horse rearing up on hind legs. The message was writ large and proud:

YOU ARE IN THE HEART OF KLAN COUNTRY
WELCOME *to* NORTH CAROLINA
JOIN THE UNITED KLANS OF AMERICA, INC.
HELP FIGHT INTEGRATION & COMMUNISM!

I slowed down while shaking Sherman, who woke up from a doze, saw the sign and said, "What the fuck is that?" Melvin the whiner stirred in the backseat, but kept sleeping, and we felt it best not to wake him. We did not stay in that state one minute longer than was necessary, but we did need to stop at a small cafe in a tiny town and went inside for breakfast. An older black man, frizzy gray hair sticking out from under his stained paper cap, was sweeping the floor and gave us a look when we sat down. After a bit came over to take our order for breakfast. It was when he gave it to the large black man who was the cook and pointed at us that I realized his surprise wasn't having a mixed race group come into the cafe, it was having a white guy come in.

Although we were not sending any more people to Vietnam as a first assignment, there were still plenty of 90-179 day Temporary Duty (TDY) assignments there, or more likely, because of troop strength ceilings, to one of five airbases in Thailand. In 1969 there were more airmen in Thailand than in Vietnam. Guys from MacDill would be sent there as the need for new airmen to replace the other guys there on a temporary basis, so one day Airman Smith is at work at MacDill and the next day he's "gone to the Nam for 179."

An unlucky person could get stuck in a permanent TDY experience and become a base ghost, like one Staff Sergeant I met. His first assignment was to Luke AFB in Arizona. Shortly after he arrived, he was sent TDY somewhere and nobody on base ever got to know him. When that TDY was up, he came back and, when a new requirement came in for a body to go somewhere, he got tagged for the job because nobody knew him, or missed him on their flight, so he was an easy pick. That was six years earlier. Making the best use of his situation, he'd studied hard and even gotten promoted while TDY. He also managed to save over forty thousand in temporary duty pay and allowances, so he was OK with all of it because he got to meet new people all the time and leave before he got tired of them.

At the end of the 179 days Airman Smith would magically reappear at MacDill, usually much worse for the wear, mainly from partying and *running the 'ville*, in whatever village popped up near any installation.

Every airman who ever went off for six months came back bragging about having "been in the shit." This led to an abundance of "Well, there I was…" war stories, usually involving getting rocketed in Da Nang, which was fair given it was nicknamed "Rocket City."

Undiagnosed PTSD was common, heroin was cheap, and more than a few airmen got hooked when it was a five-dollar-a-day habit, one easy to maintain. Some addicts would "chip" and only use on occasion by "chasing the dragon." This involved heating the powdered heroin on the aluminum foil taken from a cigarette packet until it vaporized and then sucking up the smoke. Others preferred liquifying the smack, dripping it on a cigarette, letting it dry, and then smoking it.

Didn't matter how they did it, sooner or later they had a monkey on their back and couldn't continue. A troop who self-identified for being addicted would not be punished, instead he'd be sent off for controlled withdrawal and rehabilitation at Lowry AFB in Colorado. If successful, he could apply and return to duty.

The USAF was in a major transition period as the *Vietnamization* process, (turning over responsibility for the war to the South

Vietnamese government) got underway. By early 1972, over 400,000 US personnel had been withdrawn, virtually all combat troops. We still had plenty of Air Force and Navy people in country, but manpower planners were already beginning to look at troop reductions after three years of steady force buildups.

A lot of the guys who came into the Air Force during those four years between 1968 and 1972 did it to "hide in plain sight," to avoid the draft. Most figured it was only a matter of time until they got scooped up and, better to be in a military branch where you had to have a college degree to get killed, given pilots all had college degrees and were suffering the highest combat loss rate by occupation.

These were the guys two-years into their four-year enlistment contracts, hated the military and couldn't wait to get out, so they'd do stupid things to get thrown out, as opposed to the guys who just had criminal tendencies. Days after we arrived and while still in-processing, MacDill underwent a rash of burglaries at the golf course and at a flying squadron, where helmets and other gear were stolen. Turned out it was some cops on another shift who discovered the open doors while conducting security checks and helped themselves to the property inside, then called it in as a burglary just discovered. What they didn't know was, there was so much security on base, the only people who could do it were the cops and the investigators knew it. The entire flight was relieved from duty and eight of them were charged and sent to jail.

I was eighteen, a volunteer and happy to have a real job doing what I always wanted to do. That didn't mean I was a kiss-ass, to the contrary, I questioned stupid things all the time, things that just didn't make sense and I was usually correct, much to the consternation and irritation of the guy I called out. This showed leadership I had potential. I soon became the "go to" law enforcement airman to work the less glamorous, but higher priority security, when a security guy got busted for doing something stupid.

The first time I got sent over was because one disgruntled moron came to work and stood in guardmount formation being conducted by the Squadron Operations Officer. The Captain noticed part of a plastic baggie visible in the airman's fatigue pants pocket. When the Captain asked him what it was, that airman produced a bag of weed, saying, "It's a lid of grass, sir." He was relieved of duty and, instead of the anticipated discharge and happy return to civilian life, the weed-bearing airman became permanently assigned to "Weeds & Seeds," a storage assignment for unwanted airmen.

Airmen who failed to meet acceptable standards were designated as full-time squadron barracks janitors and general purpose "chogey-boys." That meant they were responsible for: making coffee, cleaning floors, painting walls, tending flower beds, swabbing toilets, washing cars, and any other task the First Sergeant could come up with for them to occupy their days since they could no longer be trusted to carry a weapon.

These informal assignments were necessary because, to carry a weapon and work around nukes, you had to possess a security clearance and be certified under the Personnel Reliability Program (PRP). This Department of Defense security, medical, and psychological evaluation program is designed to permit only the most trustworthy individuals access to nuclear, chemical and biological weapons. The PRP evaluates many aspects of the individual's work and home life. Any disruption of these, or severe deviation from an established norm, would be cause to deny access. The denial might be temporary or permanent. Taking a prescription dose of Sudafed was temporary. Having a bag of weed was permanent.

+++

Keep An Eye On That Nuke

After demonstrating I could work a full shift without falling asleep or discharging my weapon, I was moved on to greater responsibilities, thanks to a steady stream of security guys getting busted.

One idiot went to a scary movie before his shift and, while walking around his assigned post in an F-4 parking area for one of the flying squadrons, thought he heard something and drew his .38 revolver. Finding nothing he put it back in the holster. He heard another noise, pulled his pistol and cocked the hammer, so now just two pounds of pressure on the trigger would drop the hammer, making the shot more accurate. He put the cocked pistol back into his holster. Spooked a third time, he pulled the trigger during his quick draw and blew the bottom out of the holster. He lost a stripe and after that all the security guys had to carry an M-16 rifle with no magazine inserted.

Thanks to guys like him, I was soon in training as a security controller under the mentoring of a seasoned twenty-two year old staff sergeant. He was a veteran of a year tour in Vietnam and fifteen months in the Philippines. I'd listen to all his war stories involving Subic Bay and Alongopo City, his descriptions of all the debauchery in the many "*Dens of Iniquity*" available to airmen made me envious that I'd missed out on the best tours the USAF had to offer.

He'd recently returned from a six month stint at Rocket City so he had that cachet of being a full up combat vet going as well. I still had a few more months before I could put in for an assignment to Vietnam and, after hearing all these guys, I was keen to go because it always sounded like a great time.

The Controller was a big job because, in addition to our three flying squadrons, we also had a nuclear weapons storage area (WSA) at the back of the base, near the golf course. The facility stored nukes for the nearby **S**trategic **A**ir **C**ommand (SAC) detachment of two B-52s and a KC-135 tanker on permanent station in case the Soviets or Cubans ever got frisky, like back during the Cuban missile crisis in October of 1962.

Completely self-contained, those SAC warriors had their own support personnel, cooks, cops, and admin guys assigned full time and living out there. Each B-52 could carry eight B28 hydrogen bombs with parachutes for lay down delivery.

The number one installation priority was the safety of those weapons. They were placed in pairs in secured concrete storage vaults called igloos that were covered with dirt and grass. A double barbed wire perimeter fence surrounded the igloos, and at night a K-9 handler and his dog walked the strip between the fences and also inside and around those securely locked buildings. There was an entry controller bunker with a one way man-trap entry gate to maintain control over access. It was a revolving steel bar door like you find in any subway station. If locked it would stop entry and capture the person but always allowed unimpeded exit in the event of an emergency. People wanting entry were authorized each day and their names had to be on the hand-delivered list the controller received from operations. Incoming workers had to show their line badge with proper access areas indicated. A line badge had twenty numbered squares, ten on each side of your ID picture. If you didn't have access, the square would be blacked out. If you did, the number was visible and the holder was admitted into the **NO SMOKING** area where you couldn't bring in any device capable of making a spark or open flame. For all the high tech, it made me think nukes were quite delicate and had fuses like the "Acme Rocket" from the Road Runner cartoons. A roving three-man Security Alert Team/Quick Reaction Force was available if Cuban frogmen were ever detected coming ashore to wreak havoc.

SAC flying crews stood alert duty at MacDill for seven days out of a twenty-one day period and would fly training missions designed to keep flying skills honed to a razor's edge. A B-52 had to be airborne within three minutes of the klaxon alarm horn going off. SAC alert crew members lived apart from the support personnel in a Readiness Crew Building (RCB) known as a mole hole, adjacent to the Alert Ramp. If the klaxon sounded, those crews would exit the mole hole and run out to the waiting planes. To meet that three-minute "gear up" deadline they'd push the throttles forward and belch a cloud of black smoke visible to me at the other end of the 11,421 foot runway. Those eight relatively inefficient, and notoriously smoky, low bypass turbofan engines have water injected into them to rapidly increase thrust for takeoff. The trade off is thick black smoke pouring out and providing that thrust during takeoff.

With no time to taxi and line up into the wind, they only launched in one direction from the RCB. Depending on that wind, they might need a long take-off roll and use pretty much every foot of runway to get airborne in the dense semi-tropical air. In those cases, the tower would hit the warning lights and bells would also sound. Outbound traffic would be stopped along the access road and we'd hold up inbound traffic at the gate. There were more than a few times I'd be standing in awe as that massive airframe struggled to rise, and willing it to avoid hitting my gate shack, which was not an unreasonable concern, given the shack had been destroyed one night in early 1973 when a drunken Mexican national, who'd overstayed his visa, drove his 1968 Ford flatbed truck down US Highway 92 thinking he was heading to Miami.

US 92 ended at the gate and so did the Mexican who ran his truck directly into the yellow and black striped concrete blocks designed to protect the building and occupants from out of control cars careening into the gate shack. Those blocks might have worked if the rebar the engineering plans called for had actually been inserted by the contractor during construction. It was somehow fitting because the road was named for Capt Dale Mabry, who was piloting the Army airship *Roma*, a dirigible, when it crashed in Norfolk, Virginia on February 21, 1922, resulting in 35 deaths, then the greatest aeronautical accident of the era. This concrete highway is the main commercial access to the base and provided a never-ending vista of massage parlors, used car lots, payday loan outfits, blood & plasma banks, strip clubs, dive bars, oyster & seafood shacks, jai alai frontons, and restaurants. All these modern camp followers, a business model dating back to the Roman Legions, spring up outside of military installations globally, like toadstools after a rain.

Sherman was on duty that night and saw it coming, even telling the other guard over on the Bayshore gate, "I think this motherfucker's going to hit me!" He screamed and dropped the phone, diving out a side door as walls were collapsing. He ran a quarter mile screaming before he realized the truck had stopped. The debris was cleared away and guards were then reduced to standing on the cleared space where the shack used to be. Operations sent down a folding chair to sit on when there was no traffic and also promised saw horses with yellow blinking caution lights attached all around the hole until the civil engineers built a new shack and slapped it in place five days later.

With that event fresh in my memory, and with some trepidation, I'd watch that behemoth airframe come roaring up to me and finally, through sheer brute force, begin to rise off the concrete and slip the surly bonds. I could see the tires spinning as the landing gear retracted into the wells and I was blasted with a black cloud smelling of unburned kerosene.

Since anything could happen in the blink of an eye, and to reinforce training and keep our own skills sharp, we had practice exercises every evening to cover any and all contingencies involving nuclear surety. I learned to plot and monitor aircraft locations during air operations, perform all the necessary radio and alarm checks, understand aircraft or nuclear weapon accident responses and a host of other duties outlined in the ever present check lists prepared for any and all situations possibly arising during operations. All this was under the watchful eye of my mentor, a surfer type with bleached blonde hair. His laid back demeanor made him a natural teacher, one who made it easy to pick up the intricacies of the job.

This was a great gig for me. I was behind locked doors in an air conditioned room with a thirty-cup coffee pot, unlimited supply of high-grade government coffee and, smoking was permitted. I'd been there for two weeks and was feeling acclimated, even experienced, after the night shots were fired inside the WSA.

The interior K-9 dog handler had been busted for being drunk on duty inside the WSA a month earlier when he was caught fast asleep on top of an igloo by the security supervisor who hadn't heard from him in a while. The hungover handler had put his dog on alert and fell asleep. The dog was bored so it also fell asleep. The handler lost a stripe and was sent to Lowry, in the Rocky Mountains of Colorado, to dry out. He'd just returned to duty clean and sober, PRP cleared and was reunited with his dog, who missed him terribly. They went into the WSA and climbed back up on the igloo he'd fallen asleep on. He told the dog to sit, pulled out his .38 revolver and shot that dog dead for ruining his life. He got a year in Leavenworth and a dishonorable discharge.

It was four in the morning and I'd run out of cigarettes. I smoked Kool menthols as did my mentor, who kept his open pack sitting on the desk by the ashtray. I reached over towards them while asking, "Mind if I bum one?" Startled, he said, "No!" rather sharply as he reached across, snatched the pack up and put it in his pocket. He looked at me and said, "Sorry man, I've just got enough to get me through the shift." I was a bit surprised, but they were his cigarettes, so I dispatched a patrol to call me from the snack bar and, when he did, I had him get me a pack of Kools.

I knew some guys just didn't like getting smokes bummed off them and would tell you right up front. Some others would use a razor to cut open the bottom of the pack and leave the top sealed, so if you asked they would point to the pack and say, "Oh man, I would, but I just haven't opened this pack yet and I'm waiting." What could you say? You were asking a favor. Well, after I got hip to it, I started saying ,"You could tap one out the bottom, you cheap motherfucker," but a pack only cost a quarter and it was my fault for not having brought enough smokes. I also thought about a guy I heard in the barracks calling out a perennial mooch, saying, "If you can't afford a twenty-five cent a day jones, my man, you need to quit that shit."

The next night when I reported in, a Tech Sergeant I'd seen around was sitting in the controller's seat. He introduced himself and told me my mentor self-ID'd for heroin addiction. He'd been lacing his cigarettes to maintain a habit that only cost five bucks in the Nam, but ran $300 a day in Tampa, and he just couldn't afford it any longer.

From him I learned you never let yourself get a taste for something you might not be able to afford later.

+++

Guardmount

Being a cop meant you had to set the standard for uniforms and personal grooming. There was an inspection each and every morning before you were turned out for your shift assignment. The Air Force loved shiny things and two of those shiny things were shoes. Before each shift I would sit down with a brush, some water, cotton balls, shoe polish, edge polish and a toothbrush, then spend thirty minutes making sure my shoes were ready for inspection. I'd spend another twenty minutes ironing my uniform, but in the heat and humidity of central Florida it was simply a losing proposition. Shoes that were shiny enough for you to see your face in at six in the morning were dull and faded by noon thanks to the tropical sun beating down on the concrete where I stood. Shoe polish melts at 104°F and on sunny days the thermometer might read ninety in the shade but there wasn't any shade on that heated concrete and I'd often watch my spit shine cloud up. The same was true for all the uniforms of the time, sharp at six and wilted by ten.

Unless it was raining, guardmount was conducted outside the station house fifteen minutes prior to the beginning of each shift. The on-coming shifts formed up outside by date of rank, executed a "dress right" alignment, bringing our right elbows to the horizontal, then shuffling right until all elbows are touching all the left shoulders. The line is now aligned, so when commanded, arms drop, everybody returns to attention until told "at ease." The flight chief would always cast an eye, but sometimes the commander would pop by to conduct guardmount and get to know his airmen. Day shifts were closely inspected because that's when the commanders and senior NCOs came to work, and a spit and polish police force radiated confidence.

Of course there was always some minor violation, like "flying a Yankee pennant," a bit of thread visible from a sewing job like replacing a button, or sewing on unit patches or stripes. The fix was to spot the offending string and burn it off with a lighter, the flame sealing the edge against fraying in the process. Hair length was a constant topic, with admonishment promised for hair a bit too long and over the ears, mustache hair beyond the "vermilion border of the upper lip," or other hirsute irregularities.

The level of attention to detail and standards was dependent on the mood of the flight chief. Some chiefs were fairly relaxed and used the opportunity to read the assignments, review the rules on the use of deadly force, make general announcements of interest and ask if there were any questions. Some were hard-asses who used the time to "instill discipline" and generally see if they could make other people miserable. Regardless of temperament, the entire process normally took just ten minutes which allowed guys to grab their gear and start moving out of the parking lot before six.

The worst thing you can do in the military is be late. In fact, it's a crime called "failure to go" if somebody is late for work without excuse. This can be punished with jail time and there aren't any good excuses. My first training instructor remarked early on during basic, "Excuses are like assholes, everybody's got one and they all stink." I learned important lessons about time management as a direct result of that rule which is "the only time that mattered was the time on the flight chief's watch" and late was the moment he called the flight to attention.

One sad morning, while beginning the last day of a three day-shift cycle, I was coming up the sidewalk to the assembled flight when our newly arrived flight chief, Master Sergeant "Pops" Connor, looked at his watch and called out, "Flight, attention!" I stepped into line with the flight while Pops cheerfully announced "You're late, you've just lost one day off." This was a big hit since we only had four full days off a month. When my flight went on break, I reported to the office in green fatigues and was set to work pulling weeds from the flower beds around the station house.

My weeds and seeds co-worker was a rummy old former master sergeant who'd done something wrong because I could see the sewing stitch shadow where his four other stripes had been and which the two new A1C stripes couldn't cover. We didn't talk much, but I could smell the alcohol wafting from him, it was infused into his sweat. He was coming up on twenty years and his commander had already steadily reduced him in grade and was now using weeds and seeds as an informal drying out space. The thirty-eight-year old drunk was content to be on hold for a few more months until his retirement was finalized. Once signed out of the personnel book, he was free to take his ease in one of the nearby trailer parks and drink himself to death.

I'd read an *Air Force Times* article letting us all know that enlisted men died an average of eighteen months after retirement, the result of decades spent smoking and drinking to excess while working long hours under stressful conditions. The

Times also let us know that officers fared little better, on average lasting just thirty-six months. Everybody knew it was a hard life, but they went for the really big carrot, retirement at twenty years with fifty percent of your last salary, plus a cost of living allowance (COLA). Every time Congress passed a military pay raise, the retirees got a raise plus COLA. Free travel on military aircraft heading overseas made it easy to retire to a place where your hard-earned dollars would bring you all the fun you could ever wish for. The military even kicked in free medical for life because retirees just didn't take that long to die and, when they did, it was usually of a massive heart attack.

The next and final time I was late, was by about forty-five seconds. I lost my two days off and spent them in the heat pulling weeds, and working eighteen days straight. I was admittedly a wise-ass, a trait I came by honestly growing up in New York, and that grated on Pops. With over twenty years of service, Pops, at forty years old, was looking far older, resembling the equally tired former President, LBJ, thanks to his most recent unaccompanied assignment to the sexual fantasy land in the Philippines.

He presented himself as a by the book "no questions tolerated" supervisor and we had a severe personality clash because I saw stupid stuff being done every day and commented on it. Over the next three months I racked up five "Letters of Reprimand" and two threats of courts-martial for my insolence before we finally became great friends at a squadron party.

About once a month we held a party in a palm-frond covered bohio-style open air party room on the base beach. We'd all chip in for booze and because these were official, mandatory events, the cooks were always happy to provide trays of meats, salads, and anything else we needed. I'd walked over to my car to get a pack of cigarettes when I saw Pops hop into the back of his blue and white Plymouth station wagon with one of the strippers so I knew he was working on getting a blow job.

He'd thrown some beach towels around the rear windows for privacy and had just set to business when his twelve-year old son came riding up on a bicycle, having been sent to the beach by his mom to find Pops. The kid saw the wagon rocking back and forth and headed that way. Realizing this would be a very bad outcome I intercepted him, and in a loud voice told him his father had just left in another guy's car to go get some pizzas and would be back soon. I told him he could go and I'd give Pops the message when he got back.

The kid left and a visibly shaken up Pops came out a few minutes later. He began calling me "pardner" after that, a term he only applied to people he liked. He even started assigning me to better posts, like patrol. I responded by living up to his expectations as a patrolman.

Still seeking recruits, but finding it more difficult since the draft ended and draft dodgers quit volunteering, the USAF initiated a program where guys who signed up for six years of active duty, instead of the usual four, would get the second stripe of an Airman First Class right out of basic training and avoid the newly changed standard of remaining an Airman Basic for four months out of basic, then wait six more months as an Airman and only then being eligible to sew on Airman First.

These were important distinctions. We'd all put on our first stripes out of basic and were coming up for promotion to A1C in the next month, when along came some guy from Virginia who'd taken the deal. As an A1C he could and did order us to empty the garbage or be the guy putting down traffic cones in the morning or evening to facilitate the traffic flows while he drove the truck, jobs like that. His "authority" would continue after we sewed on A1C because he'd still be senior to all of us by virtue of his "time in grade." It was especially galling because he simply hadn't paid his dues as an airman, getting all the dirty jobs: cleaning toilets, washing the patrol cars for the entire flight, cleaning the gate shacks, emptying garbage pails, washing, striping and waxing the station house floors. It was crap work and he'd skated past it and nobody liked a skater.

He was also a shameless kiss-ass. The black guys called him "Hillbilly Pinocchio" because he was always lying about his purported virtues while sticking his nose up Pop's ass. Others maintained that Pops "should have turn signals sewn on his belt so Pinocchio would know when to turn so not to break his nose." He did nothing to disabuse anybody of this reputation because as a genuine kiss-ass he wasn't worried about contemporaries on his climb up, he had his stripes after all.

Of course the USAF insisted that, for him to keep that stripe, he had to display all those many positive leadership traits, those several very many, of which the most important trait, was to be on time. Since the Navy first said, "Time and tide wait for no man," and as my own recent experiences had affirmed, you just cannot be late for anything. An airman might be given menial labor to drive the point home, but this lesson should already have been taken to heart by any newly minted airman first class. Hillbilly Pinocchio found that out one day when the piece of crap lemon yellow Pontiac he'd bought for seventy-five dollars at a car lot just outside the main gate died after dropping a date off from a magical day at the newly opened Disney World. This made him one hour late for guardmount which pissed Pops off, but this golden child had never been a problem and his excuse was legitimate. Still, Pops put him on clear notice not to ever be late again or he'd be losing that stripe.

I was assigned to work the Dale Mabry gate with Pinocchio that day and not only did he not pull his weight by choosing to sit on his ass and just issue vehicle passes, he made a further point of addressing me only as "Airman."

The next morning I got up at four to get ready for the day. I left my room and headed for the showers down the hallway. I passed the electrical panel, opened it, found his room number, flipped the breaker and shut off the power. I finished getting ready forty-five minutes later, restored the power and closed the panel door as I went back to my room.

Pops had to send a patrol to wake him up and wasn't having any excuses, this blatant offense being just one day after his warning. Pinocchio was instantly labeled "chronic" and a guy just not getting it. He lost that stripe and still had to serve six years. He also had to wait six humiliating months for promotion back to A1C. Of course he was now junior to me and everybody else who hated him, as we reminded him of that for those next six months as we piled on all those jobs he'd missed experiencing.

+++

The Climbing Man

Florida gets hot in July, most days see ninety by mid-morning and the humidity can be stifling. There wasn't a lot of relief when that red fireball vanished below the horizon because the overnight low might finally get to seventy-five by four and stay pleasant until dawn, but until then, with not a breeze stirring, it remained too warm and humid, so the sweat continued to roll. Once the sun's up, you know it every minute you aren't under shade or in an air conditioned room. Some security guys would get tired of walking around planes because the vast concrete parking area continued to radiate heat long after sundown and compounded their misery.

In those days, before Pops and I overcame our differences and I'd demonstrated my discretion sufficiently, there were fewer tender moments at guardmount. After inspection big Air Force announcements followed, then any new local orders or rule changes, and finally notes of interest like squadron activities available if anybody had any free time, which none of us young airmen ever did. Those activities were geared toward career personnel, the lifers, the ones who stayed after the first four-year tour. They were the ones filling slots in the back offices; the investigators, training guys, and others, all soft jobs, normal duty hours with weekends and holidays free.

Before it gets hot, however, there is that short period of time, an hour or so, when the light from a not yet visible sun illuminates the world. Slowly at first, the light becomes stronger and brighter making it easier to see people and places. This is sometimes referred to as a "golden hour" by photographers, a time when the lighting is just perfect, bestowing a flattering golden or rose hue on people, and no shadows are cast. It was in just such a light that our flight lined up off the side of the station house and facing west, towards the flight line. We were looking across an open field and at the water tower.

Stateside USAF bases always paint their water tanks in a red and white checked pattern for greater visibility by aviators. On top is a rotating beacon that flashes a white light followed by a two-blink green light to distinguish the air field as military. The towers are protected by a chain link fence and access is through a padlocked gate. A steel maintenance ladder is attached to one leg and a metal catwalk ran the circumference of the tank.

I was looking idly at that water tank while Pops read off some official piece of news, and I watched as a figure in green fatigues with an M-16 rifle slung over his shoulder walked up to the fence, tossed his rifle inside and began to climb the fence. I was concerned about his intentions because just six years earlier, twenty-five year old Charles Whitman, of Austin, Texas, spent his morning murdering his mother and wife and spent the afternoon with several rifles atop the twenty-eighth floor observation deck at the University of Texas Austin Tower sniping passersby. Over the next hour and a half, he killed fourteen people and wounded thirty-one before being shot and killed by two Austin PD officers, McCoy and Martinez. Once my climber left his rifle on the grass, I felt relief as I watched him climb, knowing he wasn't going to be some kind of later-day Whitman.

I nudged the guy next to me and pointed with my jaw. He just smirked. The climbing man was then about fifteen feet off the ground and showed no signs of stopping. I decided I needed to tell Pops about this and raised my hand, but Pops was focused on the info sheet and telling us about the base bowling leagues forming, so when I said, "Excuse me…" and before I could get any further, a clearly irritated Pops yelled at me "I don't want to hear another goddamn word from you, so just shut the fuck up until I'm finished!"

Properly chastened I stepped back into formation. Pops got through about one minute later and said to me "Now what's so goddamn important?" I pointed towards the tower and the climbing man and said, "I thought you'd want to know about this."

Pops looked up, puffed his cheeks and exploded, yelling "Why the fuck didn't you say something sooner?" I didn't bother to answer and just waited along with everybody else. Pops just stared at the scene, open mouthed, as he thought about his response. Finally, he turned to me and said, "OK, you reported it, you work it." He passed it off like it was any other call. I looked at him and said, “You’re kidding, right? What do you want me to do? Shoot him down?” Pops didn’t care. He turned on his heel and walked back into the office.

I was partnered with Sherman, of collapsing gatehouse fame, who was fun to hang out with and run the bars and strip clubs on Dale Mabry, but was also a no bullshit cop. There was a lot of societal pressure on black cops to “cut a brother some slack” but that wasn’t Sherman’s way as he’d explained to many a disappointed airman while he wrote out a citation, even causing one to ask, “Can I have the white dude instead of you?” Sherman was married but his wife wasn’t arriving for another six months so he lived next door to me in the barracks. We were often partnered on patrol and worked well together. We ambled over to the tower and looked up at the climber who had reached the cat walk and was now sitting with his legs dangling over the edge while he took in the view.

I looked at Sherm who said, “Don’t look at me! Pops said this one’s all yours, I’m just the muscle!” With that he curled his right bicep so I could see the softball he had sewn in there.

I looked up and yelled “Hey! Come down!” and the immediate response was “No!” The climber went on to tell us how much he hated the flight line and he hated walking around planes and the job really sucked. I had to admit he had a point. Just then Sherm yelled up “Then jump, you stupid motherfucker, and quit wasting our time!” After we stopped laughing, I said, “Well, we aren’t going to get him to come down, so what do you want to do?” Sherm just smiled and said, “That stupid motherfucker doesn’t see that sun coming up? He’ll be down before nine.”

And he was. Down at half past eight, two hours past sunrise.

The USAF wasn’t interested in losing this guy because he’d been a good performer, but they were interested in motivating him to becoming a better troop. He was assigned to weeds and seeds, from eight to five. After being issued a lightweight USAF regulation pith helmet, like they wear on an African safari, he became the first guy I ever saw get assigned a lawn mower. He was then ordered to start mowing the infield on the flight line, a huge expanse of grass separating the 11,000+ foot runway from active taxi ways.

In about a week, he'd recognized the error of his ways, and the foolishness of his complaints, and returned re-energized and committed to excellence.

+++

The King And Al

Al was the alternate desk sergeant, switching off with a Staff Sergeant named Oliver. A six-year buck sergeant, Al had no time overseas. He hailed from outside of Jacksonville, Florida, the only son of a fire-breathing hard-shell primitive Baptist preacher, the kind who held revival meetings in a tent in the woods. Al worked for the railroad for a few years before answering the nation's call so he carried a silver pocket watch from those earlier times. He looked like a train conductor when he'd consult it. He stood about six foot even and was solidly built, with a deep affection for Krystal burgers and "hot and fresh" Krispy Kreme doughnuts when they came in each morning.

Meanwhile, Oliver was a veteran with multiple overseas tours, mainly in South East Asia, and a steady, no bullshit demeanor which was important when you were working the operations desk. Up on that desk phones were constantly ringing with all manner of requests for services, or emergencies, plus maintaining communications with the Wing Command Post, the central point for all emergency operations during any emergency, nuclear or biological. It was rumored he'd worked at the infamous Long Binh jail in Vietnam, a miserable shit hole no troop ever wanted to get stuck in.

Oliver's training and experience showed one hot and humid summer night when a disturbance broke out in the twelve-cell confinement facility next door. With ten prisoners and no air conditioning things just went south. McCoomb, the A1C jailer, left the cell block area, locked the front door of the jail, and then came over to tell Oliver about the riot, as if he couldn't hear the bedlam through the jail access door just a few feet away.

Oliver unlocked the wooden door, opened it and shouted through the jail-side metal door "You'all need to knock this crap off right now or I'm going to gas you!" The rioters shouted back varied and sundry obscenities, so after three minutes Oliver pulled out one M7A3 RIOT CS gas grenade from a case of six stored under the desk. He pulled the pin, let the spoon fly and tossed it into the cell block area, then closed the wooden door. After fifteen minutes, he asked the fire department guys, in their station on the opposite side of the jail, to put some ventilating fans up while coughing and gagging prisoners were brought outside under guard. There were no more incidents after that. Not many more prisoners either, because word got around that the jail didn't play.

Meanwhile, Al lived by a rule of kindness and acceptance. This included his treatment of all of God's gentle creatures which must have worked pretty well for him, a Baptist St. Francis of Assisi as it were. At least it worked well until the day Al met King, the recovering sentry dog.

During Vietnam, US forces trained dogs, primarily German Shepherds, to be sentry dogs given their ferocious demeanor and solid bite exerting 238 pounds of pressure, more than enough to snap a bone. These ferocious man-killing dogs were trained to find and destroy anything human ahead of them. Put on the perimeter of our air bases, it was heaven help anybody in front of one. The dog only knew one master and the general rule was to euthanize the beasts at the end of the handler's tour because once they'd been blooded they were simply too dangerous to keep around. If the handler was injured or killed, the dog was immediately destroyed as well.

In the summer of 1972, somebody somewhere approved a test program to see if sentry dogs could be successfully re-educated for law enforcement purposes, like explosives or drug detection. The dogs had already undergone an intensive selection process at some considerable expense, so if the experiment was a success a lot of loyal dogs could be recovered and saved.

I'd turned down the opportunity to be a dog handler at the academy. At that time, there wasn't any glory in being a "puppy pusher" and there was all that off-duty time spent maintaining your animal, including Christmas and New Years, so I satisfied any itch by watching the handlers work with and train their dogs. Word had come down that a sentry dog was coming, a crazy mean dog, and anybody who wasn't working went to the kennels to see how this would all turn out. The dog would either immediately respond to the training or it would be put down and the test concluded.

The kennels had six compartments on either side of the central run allowing room for twelve dogs. There were just six currently assigned to the base so, given the reputation of sentry dogs, a decision was made to put the animal in the furthest cage. Unloaded from the truck cage and into his new home, a larger pen, he was snapping and snarling as he paced along the chain link fence, checking out the new territory. The other dogs were hanging back in their cages, clearly convinced a new Alpha dog had arrived.

The kennel master was a buck sergeant, a blonde haired, blued-eyed, corn-fed big old boy from central Georgia named Cody. He entered the central run wearing only an arm throw, even though a full body suit was available. A dog in training learns to attack the closest bit of meat to it and that thick piece of foam wrapped in leather allows a handler to let the dog experience taking a bite while protecting the trainer from those bone-snapping teeth.

Cody told another handler to slide open the door that would allow the dog into the run with him. He came boiling out and made straight for Cody's outstretched arm. The dog launched itself and as its teeth sunk into the leather, Cody used judo technique, borrowing the flying dog's kinetic energy to slam it into the ground where it let our a yelp of pain but turned to renew the attack. It was pretty close quarters and that wildly aggressive dog came off the concrete floor, intent on making a meal of Cody's junk, but was instead, like poor old Ed on that dust-off helo, introduced to Cody's size twelve black leather combat boot. That boot tip caught that unsuspecting beast right below the chin, flipping him backwards while the dog howled and cried in pain as is slammed into the floor.

The dog had had enough at that point and slunk back to his cage but the door was closed and Cody was advancing. The dog lunged for the wrap again and Cody slammed him into the ground, then physically pinned the now terrorized dog. Ordering the door opened, Cody grabbed that terrified animal up by the neck and threw it inside to lick its wounds.

The next day Cody came to the kennel and called for the door to be opened. The dog came out, saw Cody and stayed inside. Cody walked into the cage and beat the crap out of that cowering and crying dog to complete his domination of the now docile and subservient creature. Next thing you know, they were buddies and the newly christened "King" was certified as ready to begin law enforcement training.

I'd seen the training and watched as Cody and King rode patrol together and it seemed like they had a good relationship, but to my mind, I didn't trust that dog as far as I could throw it. Given it weighed one hundred pounds, I couldn't throw it from here to there.

Oliver had gotten an assignment and, given my performance on the security side of the flight line, I was brought up to be the radio operator/dispatcher and alarm monitor while Al assumed the title of Desk Sergeant and directed any response as the situation dictated. Air Force installations contain an astonishing amount of terribly expensive and highly classified equipment and systems. All of those buildings and many rooms within buildings were alarmed against entry. Any activation required checking for a fault and if none was detected, dispatching a patrol, as well as waking up the owner of the facility, for them to come down to see what the problem was. The pace of activity could go from dead slow to "hair fully ablaze" in less than a minute, like when a student pilot crashes an F-4 phantom jet into another F-4 over the training range, or a car accident with injuries occurs or an alarm goes off at the bank, so two people were necessary.

The station house was a large two-story building, whitewashed with orange tile roofing, done in the art deco style favored when the base was built in the early 1930s and set at an intersection that would allow police cars and trucks to exit and immediately be oriented in any direction, as this greatly aided in response times.

Walking in the front door, a visitor passed the Superintendent's office, the senior NCO overseeing all law enforcement operations and personnel. He had a board in his office with a laminated ID card photo of each airman, where they were assigned, and duty status, so he could always reach out for anybody he needed. The office opposite belonged to the **O**fficer **i**n **C**harge (OIC), a figure rarely seen. A first lieutenant, he'd been a scratch golfer in college and could make a 470-yard hole in just two strokes. That drive made him popular whenever any general was playing a round, because MacDill, having no fewer than thirteen general officers assigned at the time, and two of them four-star generals, were all happy to have the young officer in their foursome. After a round they'd all let him know it while they unwound at the base Marina and Yacht club. He was generally carried on the status board as assigned "personal security protection."

This was nothing unusual in the early seventies, because we also had assigned the youngest Army Brigadier General, then forty-two years old, who was famous for having hookers come out to the base. The first time several showed up in one car and said they were there to visit, I followed protocol and called his house to verify they were his intended guests. He vouched for them, adding, "Come out when you get off duty!" I declined, but I admired his style. I also declined the pimp's offer to drive his ladies, opting instead to have a patrol take the girls to his quarters on the golf course and return them when the social event was finished. I thought his "Superfly-styled" pimpmobile a mobile advertisement for his services and best not admitted on the installation.

Along the wall, just before stairs leading up to the investigations office, was a steel gray Westinghouse stand-alone refrigerated water fountain that had been installed when the building was new in 1934. It had a push button, but also a foot pedal in case your hands were full.

I was on the desk that morning. To my left was a bank of black paneled alarms; each had a voltage meter, amber, red, and green function light, an annunciator that would squawk to get your attention, plus a toggle switch to reset or deactivate the system. In front of me was a rotary dial multi-line phone with fifteen lines. One was the emergency line, another only for bomb threats, three non-emergency lines, the squadron intercom system and direct lines to the Command Post, Wing Commander's office, Base Commander's office, Fire Department, Emergency Room, Tower, Base Operations and the two gates.

This was the Vietnam Air Force after all and we had plenty of telecommunications technicians killing time until their next TDY. I realized this while drinking beers at the grass shack marina bar at two in the afternoon after pistol team practice ended. I saw a Chief Master Sergeant, in his blues, sitting on a stool drinking and having a great time. A black, no dial, direct line phone was attached to one of the poles in the Tiki-hut-themed bar and if it ever rang he'd walk over and answer it. I inquired and he freely shared that he was the Chief in charge of the base personnel/assignments office and proudly declared his office could run very well without him, so not wishing to sit in an empty office all day, he called his Chief buddy at the Comm squadron and had the direct line installed.

My seat on the elevated desk afforded me a clear view of the entrance and stairs. On the other side of the alarm panel was a small open room with coffee maker and couch for complainants or suspects who came in. To my right sat Al and in front of him a Remington manual typewriter and identical multi-line phone. The desk was elevated in traditional police fashion and the two wooden steps were just to Al's right. The distance to the jail access door was less than ten feet and the box of gas grenades were still under the counter, minus the one.

It was mid-morning and pleasant owing to all the administrators being out of their offices and wandering about the base. The superintendent was out for coffee while the OIC was teeing off with some admiral. The rising sun's rays were just slanting on to the shiny black and white linoleum tile floors that had been cleaned just a few hours earlier by some new guy on midnight shifts. Everything was going fine until the very large frame of Cody filled the doorway. He was accompanied by King, now declared to be an agent of law enforcement and protector of human friends.

I didn't trust that dog. There was something in its eyes that said, "I might have to kiss this big dope's ass, but I can sure as hell tear yours up!" Of that I had no doubt and pushed my chair back a bit while slowly unsnapping a strap and freeing the Smith and Wesson revolver currently holstered on my right hip.

I'd seen that dog in action and knew I'd put all six bullets into him just to make certain he was absolutely dead if he got away from Cody. As they came in, Cody tapped the top of the fountain while stepping on the plate. He took a drink and then tapped it again for King to have a drink. The dog stood on hind legs and began slobbering, slurping and sending rehydrated dog drool flying all over and mainly on the formerly clean floor. I stood up and yelled at him, "Hey! Get that goddamn dog off the fountain —its for humans, and then get it the fuck out of here before I shoot it." Cody tried to calm me down by saying, "Hey, his mouth is cleaner than yours and I got him, he'll obey me."

I wasn't buying it and verbalized my self-defense argument and use of deadly force justification by telling him to make sure he kept tight control on that dog. I told him I'd kill it because it scared the hell out of me and I had no where to go if it came up those steps.

Right then Sergeant Al of Assisi got inspired, and being a hard-shell, slap-happy, primitive-Baptist, he believed that all can be redeemed, a philosophy he'd share while trying to recruit me to go to yet another revival meeting. He turned in his chair and now facing the steps said, "Come here, King, come here, that's a good boy," and Cody let the lead loose. King wandered over and started licking Al's outstretched right hand, being all friendly and letting Al scratch behind his ear. I had my hand on the checkered wooden grip of my pistol to draw it in a flash, and I wasn't taking my eyes off that monster until it went back out the door.

Al twisted halfway back towards me and was absently stroking King's muzzle while telling me, "See? He's all better now and a really good boy, who's a good boy?..." and I couldn't tell, but maybe he stuck King in the eye, because something triggered that psychotic mutt and it starting snacking on Al's forearm while Al screamed. I screamed while snatching my pistol from the holster, ready to kill that dog as soon as I had either a clear shot or it killed Al and dragged him down the steps like some overfed Raggedy-Andy doll.

I'd pulled back the hammer when Cody snapped the lead and choked the stupid dog out so it would finally let go of Al. I called Pops and had a patrol take Al to the emergency room where he required a bunch of stitches and cast for his fractured wrist, but was otherwise OK. I told Pops what happened; he called Cody and told him he was banned from the desk area and that was good enough for me.

We finished the cycle and went into days off. When we came back from our three days off and began three swing shift tours, Al was back on limited duty and wearing his right arm in a sling. I welcomed him back and told him he was a goofy bastard to want to try to make friends with a dog about as crazy as a shit-house rat. He told me kindly that King was simply misunderstood. I liked that, misunderstood. I'd grown up with Stuart, a terribly "misunderstood" kid, so I knew crazy, and had no misunderstanding about that dog being just as crazy as Stuart ever was.

The weather was still pleasant, but getting warmer, and the sun's rays were now creeping slowly back down the hallway to the entrance, when the doorway again filled with Cody's massive frame and that frightening hell-hound. I immediately stood up, unsnapped my holster and put my hand on the pistol grip saying, "You aren't supposed to be here and need to take that nasty-ass killing machine with you before I kill it!"

Cody pulled up the lead and was ready to take the dog out when Al said, "I asked him to come by. I know that King is sorry about what he did and I want to show you that he's not a bad dog."

It was Al's show, he was an NCO, so I put my back against the wall and waited. Al turned in his seat a full ninety degrees to face King head on. I watched that dog's eyes soften as he put his head on Al's right thigh, Al's left hand now stroking his muzzle.

An alarm panel annunciator went off at that moment, startling me and Al, but mainly King who took it out on Al's left hand, although in fairness, Cody had King choked out very quickly and this time Al only needed a couple of stitches.

+++

The Hazards Of Cross Cultural Sexual Advice

It was early Friday afternoon and I was walking down the hallway of our barracks to the showers when I passed the open doorway of Eddie, a black guy I knew by sight and to nod at. I tossed in a greeting, saying, "Hey, what's going on?" and ordinarily getting a response like "It ain't nothing but a thing…" or my favorite, "Time in grade and the rent, motherfucker."

Eddie worked another shift so I just tossed in a greeting, but in that moment, flash frozen in my memory, was Eddie, naked and sitting on a chair, with his legs splayed and presenting, for my astonishment, a remarkably large ebony penis, well, the largest penis that ever hung right in front of me, and in the military, communal showers guarantee a lot of penis-noticing. It certainly went the distance in supporting the stereotype of black guys having big dicks.

Before I could say anything, and while running the mental check list of all the things I could not say, keeping in mind the ever present not-to-be-crossed-inference and never-alleged line of homosexuality. I also noticed that he was holding his flaccid member in one palm while stoking it gently with a cotton ball. I saw the open bottle of isopropyl rubbing alcohol and shot him a "What the fuck are you doing to your dick?" look. Eddie picked up the cue and said, "Taking care of the equipment, got to be ready when the ladies call."

I couldn't argue with the truth of that statement but thought it not a good idea for him to be hanging a cigarette in his mouth (like he was.) Before I could remark he said, "I heard you be laying up in some bitch's crib downtown, my MAN!" I had a reputation. Who knew? I acknowledged his accolade and to return the compliment said, "Yeah, she's all right, but we need to change it up, you got any tips or pointers?"

To my great relief, Eddie stopped stroking his sizable unit and gave me a thoughtful look, well as thoughtful as a guy can be who's holding his schlong in his left hand. He tossed the cotton ball and, taking the cigarette from his lips, said these exact words: "Ice is nice." I heard him but I shook my head and asked him to repeat that. He leaned forward and said, "Ice. Is. Nice." That said, he took a big drag off his Kool and laid back in the chair. Taking that cue to mean my audience with our in-residence sexual Mister Wizard was at an end, I was free to go and use that knowledge.

Truth was I'd been dating a college girl for a couple of months, since the beginning of the summer; a sexually liberated wild hippie from Miami. With her shiny black tresses, bright blue eyes, full figure and willingness to try new things, she alone robbed me of my virginity when all the painted women of Ciudad Acuña could not, and now, just like a dog who'd been befriended, I'd become quite emotionally enamored of her as well. As it happened, I was working afternoon shifts, getting off at ten so I could be at her apartment by ten thirty, in time for some fun.

I got there shortly after eleven, watched some TV and had a drink before going to bed. It was hot in the apartment; her roommate had gone home for the summer, and she couldn't afford to run the air conditioning so we slept with all the windows open to try to catch any breeze. It was warm, now early Saturday morning, sometime after three, when I woke up from my doze covered in sweat despite having taken a cooling shower following our congress.

I heard the old guy across the cobblestone street get out of a cab and begin to hobble up a bleached-out navy-gray termite-riddled wooden staircase that looked about half ready to collapse. His wife always threw the bolt when she went to bed. This was smart, because although lacking a formal education, and many of her teeth, she saw the ship of Tampa's favorite Pirate, José Gaspar, docked a few blocks away and knew it encouraged her husband's bad behavior. She also rented her downstairs screened-in sleeping porch to a couple of carnies in town for a month of work at the State Fair, over near the University of Tampa, and you just never knew about those people. She also knew that campus was full of New York hippies and so was the party house on the corner, with drunken frat boys carrying on at all hours, so who knew what kind of people who might be up to no good, were out and about at night?

In fairness, there was significant criminal activity in the Hyde Park district of Tampa in 1972, but given the multiple ailments requiring her to huff from a portable oxygen tank, it just seemed unlikely any rapist would climb those rickety stairs to take advantage of her breathless beauty. This was just a weekly comic farce put on for any inadvertent audience. He would climb those darkened stairs slowly, sometimes muttering when he stumbled on a loose stair, or cursing when he picked up a new splinter from the equally deteriorated handrails, before finally reaching the top. Always the optimist, he'd toss open the screen door and try the front door which would always be bolted so he'd bang on it while yelling her name. A few moments later, the hundred watt yellow bug light would come on a few feet from his head and startling him, while she'd yell, "Who is it?" loud enough for us to hear across the street. He'd yell back that it was her husband and, finally convinced, she'd open the door for him to come in, but when she smelled the liquor on him, she'd start yelling at him all over again. Sometimes she let him come all the way in unmolested, other nights she'd throw him out, and once even got him rolling down a few steps. Tonight was just a bit of yelling before she let that poor bastard come inside to sleep it off.

It was hot and when it got too hot there just wasn't any meaningful sleep to be had. It wasn't like you could go out on the screened porch and take in the night air because there wasn't any porch, just a balcony with rusted hand rails and a view that was the parking lot. Even the drunken bacchanal that was the annual Gasparilla Day parade, which started at the pier just two blocks away, ignored our street, Hyde Park Place. Those pirates from the Gaspar preferred to begin their sack of Tampa on foot, and one block over, on Magnolia Street, before joining the fleet in front of the conveniently named Magnolia Street Bar and Grill, and thence on to the campus.

I couldn't sleep. I tried but was just tossing and turning, so much so that my girlfriend half woke up and said, "What's the matter?" I told her I was up and to just go back to sleep. I slipped out of the bed, walked into the kitchen and poured a glass of tap water. I opened the freezer and pulled out the aluminum ice tray. It was filled and to get those cubes I pulled the sides alway from the ice, then lifted the handle on top that cracked the ice into manageable cubes and put three in my drink.

Right then my girlfriend yelled "*What are you doing in there*?" This phrase has been directed at me by every woman who had ever entered my life. I first heard my Aunt Lizzie yelling at Uncle Dom if he stepped out of the room for more than a minute. She did this even if he was going to the bathroom. One day he finally had enough and said, "Whattaya think I'm gonna do, Liz? I'm goin' to New Jersey to use the bathroom so I'll be gone for a while." After that, when I noticed my mother asking the same question, I began to answer, "I'm going to Jersey."

Of course I couldn't say that and risk annoying my girlfriend, given I was just eighteen and newly initiated into the joys of sex. I was restless, bored, and perpetually horny, which was fine, but as I was likewise woefully unsophisticated in the ways of romantic love, Eddie's words came to me unbidden. Newly armed with great clarity of purpose, I drank the water but took those somewhat melted and rounded cubes with me.

I was ready to go as soon as I walked back in the door. She was still dozing, but laying on her back, atop the sheets, she presenting a vision in the mottled light of a street lamp filtered through palm fronds. I took two steps forward and upon reaching the edge of the mattress, knelt on the bed and began my seduction. She started to protest but, trusting Eddie, I said, "Sshhhhh, you're gonna like this a lot." I grabbed one of the smooth cubes from my glass to begin as Eddie the Lothario had instructed.

I never even got close.

In fact I wound up getting both injured and estranged. Some water dripped from my hand and splattered somewhere on her mid-thigh. Even though asleep, the frigid water signaled her brain, resulting in an instantaneous bucking I then mistakenly interpreted for Eddie's promised sexual arousal. When her left knee drew up as she rolled to toss me off, she hit me where it hurt. The pain was incredible as I fell off the bed and on to the floor. She was screaming and threw me out of the apartment. I quickly dressed and drove back to the base, took a shower and went to bed in my air conditioned room where all I could do was wonder how I went wrong.

A few days later I was walking past Eddie's room where he was mercifully just shining his shoes and I confronted him with, "What the fuck were you talking about? Fucking ice is nice bullshit!"

Eddie drew back, looking wounded. "What are you talking about? What happened?" I gave him the full report and he laughed, then called over another guy, and telling him, and that guy started laughing. All Eddie could say was "Sorry, my man, I thought you'd understand you just put an ice chip on your tongue so you thrill her and chill her when you take it to her going down. You dig?"

I got it. I was also cut off for the foreseeable future, but after that I always made sure I understood exactly what somebody was telling me.

+++

Burl And The Fat Man

Burl was an angry black guy from Philadelphia. He never said why he came in the Air Force but, most of the time I worked with him, he was complaining about "the man" who had been responsible for all of the wrong that had befallen him. His efforts at fighting the power consisted of letting his afro grow longer than regulations permitted. Air Force Regulations directed that an afro could not extend more than two inches from the skull and Jamaican dread locks were banned outright. Like many other black guys at the time, Burl would crank his 'fro down and stuff it under a *do-rag*, a piece of nylon stocking used to cover the top of his head. This "skullcap" compacted his hair so it fit under his white duty hat. He put that hat on when he left the barracks and only released his hair from it's prison at the end of a shift when back in the barracks.

For a long time, our Wing Commander, unimpressed by the lax grooming standards he found on flight line maintenance troops, tasked us with standing outside the dining hall for five minutes before and after we ate. Our job was monitoring dress and appearance standards, making on the spot corrections as needed and sending a notice of infraction to Command. Hands in pocket, jacket unzipped, shoes not shined, all were noted on a small blue chit, a DD Form 341, and sent to the offender's unit for action. We even used a ruler to measure afro hair length. Because we were armed and first responders with only twenty minutes to eat, we would go to the front of the line. We'd pass all those guys we just wrote up which made us even less popular.

One of our group, Johnny, was a native Floridian, from South Bay, just below Lake Okeechobee. He made the mistake of writing up a recently promoted A1C cook who was coming back from a smoke break. Johnny got into the chow line and that cook switched places with another server, taking over the spaghetti station. He made a big plate of pasta, sauced it up, and when Johnny slid his tray on by, put the plate on the serving counter, then quickly flipped it on Johnny, splattering his uniform with that hot saucy mess. At his hearing in front of his commander, that cook claimed it was an accident, but his commander disagreed and took both his stripes to make an example not to screw with cops just doing their jobs.

One day, while working the Dale Mabry gate, Burl told me he was a member of the Black Panther Party, a revolutionary black nationalist and socialist organization. I told him I remembered answering a question about belonging to any groups calling for the violent overthrow of the American way of life on the initial entry security clearance application form. I reminded him this was a form he must have filled out when he enlisted, adding, "You know the OSI (Office of Special Investigations) checks those things don't you?" He didn't and when that realization hit him, he said he had to sit down. That was the end of his claim to being a Panther. The next day he got a fresh tight haircut and a do-rag was no longer in his wardrobe.

Burl and I got along and sometimes we were directed to be a two-man patrol responsible for building security checks and any cash escorts requiring armed guards, because cash was still king in the early seventies. Airmen and retirees would get their checks in the mail and cash them at the bank or credit union, then spend that cash at the Base Exchange (BX) department store or the Commissary, a non-profit grocery store. On any payday, the receipts could be in the hundreds of thousands of dollars. Those dollars now had to go from the Commissary to the accounting and finance office where the paperwork would be dropped off. From there it was across the street, on foot, to the commercial bank for deposit, this small journey necessitating the use of a two-manned armed escort.

The last afternoon Burl worked escort duty, we'd been dispatched to escort the Commissary Manager making a cash drop. We drove up to the rear entrance, walked through the warehouse and into the manager's office. An amiable fellow from Alabama, this man was courtly and used "sir" when talking to people. In addition to a rather thick southern accent, he also possessed a remarkably pronounced butt, no doubt a genetic trait, but one very much larger than his chest. This gave him a more than passing resemblance to a large pear on stick legs. He greeted us with a nod and took his time getting ready.

He was authorized to be armed, so he reached into his gunmetal gray government issued desk and pulled out a green fabric web belt and dark brown leather holster that held the .45 caliber semiautomatic pistol he wore on his right hip. His butt made the pistol point out more than down, so I always walked to his left. After picking up his two lockable leather and fabric sacks packed with cash, Burl and I made our way back to the loading dock and the manager's car. Burl peeled off to get our patrol car and bring it up and behind him while I kept an overwatch on the area.

We successfully followed him on the short drive past the flying squadron hangers and orange tile-roofed support buildings, turning left on to the main road through the base before finally pulling in to the finance office parking lot. Getting out of our cars we followed him inside and waited while he conducted the business there, then followed him back outside to walk across the street where he would drop the cash at the bank.

As we came outside, he asked me, "Sir, now what would you do if a car with some gunmen pulled up and demanded these bags?" I told him it depended on the circumstances, but this was only money, and not mine, so no sense dying, besides, they'd never get off the base. He appeared satisfied and then turned to Burl saying, "What would you do, boy?"

I knew it was that word "boy" that elicited Burl's response and I made a point of sharing that with the OIC later, but in that moment, as we walked and the manager's arms stood out at almost thirty-five degrees, holding those bags, swaying as he waddled across the street at a rapid pace, I knew this would be good.

Burl just looked back at him and said evenly, "I'd knock your fat ass down and use your big butt as a barricade."

+++

I'll Be The Doctor, Thanks

I was working patrol, dispatched to the Bayshore Gate to provide an escort for a civilian ambulance carrying an airman who'd been involved in a motorcycle accident off base. I led the ambulance to the Base Hospital, then followed the attendants as they wheeled a gurney, with a sheet covering the body, into the ER as a newly assigned doctor walked up quickly while undoing the stethoscope from around his neck. The driver said, "No hurry, Doc, this guy's dead." The doctor looked at him and snorted in derision, "Oh really? You a doctor now? Because I am and I'll make that determination, thank you very much."

The doc drew up and pulled the sheet back to reveal the body of the unfortunate airman whose head was neatly tucked into the crook of his right elbow.

The doc's eyes grew wide, but all he said was, "Everybody gets lucky once."

+++

Morning, Lick My Dick.

Airman First Class Roach was another one of those guys who hated the USAF and made no secret of it. A committed draft dodger, he'd signed up two years earlier and was still in his first assignment at MacDill. Lacking any motivation, his promotion to sergeant had been denied so he was just waiting for his time to be up. He was a perennial gate guard because none of the other guys ever wanted to work with him on patrol. A noxious complainer, he took every opportunity to share not only how bad his life was now, but how bad it was going to become after he got out, because life always sucked for him.

He was especially resentful of the young pilots in training because they always had beautiful wives or girlfriends who were playing tennis on the courts by the beach wearing short white skirts. He spent so much time maintaining the security of those courts that, after enough complaints of "some creepy cop always watching us through binoculars," management put in green privacy slats and Roach was permanently and forever assigned gate duty.

Being a gate guard was pretty simple. Look for the DoD decal on the bumper or windshield, note the color code, then wave the person in. Blue is an officer, so smile and render a salute while saying, "Good morning, Sir or Ma'am." Yellow is an NCO, red is enlisted, white is civilian, and for them it was a smile and a cheerful "Good Morning!" If you called an NCO "sir" the usual response was "Don't sir me, I work for a living." If there was no decal and no military ID, they'd be pulled over and the other guard would issue a pass or deny entry. You waved traffic for thirty minutes and then went on break. You could read the paper, but there were always those moments when karma would smile, delivering a carload of pretty eighteen year-old bikini-clad daughters of senior officers or NCOs who wanted to use the base beach and were in a friend's car with no decal. Those passes took much longer to write.

In late December it was getting cool at night. Some days frost was visible on the cars coming on base and most drivers had their windows rolled up and the heaters on, so they couldn't hear your greeting if you gave one. I was working with Roach at the Bayshore gate and he was complaining about having to give any greetings at all, while I was more interested in sitting next to the small electric heater we had inside the art-deco styled gate shack. The small room barely held a desk, chair, Igloo water cooler and two telephones.

The boredom and routine of working the graveyard shift with nothing for company or stimulation were the greatest dangers to a gate guard. One evening I saw a crawdad making its way towards the Bay; sadly, it chose to stop in the traffic lane. When I approached, this tough bug would rise up, ready for anything. It wouldn't back down and wouldn't go away, despite me telling it to leave, so I began inching closer to the traffic lane. What that feisty crawdad didn't realize was drivers recognize a proximity around their car and subconsciously adjust to avoid striking any object. To avoid me, those cars would move slightly to the right, and within two cars passing that crawdad was road smear. This is what boredom led to.

Daytime and a significantly increased duty-day traffic volume mandated two cops on the gate, but even then there are moments of boredom, like on any Sunday, the only day people weren't expected to be in their offices. One such Sunday morning, I was working with a black guy named Mac originally from St. Louis. We'd been in the same training class and he was a part of our tight little group. The newspaper delivery guys would drop off copies of their paper for the guards to read and the Sunday papers were the biggest and best editions. Likewise, the pharmaceutical rep gave each gate a case of Mylanta antacid every month so each guy had his own bottle. This was a great kindness because around twenty-thousand cars a day came through those gates and the noise was constant. When you had just a twenty-minute lunch break during which you ate too fast, coupled with the aircraft screaming overhead all day and the unannounced alarm exercise or robbery drill, all the while working sixty-hour weeks, the Mylanta was a life saver and that representative a patriot.

That quiet Sunday was lovely, with Chamber of Commerce "post card" weather, bright and sunny with white fluffy clouds ambling by. I'd been waving traffic for thirty minutes and wanted a break for a cigarette since there was no smoking while waving. I tried to get Mac's attention and said, "Your turn," but Mac was engrossed in the comics section of the newspaper, which ran eight pages, and so he gave me an "Uh huh," and I knew he hadn't heard a word I said. I saw he was fully engaged and reading some comic strip. He'd done this before so I knew he really wanted to finish all those comics before he got up.

I gave him a few minutes to finish the page he was on. In a complete disregard of established protocols and unspoken agreements, he turned to the next page and was reading yet another comic. Seeing no traffic approaching us, I took out my official 25th Anniversary USAF engraved Zippo lighter, struck it, and lit the bottom of the page on fire. Mac was so engrossed that it took a few moments for him to realize the paper was burning. He spotted the flames as they engulfed Alley Oop, a time traveling caveman. He jumped up yelling, "What the fuck?" as he swatted out the flames and I lit a smoke.

It was still the sexual revolution in America and we were often the happy recipients of women exercising a newly found sexual liberation. One young woman, a hard-shell Baptist named Charleen, would come to the Bayshore gate on Tuesday evenings driving her 1969 powder blue Mercury Cougar convertible, wearing peach-colored hot pants with white knee-high go-go boots. Her dark blonde hair was perfectly coifed in a french bun, not a hair out of place, thanks to generous applications of CFC-laden hairspray. She came with the idea of finding lost souls, and possibly a husband in search of salvation, and where better to look than a military base with nothing but a bunch of lonely young guys who needed saving?

In order to achieve her goal, Charleen, a comely salesman for Jesus, would use her abundant good looks to capture the attention of many a lonely young airman. She'd get out of her car, strolling by and asking if anybody wanted to take a ride to the beach and talk about Jesus. Once at the beach, she switched to giving "Blowjobs for Jesus" in return for a promise to attend church with her on a Sunday. She was so committed to her cause that it became a matter of routine to see her coming and call the desk to request a thirty minute relief break. A patrol vehicle would come by to step in and the relieved guard would go with Charlene for that ride while she would proselytize as best she knew how. Although many were called, none were saved, but all were better for the experience.

And so it was that cold winter morning when Roach became bored with the routine and decided to change things up. He'd wave traffic through while rendering the appropriate honors to the occupant of the car, always saying, "Good Morning" as required. He decided it'd be fun when seeing a good-looking woman sitting alone behind the wheel with the window up to cheerfully say, "Good morning, lick my dick!"

Seated at the desk, I could look out the casement window and see him waist level and also the cars passing by. I knew this was a bad idea and told him to knock it off, but he paid no heed. He'd say it and laugh and was now twenty minutes into his second wave period when a green Volkswagen beetle came puttering up. A blue officer's decal was visible on the windshield and the car was being driven by a remarkably attractive woman. Roach had straightened to attention, brought his right arm up to the shiny black brim of the white hat identifying his police function and said happily, "Good morning, ma'am, lick my dick!" as he completed the wave thru motion.

The VW had been in neutral while coasting past Roach and instead of the clutch being engaged and the car picking up speed, I heard a sharp chirp as the brakes locked the four tires in place. I stood up and went out the rear entrance so I was closer to the car than Roach, who was now stopping traffic.

The window came rolling down and this stunning woman with dark brown hair and very blue eyes stuck her head out the window and looked straight at Roach saying, "Did you know I could read lips and a name tag, Airman Roach?" and with that she was gone in a puff of light blue smoke from her exhaust pipe.

The phone rang an hour later, right around the time a patrol vehicle was arriving with his replacement.

What Roach didn't know until his Article 15 non-judicial punishment hearing was that the woman was the wife of a pilot who had grown up with a deaf brother. Now a one stripe airman, Roach was deemed non-recoverable and assigned to base weeds and seeds, never to be seen again.

+++

CHAPTER FOUR

Time To Roll

This Isn't What You Think

It was January 1973. I'd flown home for Christmas and New Years as a surprise for my mother and had just returned. After unpacking, I hopped into the car to visit my girlfriend. I drove those seven miles with a smile as I patted the ring box in my pocket. In retrospect, I probably should have called, but didn't. When I got to her apartment, I ran up those stairs, still kicking around how I was going to word the proposal. I went inside and saw the empty living room and saw her bedroom door was closed. I walked down the hallway and threw the door open wide while taking a deep breath, only to witness her engaged in some intimate and animated activities with two guys from the frat house next door.

Now relieved of having to make any sort of coherent speech pledging fidelity and affection while I offered the ring, I sat on the living room couch and was treated to witness two guys sheepishly walking out while tugging on their shirts. Shortly thereafter, my now demure soon-to-be former girlfriend appeared, wrapped in a pink robe she held cinched at the neck with her right hand, while she ran her other hand through her thoroughly tousled raven locks saying, "This isn't what you think."

Not imagining what else it could be, I decided my time in the Sunshine State was coming to an end; it was time to broaden my horizons. I drove back to the base, parked my car in the barracks lot, then walked over to the personnel office and put in as an immediate volunteer for a short notice assignment to Vietnam.

The big personnel office in Denver was still sending cops to Vietnam and I had one year in at MacDill so I was eligible, and my orders to Tan Son Nhat airport in Saigon came through three days later. I called the guy I was replacing and asked if he had any advice for me regarding what to pack since I could bring a maximum of three hundred pounds of personal property. I really didn't have anything special that I wanted to take and figured I'd do like all the other Vietnam vets and buy a state of the art stereo system when I got there. There was static on the line and I thought I heard him say, "Bring cold cream." I wasn't sure I had it right, so I asked him to say it again. " Cold cream, cold cream, bring three hundred pounds of Ponds because the gooks are crazy for it!"

I was excited and ready to push off, so I called back home to share the news. My mother screamed and, when my father asked what was the matter, she told him I was going to Vietnam. All my father said was, "Be sure to use condoms."

On Jan 22, 1973, LBJ died at age 64, the last "combat-related" death in a vastly unpopular war. Having achieved their political goal, and apparently hearing I was coming, the North Vietnamese government signed the Paris Peace accords on January 27, 1973. So instead of being there for the end of Vietnam and getting that new stereo, I was still considered available by the assignment machine to go anywhere it chose. By random luck it assigned me from the **T**actical **A**ir **C**ommand (TAC) to a **M**ilitary **A**irflift **C**ommand (MAC) installation, the 1605th Air Base Group at Lajes Field in the Portuguese Azores.

My knowledge of the globe was admittedly superficial as I learned when my OIC came in from the golf course one day, inviting me into his office to fill me in about my new orders. He started by asking me if I knew where the Azores were. I told him "Isn't that where Captain Binghamton is always threatening to send McHale?," a reference to the then popular TV comedy "*McHale's Navy*" The OIC just shook his head and said, "That would be the Aleutian Islands, Dummy. The Azores are some islands in the middle Atlantic." I wasn't sure about that; the only islands I was aware of besides Long Island was Hawaii. I snorted in disbelief, adding, "Sir, there aren't any islands in the Atlantic." Suppressing a groan, he pulled down a global map and pointed to the nine-island archipelago pretty much right in the middle of the Atlantic, just like he said.

All I could do was think, "Oh shit." +++

Second Assignment — 1605th Air Base Group

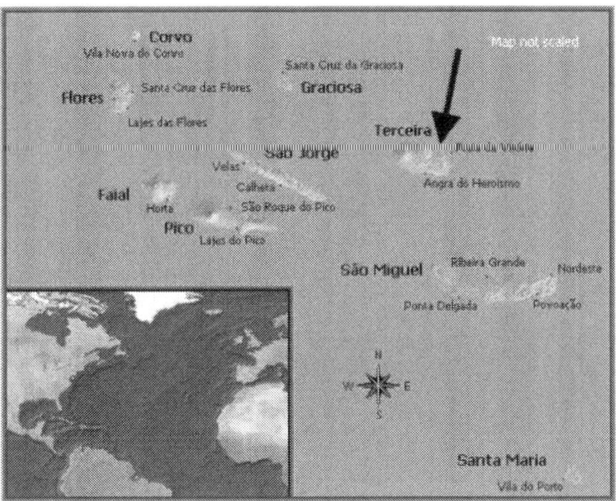

I arrived at Lajes in the summer of 1973 after a flight from McGuire Air Force Base in New Jersey. Two of my buddies from Syosset drove me the hundred miles to the base. I had to arrive six hours early to check in and wait for a flight that was usually four hours late. I reciprocated by buying them many rounds of drinks at the enlisted club, where all drinks were a quarter. They finally left shortly after eight and I processed in for the flight. The two-striper gate agent took the grooming regulation, AFR 35-10, very seriously and I was directed to trim my mustache using a disposable Bic razor. This was painful, but still better than the guy in front of me in the line who broke the zipper on his traveling pair of uniform pants and had to use a safety pin. The flight began to load around midnight and the crew announced our itinerary using a very loud public address system, as if anybody would want to stow aboard the C-141 Starlifter on a "trash hauler" flight from McGuire to Lajes to Rhein Main in Frankfurt, Germany. We were seated backwards — the best position to survive a crash, our flight attendant/load master/engineer cheerfully informed us; while another crew dog passed out the foam ear plugs. Being a cop and working on the flight line, I had my own fitted ear protection and shoved them in because one poor mommy, going to join her husband on assignment somewhere, was traveling with two little kids, and neither of them was happy and letting us all know it. The wailing from the row in front of us continued from loading until two hours into the flight. During that time, either I got used to it or they synced their wails with the engines.

I passed that flight in a state of semi-awareness because there was no stimulation, just a few dim lights, no windows, and only a couple of portholes. No thought had been given by the designers to passenger comfort and you had to stand up to look out one of the tiny portholes and then, because military jets flew higher than civilian airliners, there was less to see. Time meant nothing, we were just in a state of existence waiting for the gear to go down when we reached final approach. During the flight, you could take a break, walk the aisle and into the cargo area, or you could get coffee near the stairs to the flight deck. You had to take a visit to the on-board toilet, as cramped and spartan a design imaginable and manufactured by the lowest bidder. It was just a small toilet with waste container in a tiny box that could be wheeled on and off the plane. That is where I paid the terrible tariff for my over-indulgence at McGuire.

After several hours aloft the plane landed, taxied for a few minutes, then opened the rear cargo doors just before stopping, when the engineer said, "All Lajes passengers get out!" I stood up with two other guys, Dale and Scotty, and we walked towards the palletized cargo, pulled our duffel bags plus garment bags and walked down the ramp. We stepped well away from the aircraft, moving to the grass infield while the big plane buttoned up, having no additional cargo for Lajes.

An Air Force blue pickup truck with a lighted signboard saying, "Follow Me" came around and parked by us, as we heard the four Pratt & Whitney TF33-P-7 turbofans spool up. We watched the Starlifter lumber down the high speed taxiway to line up on the runway and depart for Germany. It turned onto the designated runway and, as it was the first (and only) plane in line for departure, instantly tore down the concrete. Its nose lifted, the gray and white bird took flight; quickly becoming a diminishing speck against the azure sky, and soon gone from sight, while the complete silence on the flight line overwhelmed me.

Once the roar of those engines faded, all that was left was the sounds of insects buzzing about the grass, and some cows peacefully grazing in a pasture just outside the barbed wire fence, marking the airbase perimeter. The "Follow Me" guy told us he'd called the Ops desk, a car was being sent, and with that he was gone, leaving the three of us to look to the Southwest and the peak of a mountain top where the clouds were resting. I could hear chickens in the nearby village and a bell tolled once, announcing the quarter hour, and for some reason I thought, "I wonder if this is what Puerto Rico looks like?" and it didn't seem so bad.

After ten minutes or so of standing in the warm mid-day sunshine, a patrol car driving very slowly came into view down the almost empty ramp, finally pulling up after a minute or so. The driver, Doug, was a taciturn Staff Sergeant, and a twenty-year vet, with fifteen of those on this island. He'd gone native, married a local girl on his first tour and just kept extending. With a pipe clenched between his teeth, he said, "Leave the bags, he barked, another unit will get them and bring them to the barracks. The Superintendent is eager to meet you." I learned that Doug wasn't comfortable shifting out of second gear as we crept off the flight line.

Oh great, I thought, I'm hung over with a raggedy mustache, but after looking at my travel companions I felt a little better. Turned out, the guy with the busted zipper was Dale, tall, white, and slender, a Mormon from Ogden, Utah. Sitting in the front seat was Scotty, a short black guy from Gary, Indiana, wearing non-regulation black platform disco shoes and sporting a small gold earring he'd put back in his ear after "that Nazi gate agent dude at McGuire" made him pull it out before being allowed to get on the flight. Even with my raggedy mustache, I'd just come off winning Base Airman of the Month at MacDill, so I figured I was OK.

The road rose rapidly as we inched along and we finally passed the entrance to Portuguese Air Base Zone 4 Command staff offices. We crested the top and I was my treated to a 220 degree view to the East, the mid-Atlantic nothing-but-endless blue water and no other spec of land to be seen amongst those vast deep blue waters. It was at that moment I caught "Island Fever," the overwhelming feeling of isolation that can develop when you internally realize you are stuck on an island and not going anywhere else without a plane or a boat. This was certainly a massive shock to my system as I'd never really contemplated what life would actually be like on a small island in the middle of the Atlantic Ocean.

We checked in with Nelson, the Senior Master Sergeant Superintendent, the senior cop with twenty-two years service. With steel gray hair and worn features, he appeared almost grandfatherly, although he was only forty. He was the guy who organized the various picnics and family activities and he was kind to little children. Despite this avuncular impression, he was a stickler for rules and this predilection caused him to focus instantly on the appearance Scotty and Dale presented. After a greeting and admonishment regarding standards and his expectations, he welcomed us, advising us to take the next ten days to process into the squadron.

And so the next few days passed with some training or other administrative activity, followed by a standing trip to the all enlisted-ranks NCO club by half past four each day. We'd come in and start drinking heavily while the Moody Blues sang "Nights in White Satin," which might well go down as the most depressing dirge ever written. Thanks in no small part to a never silent jukebox with plenty of country western and the long shots Senhor routinely poured, my funk deepened. Like any fever, it had to run its course and at the end of the ten days I'd bottomed out, accepted my fate and began to enjoy my time on the Island. This was made clear to me a few weeks later when I heard "Beyond the Blue Horizon" by Lou Christie on the radio while I drove a perimeter road offering nothing but an ocean view,

I see the new horizon
My life has only begun
Beyond the blue horizon

Lies a rising sun

And I didn't feel the isolation anymore.

I was also reminded of Winston Smith, the central character in "1984" and the last line about how "he came to love Big Brother." Well, I came to love that island, which was part of a small and hardly noticed archipelago, mountain tops really. A part of Portugal, their period of global importance had ended 500 years earlier.

Made up of nine sleepy islands, one hundred fifty-four square mile Terceira, where the base was located, was one of the larger ones. The rocky fields that had been cleared over the centuries are verdant all year long, thanks to the climate and excellent soil created by eons of volcanic ash ejected from the caldera of the inactive volcano where the valley was located. The constant clouds in the mountains create wondrous water caves to explore as well as providing abundant drinking water. Inhabited since the 1400s, it has long been a commercial fishing and commerce port, receiving goods from all over the Portuguese Empire.

By 1973, the remaining Portuguese colonies had been reduced to just Angola and Mozambique in Africa, and those two colonies were seeking independence by engaging in guerrilla warfare. The only other Portuguese possession was tiny Macau, off the coast of China, which was famous for lace and gambling. Just like in the States, many draft-age Portuguese males came into their Air Force to avoid the draft, like Luis the professional golfer who had absolutely no interest in dying and was always a happy guy because he was at Lajes, not in a jungle chasing guerrillas.

Lajes is also an excellent location for an air force base, hidden in the mid-Atlantic, about 900 miles off the coast of Portugal and 2,300 miles from New Jersey. The weather forecast was almost always the same "Lajes weather, daytime temperatures between 68 and 78 degrees, under partly cloudy skies, winds light and variable." Within days, I had that forecast memorized. Just a few weeks of winter provided a noticeable departure from that idyllic weather, with continuous ferocious ocean storms, squalls, hurricane force winds, and generally terrible weather conditions.

World War II brought the island into greater prominence. The USAF established a base near the village of Lajes to facilitate the war effort, turning the island into a giant refueling station that could, as continuously maintained, "could fuel every United Airlines flight for sixteen years." This assumed United would make a once-a-week stop like Trans Aeros Portuguese (TAP), the national airline.

By mid-1973, long range aircraft had made the support mission of this small airbase redundant. A few weeks after my arrival and just as I was embracing island life, in mid-August our entire unit was briefed about the imminent closure of this small slice of atmospheric heaven. We were told to start thinking about our next assignment.

+++

Terceira Island

What I didn't know was that the island of Terceira consists of four overlapping stratovolcanoes built over a geologic structure called the Terceira Rift: a triple junction between the Eurasian, African and North American tectonic plates. These volcanic structures rise from a depth of over five thousand feet from the floor of the Atlantic Ocean. All I was told at my inbound briefing was that the last big thing to happen here was in 1565 when the Azoreans ran the invading Spanish off the aptly named Praia de Victoria, or Victory Beach, and into the sea after loosing some bulls on them.

This historic event is celebrated over one hundred days annually with each village hosting "touradas á corda" or "rope bullfight." A bull with capped horns is brought through the street, barely controlled by the ten or so large men in white shirts and black hats who held the thick rope wrapped around the bull's neck. Of course, after being restrained and choked, the angry bull would typically just reverse course to charge the handlers, who would immediately drop the rope to run for their own lives, leaving the bull free to run amok, terrorizing the people who came to its attention. Seemingly, that was the fun of it. We newcomers celebrated this tradition by displaying an incredible lack of common sense while drinking extraordinary amounts of astonishingly cheap, but excellent quality, Mateus wine before trying our luck and running from the bull.

Finding the bull was never a problem. All you had to do was look for the crowds and listen for the screams. Once nearby, you could follow the limp rope and in short order be as close to the bull as you dared. I attended several of these roped bull fights, but my favorite time also marked our last participation, and as always, it was Spooney who made it the last, he being the singular reason why we enjoined for being allowed to do anything "fun."

Spooney hailed from Marana, Arizona, one hundred and twenty square miles of then unincorporated Pima County, Arizona, about ninety miles south of Phoenix. The census counted 1,154 souls living in that vast emptiness, hot in the summer and cold in winter, ten people per square mile, all living lonely lives among the cacti and dust. There wasn't a lot going on there and Spooney was born into poverty on the outskirts of that one horse town. He grew up looking for a way out and found relief in joining the USAF where, given his lack of demonstrable skills, he was made a cop.

Security was a dumping ground for guys who really couldn't qualify to do much else or had flunked out of whatever technical school they'd been promised as an incentive to join. I'd chosen to be a cop, I wanted law enforcement and found the academy exciting and fun. Security Police were required to present a professional appearance at all times and that meant on and off duty. You shaved every day, kept your hair cut close, boots always highly polished, uniform pressed and starched. How well people met the standard was strictly an individual's affair but, for those slower to learn, there was never ending guidance from superiors that usually involved an ass-chewing and being posted somewhere undesirable, like being stationed on top of a very large fuel storage tank during a training exercise. The stagnant water that gathered on the roof from the frequent rains bred huge numbers of hungry mosquitos.

One of "those" people who just never seemed to get it, Spooney was the proverbial round peg in the square hole. He was short, squat, and fond of his rectangular tinted "granny glasses" that were popular in 1969. In the complicated social algorithms of the late sixties, Spooney tried to maintain his former hippie persona and believed those glasses provided that. He had a clear lens model for work, but a blue lens for off duty. Part of his schtick was insisting he'd reluctantly given up that life and now was working for the man, but only until he could get enough saved to be free. He wasn't unusual; a fair number of hippies and black power advocates chose active duty because at the time it all beat the hell out being a draftee grunt in Vietnam. Those guys didn't stop enlisting until the draft ended on January 27, 1973.

Spooney had a high pitched, nasal voice that came out as a whine, no doubt the result of a miserable childhood. Paunchy and perpetually wrinkled, he had light brown hair with the tightest waves I'd ever seen on a white guy. You could not comb that hair, you could only trim it like a hedge. It always looked unruly unless under the cover of a hat and, when exposed, it seemed to flare and taper off to the left side and stand away from his head, like there was some perpetual wind blowing. The effect was to put me in mind of the cigar-chomping woodpecker mascot for Thrush mufflers, especially when he was smoking a cheap cigar with wooden tip.

Spooney was now just a suit fill. Our Vietnam participation effectively ended with the implementation of that ill-fated "Vietnamization" program where we believed their Army fully mission-capable after almost thirteen years of mentoring, training, and advising. The reality was it gave them the go-ahead to lose.

Meanwhile, the AF was starting to draw down from the massive build-up of previous years, so airmen were beginning to be separated, in many cases before the end of their contracts, and at the convenience of the government. This was seen as an opportunity to thin the ranks and, for Spooney, his "early return to parents" discharge was just waiting until he took an opportunity to self-ID as a candidate.

+++

It's Always 10 After 12 In Arizona

The nature of police work led to hours upon hours of slowly passing time just riding around waiting for something to happen, and precious little ever seemed to happen on the island, so as a result, we'd talk about pretty much anything. Spooney was senior to me for time in service and grade, but, owing to his remarkable lack of regard for any behavior that might have indicated the least bit of professionalism, he'd been "red-lined" when our commander canceled his promotion to buck sergeant by actually drawing a red-line through Spooney's name on the promotion list. That, along with his disinclination to attend to personal hygiene, and soon told tale of his legendary ill-fated performance at the running from the bulls, all worked to get him nominated for entry into the discharge processing line.

Until his discharge was approved, he was a warm body that could be planted on any post requiring zero effort. If no solo posting was available, he'd be attached to a patrol where he'd whine, bitch, wail, and moan about his fate, while sharing how he dreamed of happier days back in Marana where he could tuck a six-pack of beer between his legs, ride his motorcycle in the desert, smoke weed, and be free. He smelled pretty funky and rarely washed his uniforms, so if I was riding with him it meant keeping the window open and not running the heater because he'd begin to smell like an old wet dog.

Despite his lacking any redeeming social traits, or perhaps because of them, Spooney was our go-to guy when we needed a fourth for a game of hearts after shift. He wasn't a very good player, defensive and very thin skinned. That resulted in some animated commentary and ball breaking before we started dumping hearts on him and sending him away. He was also a warm body, often sent in alone to check trash cans for simulated bombs during exercises. We never got to evaluate how he did the job, because nobody ever wanted to be near him, since we all figured if a real bomb was ever planted, he'd be the guy to find it and shake it.

It was an early morning in September, just after finishing a midnight shift, and I was playing hearts with Spooney and two other guys when somebody was talking about Zulu time and time zones generally. Spooney opined "The time never changes in Arizona." He might have been talking about not participating in Daylight Savings Time, but we never gave him a chance to clarify his remark because we stopped playing cards and just looked at him before peppering him with questions.

"Like in all of Arizona or just Marana?" "Is it any particular time?" Do all the clocks in town always show 12:10, like the clock at the bank on the main street, and folks just alway say the same thing?"

"Say there, Billy, what time you got?"

"Well, I got 10 after 12"

"Oh my, I'm late for my appointment with the doc at 10 after 12 — see you!"

"OK, well when should I come for dinner?"

"How about 10 after 12?"

Spooney Arizona Time, or SAT, went on for some time and was incorporated into our dull and boring midnight shifts time hacks that began including "Lajes Time 0200, Zulu 0300 and 10 after 12 SAT." After a bit the Armed Force Radio DJ, who lived in our barracks and knew Spooney, picked up on it and official AFRTS time hacks, between three and four AM included the dig, "Lajes time 0342, 0442 Zulu and 10 after 12 in Spooney, Arizona, now here's Roberta Flack singing…"

Still, he was a squadron mate and, as such, we owed him a certain level of tolerance. He was on the base when I arrived and all I knew was that he'd come from assignment at Kirtland AFB, New Mexico before coming overseas and that he smelled funky. Hygiene was a constant issue. He loved hot buttered popcorn, and rather than get his fix at the movie theater on Tuesday when they had twenty-five cents "Bad British Movie Night" with free popcorn, he chose to cook it in his room. His refusal to open a window created a discernibly thicker and palpably greasy atmosphere that could be felt if, while passing his room on the way to work, you opened the door, reached inside and shook his foot to make sure he was awake. After enough complaints, the First Sergeant ordered him to take a shower, which he did, but he wore a raincoat. We finally got sick of it, tackled him, and scrubbed him with brushes and soap.

+++

Running From The Bulls

In late September several of us decided we'd join in the upcoming "Run with the Bulls" in the little village of Lajes, just outside the wire on the far side of the base. The place was packed as people came from all over the island to take part. The luckiest people were homeowners or shop keepers with a place along the cobblestone street that traced through the village. They could gaze outside at the spectacle while enjoying the comfort and relative safety of either a high window or closed door. Others chose to enjoy the festivities from inside the small bars along the route, while the poor bull was denied entry, thanks to a wooden plank placed in the center of the doorway by the owner which allowed people's entry, but stopped the massive creatures.

A plank worked pretty well except for at one bar where the plank had been used for enough decades that long exposure to the elements had finally rotted it. An annoyed bull was chasing the man who had been teasing it. The fellow thought to duck into the bar to find safety, but the bull charged the rotted plank, breaking it, and romping into the bar. General pandemonium ensued as more men pushed their way thru the other two similarly blocked doors that left them trapped them with the irate bull. The screams and sounds of destruction from the bar went on for several long minutes until enough hefty men in white shirts showed up and regained some control over the animal.

Most celebrants just found space on a low stone wall or building ledge. Sometimes a bull would charge and lower a capped horn to scrape people off the walls, which made inattentive drunks jump backwards, accounting for several minor injuries and twisted ankles. After finding a place to stand or, if feeling especially bold, getting into the thick of the action, it was every man for himself in the event of danger. I'd found a nice space on a wall; well, the leading edge of a wall anyway. My perch was just wide enough for me to get some purchase and take photographs. The bull ran by and began to work on the crowd near the fountain. Screams rang out as participants ran in all directions. One young man slipped but got up in time for the bull to scoop him up with those horns and toss him into the fountain.

I decided to see if I could get some street-action shots and if I was lucky, I could follow the local custom to try to grab the bull's tail and give it a yank to show I was unafraid. I jumped down and saw the bull tenders running towards me at great speed, the bull in pursuit of them. For reasons known only to the bull, it focused on the running men and didn't notice me. The bull stopped charging just after passing and I was getting some excellent close ups, when out of my peripheral vision I saw the tail of the bull and realized I wasn't looking through my 200 mm long-distance lens, but my regular 55 mm lens. I lowered the camera looking straight into the bull's eyes. I took off running and before I'd gone five steps heard that nasally whine calling me. I gratefully grabbed Spooney's proffered hand and he pulled me up onto the ledge he was on.

Although he'd grabbed hold of a piece of pipe, in pulling me up he threw himself off balance, he couldn't hold his seat and, losing his purchase, found himself looking at the bull.

Spooney's instincts for survival were well-honed, no doubt forged in the blistering heat of Marana all those long-ago summers, because he took off running with a speed unanticipated by any of us, including the bull. Spooney ran down that cobblestone street to a vacant lot with a waist-high lava rock retaining wall. He dove over the wall and getting back up saw the snorting bull trot up to him, stopping on the other side of the wall, just watching. Spooney was safe and he knew that in another moment the bull would become attracted to the next guy running by.

Spooney often chose to sport a men's bullhide uplander-style leather hat with an eagle feather and bear claw in the headband, owing to his affiliation in a tribe. He maintained that he had Indian blood but, given his light, almost blonde hair and blue eyes, it seemed doubtful. He'd taken to the notion after watching the movie "Billy Jack" the story of a "half-breed" American Navajo, green-beret-wearing Vietnam War veteran and hapkido master, setting right so very many social wrongs. The only tribe Spooney could have possibly been from was the "Fuckarwe" tribe — as in lost and "Where the fuck are we?"

Perhaps his fantasy and that hat gave him the confidence to confront this wild beast, because ever so slowly, he walked towards the panting bull with nothing but that stone wall between him and a 1,500 pound behemoth. Perhaps he did sense some connection with the beast on a spiritual level, given his perceived native heritage. Either way, as one McFadden sagely said later, "I'm not sure I'd have done that."

Evenly and deliberately, Spooney drew the hat off his head with his right hand and held it above his left shoulder. He locked eyes with the bull, then in a lighting move smacked that bull across the nose as hard as he could and just started laughing.

The now enraged bull took a step forward and, as its massive frame hit the wall, those carefully stacked bits of pumice stone, lacking any mortar to bind them, collapsed into a heap at Spooney's feet.

Not waiting for any further movement by the bull, Spooney turned tail and lit out for the next wall and another field. Ignoring the advice of Satchel Page, that legendary pitcher from the bygone Negro leagues, who first said, "*Don't look back. Something might be gaining on you,*" Spooney did look back and was terrified. When he hit the next wall, he managed, ahead of the bull, to throw himself over, which might have been okay, but the field was a few feet lower on that side and brambles had grown where his butt landed.

The minders grabbed the rope, dragging the bull back up the street to destroy another taverna; while we saved Spooney from that briar patch. He was in a great deal of pain so we hired a taxi to take us up to the hospital where Al, the med tech on evenings, spent the next hour or so going over Spooney's body pulling out nettles and thorns. Word got back to the Safety Office and running from the bulls was immediately prohibited which was really okay since we could still have a good time drinking.

I did manage to grab that bull's tail while the minders were dragging it away and learned that sometimes all you get for your best efforts is some bullshit.

+++

OPERATION NICKEL GRASS

Nobody really saw it coming, it was early October after all and the days were still fine. I was working night shifts and it seemed like my flight was always working night shifts. Nine of us were assigned to our permanent flight. Led by Tech Sergeant Nate Edwards, known by his nom de guerre, OBM, or **O**ld **B**lack **M**an, who, although only 37 years old, was thought to be pretty old by guys who were just 20. He got the name from a new arrival, a stuttering black guy named Ricky from St. Louis who was a former youth Golden Gloves boxer. He'd taken a fair number of blows to the head during those fights, which made him a bit stunad and bad with names. When looking for Nate one day shortly after he arrived, Ricky passed the desk area just before guardmount and asked the assembled group, "Anybody know where that Old Black Man is?" It stuck. OBM's assistant was a Staff Sergeant named Iowa Mike, son of a pig farmer who came out on a post check one night and asked me "Have you ever fucked a pig?" When I looked at him in disbelief he said, "You don't know what you're missing." Next in line was another "Chuck the Desk Sergeant," then me, Mac, Ricky, McSpadden, Spooney and Lazaroni, the only married guy. He lived off base and threw a lot of parties to make up for his habit of screwing up and landing us all in the doghouse. Two guys were always off, so we had seven cops on duty at any one time which allowed us to post a flight chief, three patrols, an off-base town patrol, ramp security supervisor and a desk sergeant.

Meanwhile in the Middle East, a coalition of Arab forces gathered, hoping to win back territory lost to Israel during the second Arab-Israeli war in 1967. Egyptian and Syrian forces launched a coordinated attack against Israel on October 6, the start of Yom Kippur, the holiest day in the Jewish calendar. Taking the Israeli Defense Forces by surprise, Egyptian troops swept deep into the Sinai Peninsula, while Syria struggled to throw occupying Israeli troops out of the Golan Heights.

In response to an urgent request from Israeli Prime Minister Golda Meir, President Richard Nixon directed the immediate and unlimited arms and ammunition resupply by air operations to Israel. Beginning seven days later, on the early morning of October 14, 1973, and for the next thirty-two days, MAC C-141 and C-5 cargo transports streamed daily into Lod International Airport at Tel Aviv carrying urgently needed war materials.

This resupply was conducted with an en-route stop at Lajes, since it was conveniently located approximately one half of the 6,450 nautical miles distance form America to Israel. Given the diplomatic sensitivities associated with so much of the world's dependence on Arab oil, the flight routes over the Mediterranean carefully avoided the airspace of all nations in the region. The first mission was completed when a C-5 landed at Lod Airport on October 14 with 186,200 pounds of cargo. The command's airlift planners scheduled the flights into Lod at the rate of four C-5s and 12 C-141s daily. Nine days later, the intensity slackened as sealift began to take over the bulk of the resupply operations.

By the time the shooting stopped on November 2, MAC airlift had completed 567 missions and racked up 18,414 hours flying time. In 145 missions, C-5s carried half the tonnage, while those workhorse C-141s accounted for moving the remaining 10,754 tons over 422 missions. Meanwhile, the Soviet Air Force's small cargo fleet hauled just 15,000 tons on 935 missions. What made MAC's performance all the more noteworthy was that USAF cargo was hauled 6,450 nautical miles compared with an average of 1,700 nautical miles flown by the Soviets.

Those C-5s transported outsized cargo including 155 mm howitzers, 175 mm cannons, M-60 and M-48 battle tanks, Sikorsky CH-53D helicopters, and McDonnell-Douglas A-4 Skyhawk aircraft fuselages. No other aircraft had that capability.

While the Israeli Airlift confirmed the importance of maintaining the base at Lajes, the snub by our NATO allies renewed interest in developing the C-5's aerial refueling capability. Had Portugal declined the $80 million offered for landing rights and not made Lajes available, MAC would have been hard pressed to execute any airlift and the outcome of that war could have become a nuclear engagement.

What nobody knew was during the first three days of battle, Israeli defense forces lost 500 tanks and 50 combat aircraft. These were unsustainable losses that put air superiority at risk, and without it defeat and total destruction of the state of Israel was unavoidable. It was Moshe Dayan, Israel's most famous general, who gave that bleak assessment and recommended Prime Minister Golda Meir consider a nuclear option. Israeli defense forces had gravity-drop nuclear bombs and dual-capable F-4 Phantoms that could deliver them. It was Mrs. Meir who convinced Secretary of State Henry Kissinger of her willingness to use those bombs and he got the President to sign off on the massive arms resupply.

For our small piece of this herculean effort to avoid this nuclear armageddon, the 1605th Air Base Wing earned the Air Force Outstanding Unit Award for its efforts during Operation Nickel Grass.

The dawn of the airlift gave no indication of the scope of this enormous logistical undertaking, an airlift demonstration not matched until Desert Storm in 1991. On that first morning, I was sitting in a pickup truck providing "close watch" on two McDonald-Douglas F-4E Phantoms parked overnight. One bore a tail number 11791(the Syosset zip code), and was bound for Iran in a few hours as part of Foreign Military Sales (FMS).

The runway at Lajes is oriented at 15/33, south/southeast and north/northwest, over the ocean. It was still dark, in that time of deepest night when anybody with a lick of sense is asleep. The stars shone brightly in the night sky and I was absently gazing towards the 15 end and the sleeping village outside the wire when I recognized some aircraft landing lights standing out amidst all the other stars.

Every aircraft has a signature landing light configuration. After months of watching aircraft depart at night in Florida and all the transient traffic through Lajes, I knew those configurations the same way any kid could tell you the type of automobile from looking at the grille or tail lights. I recognized the configuration as belonging to an inbound C-5 Galaxy, a high value aircraft costing $65 million a copy and given Category B status requiring the parked aircraft be cordoned off into a restricted area with a guard posted. Since we had no "red lines" to denote the security boundaries, we used pails filled with concrete and a metal rod stanchion with eyelets. We ran a yellow nylon line through those eyelets to define the perimeter, something that always seemed unnecessary because, other than the base bird, we usually only had one plane on the ramp at any time, but we set it up anyway.

I left the lower priority F-4s and manned the C-5 Entry Control Point (ECP). I'd just taken up my position when a second Galaxy's landing lights lit up in the now brightening sky. It was parked and we ran out of rope halfway through, and then, after noticing another C-5 on inbound, we simply moved the ECPs to the flight line access roads and began a base recall. By dawn a string of aircraft were in the pattern and we soon found ourselves at the busiest airport in the world. All fifty cops assigned to our small division would be pressed into twenty-four hour operations that meant some grinding sixteen-hour shifts until relief could be brought in TDY. It would be seventy-two hours of a constantly evolving security mission before we'd see relief, and when it came, it came.

+++

Hook And The Tank

In the Vietnam era there really were no weight or fitness standards enforced in the USAF because if you could show up and the uniform fit, you were "good to go." Vietnam had already ruined many lives and good people were getting out after one hitch, while some would stay as long as the USAF would care to have them, and thus it came to be that I met Hook four days after the airlift began. I'd just finished another sixteen-hour shift on day three of the operation and gave no thought to playing cards to relax, opting instead to just take off my clothes and fall into the bottom rack of my two-tiered bunk bed.

A few seconds after I passed out, I was rudely awakened by a loud and insistent banging on the door, accompanied by the thin and reedy voice of Airman Niceler, our admin troop, begging me to open the door. He was a genuinely nice and pleasant fellow, but I hated him because the last time he banged on my door, twenty minutes after I'd gone to bed, was to tell me I had to report to the hospital immediately to give a urine sample, part of random drug testing.

I told him to fuck off and was plumping up my pillow when he said, "Please open the door, I've got a new guy here on TDY and the first sergeant says he's your roommate, so please let him in." I got up, groggy and dopey, went to the door, pulled the security chain that had been holding Niceler back, grunted, waved at whoever it was and stumbled back into my rack.

Our first sergeant was a Chief Master Sergeant, the highest enlisted rank and a man riding out the time until he had his thirty years and could retire at three-quarter pay. He was very squared away, every bit the Chief. He'd overseen the design and fitting out of all the rooms in all the dorms which meant only two types of room designs, because there were only two buildings, the old dorms and new dorms. Furnishings were not permitted to be moved or otherwise rearranged or added to. This was never a concern because every floor had two houseboy/cleaners assigned. Mine was named Dinis, which is Portuguese meaning "follower of Dionysos" the god of the grape harvest, wine, ritual madness, and fertility. The other houseboy was Manoel, Portuguese for Emmanuel, meaning "God is with us."

Every airman paid two hundred and twelve Escudos, or six dollars, each month for their services and each houseboy serviced ten rooms. The houseboys were responsible for the maintenance of the Chief's home interior vision, as well as doing the laundry, and shining shoes. Our rooms were rated from **A** to **C** depending on cleanliness. An **A** room was never inspected, a **B** room once a week and a **C** room was inspected daily. Spooney had the only **C** room I ever saw, since none of the houseboys could keep up with him.

I lay on my thin single mattress atop the metal wire support frame, grabbed the soft pillow more tightly around my face to block the light and muffle the sounds of the unknown new guy unpacking, but my return to slumber was interrupted by a fairly steady banging and shifting of large items. I rolled over and away from the wall to see exactly what was going on. To my immediate horror, I was looking into a green wall of the largest ass in the biggest expanse of green fatigue pants I'd seen since the Commissary guy. The wall was vigorously moving in small semi-circles as my new roommate, a career Staff Sergeant named Hook, late of Norton AFB in beautiful sunny California, began the process of settling in. His girth kept knocking over the small coffee table assigned to the center of the room which necessitated moving it to a corner and risking the wrath of our first sergeant if our houseboy ratted us out, but Dinis knew exactly where his extra two hundred and twelve Escudos, and perhaps a bonus, was coming from that month.

Dinis rarely spoke, although his English was quite good thanks to watching "Sesame Street" on AFRTS (**A**rmed **F**orces **R**adio and **T**elevision **S**ervice) the non-commercial military channel on TV in the dayroom while on his breaks. I learned this one day when he screwed something up and I said, "God damn you, Dinis!" and he said, "God damn you!" I looked at him, pointed and said, "No, God damn you!" The lightbulb came on as he replied while pointing at me, "God damn you" then at himself, "God damn me," then waving his finger in an inclusive gesture, "God damn everybody!" with a big smile on his face having just successfully ran the gamut of first, second, and third person pronouns.

I turned back over and tried to sleep while Hook began to climb up to his rack on top. He stood on a chair, lifted a massive leg to the top of the dresser, then heaved over and onto the mattress. This move flattened the wire support frame, which stretched wildly, making a high pitched scree as the metal took on the load. The metal frame seemed to drop precipitously close to my head, because it shouldn't have stretched at all. I finally drifted off imagining I'd hear nothing, not even the final creak before the fatigued metal suffered a catastrophic failure bringing itself and Hook crashing down on me. I imagined being on the autopsy table and the pathologist making note of the criss-cross ##### pattern forever tattooed on my crushed skull and I'd leave this planet looking like the comic character Archie. I slept poorly and the next day I switched to the top bunk over Hook's half-hearted protest, but I prevailed by insisting that his superior rank made him deserve the ease of the lower bunk. Thus Hook settled into his new temporary assignment with our unit as our operations tempo increased.

Thanks to the airlift, the IDF was able to call up their national reserves and deploy them brilliantly, their forces rapidly overrunning frontline positions with hardly firing a shot, as the retreating forces fled in disarray. That rapid departure allowed the IDF to capture a treasure trove of latest generation Soviet equipment and avionics. Whole Surface to Air (SAM) Radar systems, other classified communications systems, and some intact MiG aircraft were packed up and loaded aboard those same C-5s and C-141s and flown back to Lajes, then points beyond. Some cargo came with an Uzi-toting Israeli security guard dressed in a sports shirt, shorts, sandals, and a yarmulke, but not this night.

I was on foot patrol walking between the scattered posts. I'd stop to chat with the static guards and make sure they were awake or relieve them if they needed to use the bathroom. I could make a standard circuit around the loop in about two hours. It was nice that evening, a departure from the usual rain. Lajes is at the base of a valley, part of a caldera that rises from the ocean. During the day the sun's rays warmed up both the cultivated valley and the ten-thousand-foot runway and that radiant heat kept the clouds and their rain up in the mountains. Many nights, when the sun went down and the runway cooled, those clouds came drifting down and the rains began, only to clear up at sunrise leaving the streets clean and fresh for the enjoyment of all the day shift workers. In winter, the clouds came down from the mountains and regularly rained during the day and almost every evening.

On this evening, I was walking along the grassy infield area when I saw the outline of a C-5 Galaxy but more curiously, an ECP manned by my buddy Danny, a buck sergeant. It was unusual to put an NCO as a plane guard, so the cargo had to be something really cool. I asked him, "Hey, whattcha got?" Danny pushed the black-rimmed BCGs back up the bridge of his nose and said, "A Russian tank!"

A tank was a big ticket item. Nobody cared much about electronics, but in the USAF you rarely get to see a tank and most airmen never get to see a Russian tank, so if that opportunity occurs, you just have to take advantage of it. It was dark and lifeless inside the massive aircraft. The wind was blowing through the nacelles of the port side General Electric turbofans making a racket, but that was a normal sound. Vehicular traffic was confined to aircraft parked on the apron in front of base operations and this bird had been sequestered on an inactive runway near the infamous cliffside garbage disposal tip while they organized a crew to fly her home to America.

I didn't like that tip after one afternoon with Spooney. Whatever trash was generated in our office was taken to this garbage tip — a concrete ramp built out over the cliff. You just tossed the trash, all paper, and coffee grounds, into the ocean and let nature take it. There were opportunistic Portuguese who scavenged down below despite the risks of falling into the ocean or getting caught in a rising tide or rogue wave.

As an A1C, I still drew maintenance details, and on those days, I was partnered with Spooney to keep an eye on him. One day we took four fully loaded gray government-issued trash cans produced at Ft. Leavenworth, Kansas, by military prisoners, and now containing all the day's rubbish from our office. We drove to the point and I parked about twenty feet from the edge, lacking confidence that the tip would hold a pickup truck and with no desire to find out. I picked up a can, walked to the edge and shook it out. I turned and walked back, passing Spooney who was holding two cans, one under each arm. I kept walking, got the other can, then turned to walk back and saw Spooney laughing and holding himself. I drew up and asked, "What's up?" and he pointed over the side. I looked over and saw far below some Portuguese guys shaking their fists and yelling something I couldn't hear, their voices taken by the wind. I looked back at Spooney and said, "What the fuck is this about?" and he held up a finger for me to watch him. I stood there as he picked up his other pail and dropped it over the side. I moved to the edge and saw those guys below scattering and shouting while Spooney wiped away tears of laughter from his eyes. Pissed, I told him if he ever did that again I'd see him charged. He might not have been long for the USAF, but he also knew jail would delay his return to Marana.

Now here was Danny, excited about showing me the tank, so we both went up the stairs and entered the cargo bay. I turned on my flashlight and sure enough, there was a no-kidding Russian T-72 main battle tank. I started to climb up when Danny called me back because a patrol vehicle was approaching us at creep speed. Turned out it was Hook.

Given his girth, Hook wasn't able to stand for long periods of time, so he'd been appointed "coffee guy" and spent his evenings driving a pickup truck delivering fresh coffee, box lunches, and a bit of cheer. Affable and living up to the stereotype of being a "jolly fat man" he always pulled up while shouting in Portuguese "Bom dia!" which meant "Good day" but that meant nothing to Hook; he just loved bellowing the words. He had a terrible memory for names so he called everybody "Matey" and always had a story about his time in Vietnam.

We got our coffee from the giant industrial Igloo jug set on the tailgate. Hook took great pride in his job and there were plenty of sugar and creamer packets as well as a surprising cache of condiment packets; mayo, mustard, ketchup, and chopped green pickle relish he'd salvaged from the box lunches he delivered and later collected the remnants from. Mysteriously, there were never any box lunch ham sandwiches or cold fried chicken left uneaten by a finicky troop. The glazed doughnuts also never made it out of the ops center. Would any that might survive that gauntlet ever come our way?

With Hook, we knew where those doughnuts went and judging by the powdered sugar on his chest, it wasn't into the ocean. He even had a collection of clean plastic spoons if we lacked one, because people would put spoons in the pencil holder on the left sleeve of the MA-1 flight jacket for later reuse. Ignoring this breach of uniform wear imbued a person with a certain sense of élan and authority, something I'd seen first hand when I was dispatched to pick up a first lieutenant aircraft commander who was still in his quarters. The plane was loaded and ready so my orders were to bring him plane side on the double quick so it could leave. I banged on the door and he opened it, hung over, but in his flight suit and drinking a cup of coffee. I told him I'd been dispatched to take him to his plane and "They said to tell you to get a move on, Sir." He smiled and pointed to the spoon in his sleeve pocket saying, "See that spoon, Airman? That means the plane don't go till I get there, OK?"

Hook wasted no time grilling Danny about the cargo and Danny answered him. Hook got very excited and pulled himself right up those thirty or so metal steps and entered the cargo bay. We all had our flashlights lit as we scampered aboard and began looking into both open hatches. Danny was a skinny little guy and climbed right in, rummaging around and calling out what he saw, random pieces of clothing, a canteen and some Arab flat bread, all that remained after the crew had departed.

I jumped off the tank and stood in the doorway because somebody had to watch the area for Commies or, as our threat assessment briefer opined, "Black September terrorists parachuting from a Cessna aircraft launched from Morocco." A bit ambitious, but this was after all just a little over a year since those terrorists took hostages at the Munich Olympics and killed eleven Israeli athletes and a West German police officer, before being stopped.

Mainly I was looking out for the most immediate threat, which was our new TDY flight chief, Tech Sergeant Action Jackson. He was a black man named Jackson, about five and half feet tall, slightly built, who maintained a pencil thin mustache and a compact, but graying, afro. He had a clipped way of talking that could make a commendation or reprimand sound pretty much the same. He also wore very thick magnifying lens glasses to correct his farsightedness or hypermetropia, that defect of vision in which closer objects appear to be blurred. Sadly, this made him look a lot like Mr. Magoo, the popular cartoon character. However, in 1971 the Mego Corporation released an "*Action Jackson*" doll for boys to rival Mattel's G.I Joe, who was currently kicking boy-doll ass. Mego's doll came out in three varieties: two Caucasian, one with a beard and one without, and a clean shaven African-American model, hence, the nickname. Our version was a man who loved to creep around at night to see if the troops were alert and behaving.

Although not used to working together as a team, security forces rapidly develop alternative communications systems for defeating just such a threat, a series of microphone clicks. Action was not an "organic" Lajes Field guy and a bit of a hard ass, so Chuck, the organic desk sergeant, would conduct a "time hack" by hitting his microphone and alerting all posts and patrols to the exact time both local and Zulu, surreptitiously signaling the start of a post check. Time hacks were usually on demand for an airman to set his watch and differed from fifteen minute radio checks pushed out to the troops every quarter hour to keep them awake. Normally, getting caught asleep on post meant a letter of reprimand and some miserable jobs for the next few weeks, not to mention the hatred of your buddies because vehicles to sit in while posted were always taken away to teach everyone to stay awake. During this operation it couldn't happen at all and if it did, there would be a court-martial and some serious jail time.

From then on there would be a series of clicks as sentries depressed the transmission buttons on their hand held radios when he finished his visit and again when he came into sight of the next post. When Action was out on a post check, he'd visit each guard who would then deliver a post report. Each post came with set of "post orders" that identified the post, its boundaries and limitations, a standard radio call sign and copy of the 10-series code for answering and reporting over the radio. Standardization made it easy to pluck an airman from anywhere on the planet and pop him into any location and he could be up and operating as soon as he stepped off the plane.

The reporting process was pretty straight forward. When a supervisor approached, you came to attention, rendered a salute and said, "Airman First Class Sciales reports Post 17 all secured. I am armed with an M-16 rifle and carrying a standard combat load of 108 rounds of 5.56 caliber ball ammunition" and so on, a litany describing your readiness and upon completion, he'd return your salute and either chat for a few minutes or glide off into the night. There were a bunch of posts and each check took about five to ten minutes, depending on Action's mood or the charisma of the sentry. It was up to the individual guard screwing off or dozing to stay on top of his movements.

Danny popped out of the top and yelled, "It's really cool, you gotta see this!" and climbed down from the turret to relieve me. At that same time, Hook decided to check it out. It looked to be a bit tight so he took off his web belt and went in wearing just his fatigues. Before Danny could relieve me, a click told us Action had finished up a post check down the line and was now moving in our general direction, so it was time to knock it off and come down.

Danny yelled up to Hook to get his ass out of the tank, so Hook stood on the commander's chair and pushed up. Incredibly, he didn't have the strength to pull his pear-shaped body back through the hatch; there was simply a little too much Hook. Gravity did *its* job getting him inside, but it was going to take both Danny and me to get him out. We scrambled back up and took a hold under both arms and strained, but Hook wasn't coming despite our considerable efforts. Danny said, "Go and get some of those mayo packets — we'll grease the lip and see if it helps."

Under the "can't hurt" rule, I went downstairs and to the truck, scooped up as many packets as he had, stuffed them into my flight jacket pockets, and went back up. We lubed as much of the opening as we could. It wasn't exactly round, especially by the hatch pin and our lights were just bobbing around, so we did the best we could, using every mayo packet before telling Hook to push on up. We heard another radio click and that just heightened our alarm. All that adrenaline worked because just like the first big kosher dill leaving a pickle jar, Hook popped up and was free. It was only later that we discovered you could raise the seat height.

We all moved smartly off the tank and down the stairs. I caught sight of Action's car silhouetted against the blue taxiway lights and saw it turn on to this unused runway. He'd be on us shortly, so it was better to look like we all had just started a break. Danny and I lit cigarettes while Hook poured us some fresh coffee.

Action rolled up and Danny reported the post while Hook and I stood by. Action didn't care about the cargo, he wanted a cup of coffee and a doughnut. For as long as the USAF had been at

Lajes Field, every morning at two, the off-base town patrol would stop in front of a private house in the small village of Lajes and pick up a Portuguese civilian, the baker who made the doughnuts. Every morning at five, that same patrol would pick up the two dozen hot glazed doughnuts from the small doughnut shop on base and deliver them to Operations, where the Desk Sergeant would parcel out the remainder of the first dozen. The second dozen was always up for grabs by the on-coming shift or administrative command staff. Even though the baker was a true friend of America and had increased his tribute to six dozen daily, with over thirty guys on a shift the doughnuts simply didn't last. Action knew at least a dozen had gone out to the troops and he was going to see how far the distribution got.

He hopped out of the car, walked over to the pickup truck and shined his light in the bed saying, "Daaaaaamn Hook! Where the fuck are all the doughnuts?" Before Hook could answer, Action turned his flashlight on him and saw a light dusting of powdered sugar above Hook's name tag. The bright light startled Hook, causing him to spill coffee on his uniform. Action followed the dribble with his beam and saw the wide grease stain across the considerable expanse of Hook's fatigues, only partially covered by the added web belt. A look of bewilderment crossed Action's ebony brow. He shook his head slightly and said, "Daaaamn, Hook, you just a slob!"

Put off by Hook's slovenly appearance the mood changed and Action yelled, "All right, enough hanging out around here, get back to work. Hook, you need to get your raggedy-ass back to the barracks and change, you a damn Staff Sergeant!" Hook, delighted that there would be no further discussion nor discovery of our transgressions, smiled and waved while slapping the truck back into gear. With shouts of "Bom dia!" and "See you, mateys!" he drove off happily into the night.

+++

Merry Christmas, Shakey

The excitement of Nickel Grass had faded and Lajes, like the mythical Brigadoon, went back into relative obscurity. When the mission ended, Action, Hook, and all the other guests left and our shifts and lives went back to normal. We'd been moved from our old barracks and the new place was two blocks up and one hundred feet higher in elevation. We now resided off Rua Salazar, the installation's main street that was named after "the evil dictator Salazar," according to Senhor Luis, the senior interpreter. This move was welcomed because it meant being next door to the NCO club and on level ground to better facilitate our twice daily walks for food, drinks, the occasional event, or Commander's call, a mandatory monthly formation.

Being closer to the club greatly improved our dining options. Before the move, it was easier to walk downhill to the dining hall for midnight chow on the way to work, and again at the two AM meal break, and once again when the shift ended. Working night shifts meant eating breakfast three times a day and we soon got sick of nothing but eggs and bacon. Now, with a level sidewalk and the club being right next door, our dining options were very good. A level sidewalk was especially appreciated by the drunks walking home from the club since there was less chance of stumbling and falling downhill. This was made clear one evening while walking back to the dorm with Jerry "the unwanted Jamaican guy" from Trenton, New Jersey, who'd replaced Niceler as the orderly room guy.

Jerry was a closeted homosexual when homosexuality was a reason to get tossed out, but none of us would ever comment or care. His attention to detail and error-free processing of paperwork, like leave forms, was a talent rarely seen in the field and clerks of his caliber were rarely assigned to a security police orderly room, a traditional dumping ground for bad clerks. All the good ones were usually snatched up by the headquarters and personnel offices, but we caught a break when two new WAFs, (Women's Air Force) both from Jamaica and beautiful, arrived at the same time and were sent up to the command headquarters staff, so now Jerry, the unwanted Jamaican dude, came to us.

Jerry was funny and charismatic, and it was because of him that we got to know all twenty of the single female administrative WAFs who'd recently been assigned to the base, including those two lovely Jamaicans who were never short for dance partners or drinks involving umbrellas sent by admirers hoping to have a dance.

Because I told jokes and never hit on them, those women always asked me to sit with them and it was my happy pleasure to do so. Guys always asked the waiters to find out what they drank and then sent a drink to them.

If a waiter came by to ask what they wanted, they usually had plenty sitting in front of them already, from other guys, so they'd ask me what I wanted to drink. Turned out a lot of guys bought me drinks and I never had to dance with any of them.

Single women were still a rare commodity and AF leadership naturally worried about consensual sexual relations. Many in leadership felt all non-TDY sex was inappropriate, and it would somehow take an airman's combat edge away, like the sexual abstinence theory old high school coaches used to preach. This societal concern only resulted in clandestine sexual liaisons or trips to the bordellos, but never abstinence.

I only got to know these young women by my association with Jerry, something that would have never happened otherwise and I didn't forget it. One night he'd gotten very drunk and we needed to get him back safely to the dorm, as we were not about to let him get injured. We walked two abreast down the narrow sidewalk when he stopped and said to all of us, "Excuse me, fellows, I think I'm going to be sick!" A moment later a little pancake-shape of vomit appeared on the sidewalk, rapidly followed by two more pancakes, and I thought, "He even pukes neatly!" That never would have happened walking back down to the old dorm; given the steep inclines, it would have splattered on the guys walking ahead of and below him.

My new room was modern and deluxe, but I was still an A1C until January, so I was given a new roommate. Shakey was a six-year buck sergeant from Horseheads, a small hamlet in upstate New York, around Elmira. He was here on a fifteen-month unaccompanied tour, his wife and child remaining stateside with her folks. Almost six feet tall and lean, he'd joined the USAF to escape the rural poverty so common in upstate New York. In return, he'd been assigned to Plattsburgh

AFB, a SAC base five hours north of his home and just outside Lake Placid, near the Canadian border. That's where he had met his wife, a bartender at a nearby roadside tavern where he had spent a lot of time. They both liked drinking and after she got pregnant, he married her and had a son shortly thereafter. His new bride continued to live with her parents because Plattsburgh facilitated Shake's routine 179-day deployments to Thailand, Vietnam, and the Philippines. Shakey was a good provider who sent home his salary and a lot of, but not all of, his TDY pay, because those overseas experiences left him with invisible scars and a serious thirst.

His real name was John but he picked up the nickname Shakey, or just Shake, because of his trembling hands, a hallmark of alcohol withdrawal. A high-functioning alcoholic, it wasn't that Shakey ever appeared drunk, but he was rarely seen without a drink. It was during those non-drinking duty hours, from eight to five, that the tremors would manifest, usually in late afternoon and becoming more pronounced as the duty day drew to a close. When the bosses recognized the degree of Shakey's disease, they relieved him of the burden of carrying a gun and normal patrol duties. He was installed as our full time vehicle and weapons maintenance NCO. Shakey was happy with the move, considering it a promotion because it meant evenings, weekends, and holidays free. As a result, Shakey's life was a pleasant routine consisting of working, drinking, and sleeping.

Christmas in the Azores is a lonely time since most airmen were serving unaccompanied tours and it was natural to miss family and friends back home, wherever that was. For two weeks prior to Christmas, I'd been busy schlepping downhill to the post office to pick up whatever mail had been delivered and then schlepping it back uphill to the barracks, thanks to the hump postmaster refusing to release our packages to Dinis.

As I got ready for work on Christmas Eve, I looked over at the considerable pile of presents and noticed that Shakey still had only the one gift from Mrs. Shake, a cube-shaped cardboard box, maybe eight inches square. It was gaily wrapped in thick white paper with pine tree patterns running rampant, secured by a red ribbon with gold trim. It now sat prominently atop our small refrigerator and right under a lamp, illuminated and easy to see among all my presents. Shake was off to a party at the club which offered free food and drinks, plus dancing to live music, while I was left to experience my worst Christmas Eve ever.

We were at reduced manning so the married guys could have the night off, and I was assigned to a two-man patrol with Spooney, who'd recently gotten news of his selection for early termination of contract and would be leaving for Marana shortly after the new year. Knowing his time in the USAF was drawing to a close did nothing to improve his commitment to personal hygiene and that meant another shift of keeping the heat low so he wouldn't smell like a wet dog. It also meant leaving the windows down, even when raining, because he'd also started smelling moldy recently.

We rolled out of the parking lot by a quarter after eleven and following procedure, began slowly driving down every road on that base. We saw the revelers and heard all the fun going on at the NCO Club and likewise at the Officer's Club on top of the hill. We cruised the family housing area, windows providing a peek at brightly lit Christmas trees and happy families with small children enjoying the magic of that special night. The radio was tuned to AFRTS and the non-stop Christmas songs were only interrupted by updates about Santa's location from NORAD, the North American Aerospace Defense Command, broadcasting from their headquarters deep inside the mysterious Cheyenne Mountain Complex in Colorado.

NORAD is a joint US-Canadian operation and conducts aerospace control and warning as well as maritime warning in the defense of North America. This Christmas tradition was born in 1955 when a misprint gave out a department store phone number for Santa that was in fact the secret unlisted phone number for the NORAD Command Post, for use only by the SAC Commander and the President. A little girl called and asked the Colonel who answered, "Are you Santa Claus?" He went along with it, thinking somebody on staff put her up to it. As several more calls from children quickly followed, airmen were assigned to answer the phone, telling any kid who asked that Santa was busy flying around delivering presents. It turned out Santa tended to only visit air force bases in the US and Canada.

We'd gone to midnight chow and learned there was no special meal, just the regular breakfast buffet and a half-hearted attempt at hanging non-offensive seasonal decorations which only added to the overall air of depression that comes from working alone and far away on the one night of the year almost everyone thinks of family.

We drove through the night and, while slowly creeping down an empty flight line, Spooney began to tell me tragic tales of Christmas past. I'd had some pretty economically lean Christmas experiences as a child, like the year I got a Hopi Indian kachina doll. Just that doll. My parents hadn't been out west and at age seven I realized it must have been a regift and was bummed. So while I really didn't care to reminisce, Spooney did, and for the next several hours I was an unwilling aural witness to a sad testimonial about just how poor his childhood was. He won the prize just before the dawn when he shared how one year all he'd received was an old cigar box with some colored rock chips glued inside like a display. As we crested the inactive runway near the garbage tip, I watched the sun rising out of the ocean haze, red and small, and knew the day looked to be fine, a beautiful morning as befitting the birth of the little baby Jesus. I also took great comfort in the certain knowledge that this depressing night was going to end in an hour and that gave me the inner strength to not kill Spooney, or myself, just for the sweet release.

That shift ended with no shot at getting a drink after work because the club was closed until four that afternoon so that all the staff could enjoy the day with their families, so I went to breakfast with some of the guys. We lingered over coffee and cigarettes until a quarter past eight, then walked back to the barracks and up the three flights to our floor. I quietly opened the unlocked door and heard Shake sound asleep in his bunk. Sometimes he'd do some serious sleep-talking and I'd get a rundown of some event or the other like, "Tell me again that dome light isn't working and I'll show them…" so I always thought it best to let him sleep.

On this morning I was surprised when a few minutes later Shake woke up, wiping the sleep from his eyes and saying,"Merry

Christmas, Babe!" He called everybody Babe, it was just easier than remembering names, and I responded with the basic "Merry Christmas, Shake!" He sat up in bed and stretched while yawning and smacking his lips. I took that as a cue and while reaching towards the small refrigerator and asked,"You want a beer?" Shake finished the stretch and scratched his head. After a few moments of consideration he said, "No Babe, I don't think I'll be drinking today." Meanwhile, I'd been thinking about nothing but having a large glass of whisky after the night I'd just had, but I had to admire his spirit, so I took our coffee mugs to the central dayroom to fill them. This lounge had an ocean view, large TV, pool table, two card tables and a thirty-cup coffee maker. Sitting on the condiments table along the wall was a small faux Christmas tree with some generic ornaments, a nativity scene display and, next to that, an electric menorah for the one Jewish guy. He'd scored a bunch of kosher delicacies and jars of soup from the supporting chaplain in Germany and some Jewish veterans group back home. It was just too much for one guy, so he set it all out when Hanukkah started six days earlier and it was now pretty well picked over.

By the time I got back, Shake was up and ready for Christmas. He'd combed his hair and washed his face in the room's sink and now sat in the one lounge chair while I took the wooden desk chair. Shake insisted I open all my presents and we'd open his last. With a flurry of wrapping papers, I uncovered joke and puzzle books, underwear, and playing cards, all of which made me believe my family thought I was stationed on a lighthouse. The last package was what I really wanted, two Travis McGee novels by prolific author John D. McDonald. Shake hadn't gotten any more presents, so I'd asked my sister for them, based on Shake's glowing description of salvage recovery expert, Travis McGee, the hero in twenty-one novels. One of Shake's more frequent remarks was "That Travis McGee is a bad motherfucker!," as he reread one of his favorites. I thought that if nothing else he'd enjoy reading a few new ones while I was at work.

We were down to the last gift, the one from Shakey's wife that sat atop the refrigerator and under the lamp, just as it'd been sitting since the week after Thanksgiving. I picked it up and saw the small paper tag reading "To John." I passed it to him and he slowly undid the ribbon and carefully peeled away the tape securing the expensive wrapping paper. He opened the plain brown box and pulled out a pine cone sprinkled with silver glitter and sporting a red banner with gold script letters proclaiming, "Merry Christmas from Myrtle Beach South Carolina!" There was another card inside the box so he opened it and read, " The kid is with my folks. I want a divorce."

I reached over and opened the refrigerator.

+++

You Got A Smoke?

It was two in the morning and I'd started my shift as ramp security supervisor, once again in charge of making sure the runway and empty aircraft parking areas were still there the next morning. That had changed an hour earlier when a Boeing 707, part of the Special Air Services squadron assigned to the 89th Wing at Andrews AFB in Maryland, was declared inbound with a VIP on board. I was instructed to provide security for the aircraft while it was on the ground, taking aboard fuel, and some high priority cargo.

The big plane pulled up and shut down, and the service vehicles moved forward. I was informed the VIP would be remaining on board while I stayed close to provide overwatch. I parked just past the port wing tip where I could see the refueling technicians and watch any cargo being loaded. There is a certain amount of paperwork involved with transient aircraft requiring dedicated security, so I switched on my dome light and began to fill in the multiple sheets of paper. I'd parked far enough away so I could smoke without presenting a hazard to the refueling ops and was engrossed in my writing.

I flinched when the sharp rapping on my window began and was startled to see a tall, blonde-haired woman in a dark dress standing before me. I rolled down the window and recognized her from newspapers and TV; it was Nancy Kissinger, the wife of Henry, then the Secretary of State. Before I could figure out what to say, she pointed at my cigarette and asked, "You got another one of those? They won't let me smoke on the plane during refueling."

My initial surprise passed, I pulled the pack from my pocket and shook one out. She took it and I was pulling out my lighter when she said, "Do you mind if I sit with you? It's really windy out here and my hair is already a mess." All I could do was say, "Please do," as I picked up my papers from the passenger seat and unlocked the door. She climbed inside and for a moment I idly wondered how this would have played out if Spooney had still been around.

Nancy smoked her cigarette and declined my offer of dining hall coffee. She asked me where I was from and we made small conversation while watching a forklift taking a pallet off a nearby truck and began moving it towards the now opened cargo hatch. She offered, "Once Henry found out we'd be stopping here for fuel, he asked if we could get a few cases of Mateus wine because it's only one dollar a bottle. We just can't match that price at home and entertaining is *so* expensive these days." I could offer nothing except to nod in agreement and try to commiserate with her troubles, as the club had recently raised the price of a pitcher of beer by ten cents. We watched as the forklift loaded the two hundred cases of recently palletized and plastic wrapped wine aboard and the crew closed the hatch.

She was just finishing a second cigarette as the re-fueling crew was disconnecting the hose when an aide appeared in the forward hatch and stood on the mobile stairs looking about. She crushed out her cigarette and nodded towards the aide, saying, "I suppose he's looking for me, so I better get back inside." She turned towards me and smiled, "Thanks for the cigarettes, it was nice meeting you and I hope you enjoy the rest of your time here."

She got out of the truck and I watched as she walked back towards those stairs, holding one hand against her head, attempting to keep the wind from tousling her hair further. She climbed aboard, the hatch was closed and the engines fired up. I pulled away to be clear of the jet blast as the big plane began rolling and in a few moments I watched those cases of Mateus depart the island while my brush with celebrity came to a close, vanishing into the night skies as it headed west.

+++

That Watershed Moment

It was a rainy four in the morning sometime in late January. Not a gentle shower, nor steady drizzle; it was a torrential ocean storm, a downpour being whipped by winds coming in off the ocean and howling down the runway. We'd clocked those winds during a category seven gale at forty mph by accelerating to twenty mph, shifting into neutral and opening the pickup's doors. We watched the speedometer climb and hold at forty until we ran out of runway. Visiting aircraft had to be chained down because the nose would lift when wind speeds passe thirty mph, and planes had been damaged when the tail smacked the concrete. It was unnerving the first time I saw a silent plane's nose begin to lift, and now here I was standing guard on a lashed down Navy EC-130, its cargo compartment filled with highly classified gear.

The rain came down in sheets and the light from the NF-2 light-all unit illuminating the plane clearly showed the shifting and swirling pattern of water driven by the wind, water that was also finding its way into the neck of my poncho. Once inside, hydrostatic pressure and gravity worked its magic to bring that water down my spine and into the crack of my butt where it would finally stop when absorbed by my cotton briefs. The collected water, chilled by the wind, began the slow and lingering process of evaporation. I now understood the old Vietnam guys when they said, "You don't know wet until you've got water running down the crack of your ass."

I had no truck to sit in because Lazaroni the idiot had been caught sleeping the night before and they took away vehicles from static guard posts. That would have been fine, but I wasn't the one who fell asleep. Laz had the next two nights off and it was just my bad luck that this Navy plane was carrying highly classified gear that required me to babysit it.

I'd just sewn on my third stripe as a buck sergeant, and was now an NCO and shouldn't have had this post, this duty traditionally for two-stripers, but the departure of Spooney dictated otherwise and I was miserable.

The NF-2 portable light-all unit threw light a fair distance beyond the aircraft and I spotted the glint off of the reflective placard reading "Security Police." It was attached to a slow-moving 1968 Air Force blue AMC Rambler station wagon driven by the OBM coming out on a post check. I began walking toward him and shining my flashlight to let him know I was awake. This was a chance to get out of the rain and maybe have a cigarette, it being impossible to smoke in this downpour. Who knows, he might have even brought some coffee.

As his car pulled up, he cracked the window a bit and released a cloud of pale blue cigarette smoke that was immediately snatched up by the gale force winds. I leaned in towards the crack and reported my post, adding, "And I'm about as wet as I can be," before standing back up and waiting for the invite out of the downpour.

I was immediately disappointed.

The OBM didn't invite me in because he didn't want to get the bench seat wet and have any water find its way into *his* cotton briefs. He leaned into the window and yelled into the maelstrom swirling around me, "Scales, scales, puppy-dog tails, mother fuck shit. Can you type?" He couldn't pronounce my name but did the best he could, so this was his standard greeting to me on a post check. The question however, was new.

I pondered the offer for about a nanosecond before it hit me that typing involves paper and typewriters, and neither can get wet, so I'd be indoors where it was always lit up at night. It also meant I was getting out of the field and brought into management and a career path. I knew in an instant that everything hinged on my answer and being able to deliver on the typing. Since I wasn't academically oriented in high school, I'd been shunted over to the business program and Charlie Nadler's typing class. Some of the typewriters had the letters visible but some, the ones for the typing test didn't. When test time came, I sat at a desk with the letters visible. I got to thirty words per minute with no errors which was good for a C, but that had been three years earlier and I'd not had much occasion to type since. Still, I'd watched Al typing before King ate him and I knew I had him beat for speed. Besides, after Nickel Grass ended nothing much ever seemed to happen at Lajes.

My moment of reflection done, I looked at him through my rain-spattered lenses, "Why, yes I *can* type! I took a course and I can type anything you'd like me to type."

He nodded and looking at me through his perpetually bloodshot eyes said, "Wear your blues tomorrow, you're gonna be a desk sergeant." Another bit of smoke from the Kool menthol cigarette dangling from his lips and he was gone.

I came in the next night and shadowed Chuck. He'd received his next assignment, was leaving in fifteen days, and I was to replace him. I learned all the applicable regulations and procedures, and, combined with my prior experience at MacDill, it all worked in my favor and at the end of that two weeks I was fully certified and ready to handle all shifts. I now dealt with the full spectrum of people: officers, NCOs, airmen, Portuguese military personnel, civilian employees, spouses and kids, always studying my betters and learning all the time. It was this opportunity that changed the entire course of my life.

I'd finally gotten it all: I'd shed my rain gear and was warm and dry while working in a brightly lit room near well-tended toilets and a perpetual thirty-cup coffee pot. On top of that, when I slept, it was between clean sheets.

I had just turned 20.

+++

The Death Of Apa

We had a problem with dogs on the island. Americans would ship over the family pet, but then decide it was kind of a pain to do the paperwork to bring him or her back. When they flew away, Sparky was left behind with a bowl of dog food and sincerest best wishes. The sponsors were unconcerned about the fate of the animal as the island had pleasant weather and they were confident the dog would make out. So instead of telling the kids Rover was at a farm upstate, they would comfort them by saying Rover had been taken in by a kindly Portuguese couple who wanted a dog that understood English.

It was, in fact, thanks to pleasant weather and plenty of food in garbage pails that those dogs would screw like crazy and, in short order, a bunch of stray and feral dogs roamed about in packs. During Nickel Grass, a pack was brazen enough to lay on the runway. We'd tried running them off because Lajes had flights coming and going all the time and aircraft couldn't land safely. The dogs kept returning which threatened the schedule and execution of the mission, so the commander authorized the use of deadly force to kill the dogs as a hazard to flight safety. Using shotguns, we wiped out the feral population around the flight line and runway, but it was a messy business and a passing Navy pickup truck sustained damage from a badly aimed shot. Now those dogs were occupying our on-base family housing area and starting to scare people, and a neighborhood with lots of kids was not a place where we could use shotguns.

To avoid another canine pogrom, and further damage to government property, our orders were to capture as many dogs as possible and cage them until they could be put down humanely by the base veterinarian. We had a six-cage kennel behind the police station and, with all three shifts working the tasking, it meant that kennel was quickly filled with almost forty dogs of every description.

One such dog was named Apa, which is a traditional greeting on the island, like "Hey!" Apa was a small, happy, energetic dog, thanks to the Jack Russell terrier in him. He was white with some black markings and a chestnut colored ring around his eye. He'd hung out by the base school where all the little kids got to know him and fed him treats. That little dog was a performer, having learned many tricks, and was now a favorite of the children. His talent and the esteem in which he was held, made little difference to Isom and Lazaroni, the twin idiots who were the designated dog catchers when we rotated to day shifts.

What we didn't know was how to catch these dogs and no training films existed. When the program first got underway, Isom, exercising some initiative, brought a block of cheese he'd lifted from the dining hall and was showing it to me and the OBM while explaining he was going to catch dogs with it. OBM finally just pushed his chair back, stood up, and scoffing, clued him in with, "Damn, you just stupid, Isom! Dogs don't eat cheese! Rats eat cheese! Go and get some goddamn meat! Didn't you have any dogs in the goddamn ghetto?" After researching the issue by asking Laz, Isom settled for those little Vienna sausages in a can, and when he approached Apa earlier in the shift with this highly processed delight the poor doomed mongrel came along willingly.

They brought the wee beast to the kennels and threw him in with the rest of the unwanted curs. Laz, still midnight shift pale, with a droopy mustache to match his perpetually sad face, reported to me. "Hey, we tossed in another dog we found hanging out at the school, but just be aware, it was recess time and all those little kids saw us and they were shouting as we left."

I thought no more about it because the sheer volume of dogs meant we had to start putting them down rapidly and today was that day. The euthanasia program was set to begin at two and right on time the Vet and his tech arrived, so I told the two dog snatchers to get ready to assist. The physical process of grabbing up scared, snapping dogs was tough on both of them. Each man wore leather work gloves and they had a loop noose on a pole. They'd run the loop around the poor creature's neck and drag it crying, kicking and flailing about from the cage and into the run, while the dogs left behind became agitated and raised a howl as if they knew the jig was up. It was equally hard on the vet tech, he had to splay the dog on the table so the doctor could quickly locate the heart and plunge a needle full of liquid nicotine directly into the chambers. The doomed dog would yip as the needle was inserted, a bit of blood drawn back to check it was firmly inside the heart and then the plunger pushed forward releasing the deadly liquid.

Death usually occurred more or less instantly, depending on the dog. One tough little pug jumped off the table and started wagging his tail before dropping like a stone. This canine death duty was especially grinding on the Vet, given that he was a dog lover. The pug's reaction unnerved him, so he stopped and said he'd come back Friday to finish off the rest. I went back inside to the desk while the dog catchers took the carcasses to the garbage tip and threw them into the ocean.

I didn't see the kids who came by after school let out. I didn't know they were visiting Apa and bringing him treats. I didn't know his detention was the subject of recess chatter. I didn't even know his name. I'd find that out on Friday.

That afternoon came and the medical team showed up at three. The killing table and associated gear was assembled inside the kennel run and they started without delay. Isom and Laz, now proficient at snatching up those terrified and doomed creatures, picked up the pace as everybody set to their grim task. It was going as well as could be expected, with maybe five dogs left when the children showed up. The island is hilly and the kennels were down at the end of a long and sloping driveway, just past the vehicle parking and maintenance area. Steps led up forty feet to a rear entrance into the operations building.

I was watching it all from the top of those steps. The windows were open and I could hear the phones if they rang and I also had a portable radio to monitor any traffic. Shaky was in the armory cleaning the rifles and he'd field any calls and could get me if needed. The children were yelling as they came marching down the street and I could see the angry little mob. I didn't want them coming down our driveway and seeing this command directed horror show.

Spooney's replacement was Jimmy, a twenty-one year old black guy from Patterson, New Jersey. He was a tough guy who always looked angry because he was. Some people thought he hated white people, but Jimmy really just hated everybody. He was a good cop though, always did his job, just lacked personal warmth. He came out of the bathroom and I yelled at him to head down the hallway and intercept those kids to keep them from coming down the driveway. He sprinted down the hallway to the far exit that would bring him out in front of those kids, while I ran down the steps towards the veterinarian, a Captain. I said, "Sir, we need to get this done pretty quick, we got all those kids up there" nodding towards Jimmy, who was now engaging the juvenile mob. He took one look and agreed. I could hear Jimmy yelling and I knew there'd be some phone calls later from parents who objected to their kids being called "motherfuckers," but right then getting this horrible job done was the priority.

While Jimmy taught the kids some new words, the vet tech directed Isom to grab the next dog, which of course, was Apa. He'd dug in his heels and Isom slid him across the concrete floor to Laz, while Apa screamed in terror. Laz took the noose off and held the trembling little dog face-forward and at high port arms, just in case he took a leak from fear. The children spotted him and began yelling "Apa! Apa! Don't hurt him! Let him go! Apa! We love you, Apa!"

Laz gave Apa to the vet tech who flipped him over while the children wailed from thirty yards away. Thanks to elevation, they had a partial view of the run and could see the vet as he plunged that needle about as fast as anybody could and then let Apa up. The dog scrambled to his feet and was wiggling around trying to make sense of what was happening. He continued dancing for almost a minute while the noise level was increasing to near hysteria from the children, and this cacophony exasperated Jimmy, whom the highly agitated mob of small children now threatened to overwhelm. Jimmy had been joined by Sam Spade, our one investigator, who came when he heard all the noise while sitting in his office engraving property and then came out to see what the matter was.

Even with his more soothing adult approach, things were going south. Both men were powerless because there was no way they could, or would, use any force to stop these kids — only adult voices. Jimmy made it known to everybody later that he'd have preferred administering beatings, something the OBM bluntly assessed when he showed up later saying, "What the fuck is wrong with you? You can't be calling kids a bunch of little motherfuckers, you stupid motherfucker."

Ignoring the hue and cry of the mob, the doc calmly told the tech to flip Apa over and he'd give him another dose. The doc filled that syringe with more than enough to do the job. When he made that final intracardiac injection he knew that Apa wasn't getting off the table, yet remarkably, that little dog got up on his feet, remaining on the table just looking dazed. The children were crying in the background and some began screaming that we were all murderers. Apa stood gamely and then slowly began to sway. His hind legs gave out first and in those final moments I lost the sounds of the children and only saw that game little dog desperately trying to pull himself forward and towards the vet, who was now backing away, terrified.

And then he just dropped dead.

We were scheduled to rotate back to the hated midnights in another week, but given the events of this day that couldn't come soon enough. All of that weekend, whenever a patrol drove through housing and passed some family event or activity, little kids would point at the car and shout, "They killed Apa!" and the patrolman would have to drive away before creating another juvenile riot.

+++

Have You Seen My Dog?

The problems with stray dogs didn't end with Apa. The children eventually forgot and they didn't scowl at us anymore, but dogs were still a big problem.

Some guys on other shifts developed different approaches. On the night shift, a two-man patrol in a pickup truck tried driving through the housing area with one cop in the bed holding out a thirty-six-inch riot baton while passing the low stone walls the dogs habitually perched on. The dogs had never reacted to passing cars, but they were stunned when hit with the baton and easy to capture. While certainly innovative, this practice came to an abrupt end when one troop beaned a stray in front of a poor local woman who'd stepped outside to smoke a cigarette, and witnessing the event, was traumatized and called in to complain about "cops beating dogs with sticks."

The solution was provided by our Chief of Police. The major was an Academy grad and an awfully good man. He liked us and so took an interest in us and we all respected him greatly. He'd done his research and on one particularly fine and early morning he dispatched me to meet a C-130 coming in from McGuire and pick up a package.

I went out to the flight line and watched the sky lightening with the dawn as the four-engine turboprop came in on its final approach from the Northwest, over the water. The plane landed and the "Follow me" truck guided the Hercules to a parking spot and chocked it. The engines shut down, the crew hatch opened and the flight engineer signaled me to wait, then brought out a rather large box. With nothing to sign, I just put it in the bed of the pickup and drove back to the station while the crew began their offload, got something to eat, and went into mandatory crew rest for the next eight hours. They'd pick up passengers and mail before taking back off for New Jersey later that afternoon.

I brought the package to the major's always spotless office where not a single piece of paper was ever out of place and the floor was freshly waxed and very shiny, thanks to the unending efforts of our janitor to curry favor. I knocked once, he looked up and smiled while motioning me in and said, "Do you know what this is?" I confessed I didn't. He told me to do a recall of all on- and off-duty troops to test our notification system and immediately following lunch have them assemble in the vehicle compound for training. This was always a welcome relief because very little happened in the Azores on any given day. We'd go for weeks at a time with no excitement other than mandatory riot control and robbery training exercises, two events that had never happened on the base. Its safe to say that nothing ever really happened during the duty day, so pulling troops in off the road and from the dormitory and back office was not going to subject the installation to pandemonium. Besides, I had Shake to monitor the phones since he didn't carry a gun anymore, just cleaned them.

Everybody reported as directed and assembled down by the now infamous kennels. Truth is most of us lost heart for culling out the strays. There were just so very many of them and confidence in our collective capabilities was seriously eroded after the debacle on the flight line and that patrol playing doggie stick ball in the housing area. Likewise the Major was not inclined to consider firearms again after I'd gotten shot by an airman trying out for the base pistol team.

The indoor range was small, just four lanes. I'd made the team after all the range time in Florida and was just putting in some practice time as were two other teammates. In the first lane was a recent arrival and pistol team aspirant, an airman named Jeff, from Travis in California. Everybody had to qualify with a pistol when they arrived and this gave us a chance to see if they were a shooter or one of those guys who'd be better off throwing the gun at a bad guy. Jeff was a skinny little guy given to bragging about his imagined capabilities and fancied shooting like a gangster. When the range instructor told him to put on some headphones, Jeff declined, saying, "I'm from LA, I'm used to gunfire."

The range was made hot and the command given to open fire. I'd drawn and taken a combat stance with my pistol extended straight out in a two-handed grip with right thumb wrapped around the back-strop. I had a good sight picture and was releasing my breath as another shooter fired. I felt like I'd been stung by a bee, a large bee. I looked down and saw the blood and couldn't understand why it was there. It finally dawned on me that I'd been shot and cease fire was called. We figured out Jeff's bullet had crossed to lane three and ricocheted off the metal bar that held a target and then again off the wall nearest me and hit me in the hand. Sadly, Jeff did not make the team and now I couldn't imagine who'd have been killed or maimed if someone like him was given carte blanche with a Remington 870 WingMaster and five rounds of 00 buckshot.

The Major was not about to leave us hanging though, and he had the tech solution to our problem. A table had been set up and displayed on it was a very handsome dart gun, but not just any dart gun. This was a breech-loaded Pneu-Dart Model 176B, a C02 cartridge-operated dart projector. Recommended for close range shooting, it came with an impressive selection of syringe darts each containing a sedative and adorned with a bright orange plume to track the flight and locate the syringe. There were a number of pre-loaded syringes, each based on the animal's weight, so from that selection you could tranquilize a poodle or an elephant, as the need arose.

The Major was an excellent shot and had been on the Academy pistol/rifle team. His office was filled with plaques and trophies attesting to his skills. He explained to us how the rifle operated and in short order it was time for a practical demonstration. The timing was bad however, the kennels had recently been emptied, and no new strays yet collected.

A recently arrived and unhappy A1C, whose name I cannot remember, was the designated assistant for setting stuff up and lifting heavy things. He reported this lack of a test subject to the Major. Never one to let a training opportunity slip away so easily, our boss cast his eyes about and saw a very attractive Irish setter wandering past our station and walking along a well-worn path that ran along the fence line. It was outside of the installation and not very far from the cliff edge where Americans were prohibited from walking for concerns of falling off. A few weeks earlier, a couple of sailors went down by where the garbage was dumped, a prohibited act. One lost his footing, fell into the water and, due to the mushroom shape of the island, worn away by ocean waves, was sucked under; his body wasn't recovered until some days later when spat back out by the ocean. Drowning wasn't the concern here because the one hundred foot fall into the water would kill anybody who went over.

This dog had a beautiful red coat — and clearly, no tag, which was required on base, so it was just another stray. The Major picked up the rifle and asked for a dart. The unrecollected airman handed him the nearest one. He took it and held it aloft, the bright orange feather making it visible to all. He inserted it, brought the rifle to his cheek and said, "Attend" not unlike the learned master marksman he in fact was.

We watched as his ramrod straight torso swiveled slowly from the left to the right, tracking the dog with deadly devotion. A soft "puff!" and the dart was away — sailing fast and true as we watched it strike flesh, embedding squarely in the dog's neck. The dog yipped, took another five or so steps and fell over, to the scattered, but polite, applause of the assembled guardians of the good order. The show being over and nothing more to be seen, I sent my unknown airman over the fence to check the animal. He picked up the head, looked at it and called back, "He's dead! What do you want me to do?"

Mindful that this completely forgettable airman could fall into the ocean and knowing I needed to keep a close eye on him, I told him to take the carcass right up to the cliff edge and toss it so I could go back up to the desk. I stayed because if he fell there was absolutely nothing to be done, but I wanted to make sure I had the time correct for any blotter entry. When I got back inside, Senhor Luis, our senior dayshift interpreter, looked up from the ten-year-old copy of "*The Stars and Stripes*" newspaper he used to cover up an even older copy of *Playboy* he was actually looking at, as I fixed a cup of coffee in the break room and went up on the desk.

Sometime later the phone rang. The conversation went like this:

"Security Police, Sergeant Sciales, can I help you, Sir?"

"Good afternoon, Sergeant," said the clipped and heavily accented voice. "This is Colonel Silva, the Portuguese Air Base Commander."

A first time caller. I sat up straighter in my chair. "Sir, how can I be of service to you today?"

"Thank you, it is about my dog. My dog is missing."

I felt the sweat starting on my forehead. "Sir, can you describe the dog? Does it wear a collar or anything?"

"No," came the disembodied voice, "the dog is very gentle, he walks by himself along the perimeter every day and has not returned, which is not his way, you see." I couldn't think of anything to say as he continued. "He is an Irish Setter, has red fur. Have you seen him?"

As the rivulets of sweat trickled down to my eyebrows, I said nothing. What could I say or do? That dog was missing for all eternity, so all I could think was to give him some hope. "Sir, I don't know, but I can certainly ask our posts and patrols to keep an eye out for him."

He thanked me and rang off. I was out of my chair and running the twenty-five steps to the commander's office. I slid past the outer doorway on that highly polished floor and caught the frame with my fingertips to stop. I pulled myself into his office. The Major looked up as I blurted out, "Sir, you killed the Portuguese Air Base Commander's dog!" and the details of that conversation spilled out over the next few seconds.

Ten minutes later, while Shake watched the desk, I was in a police car running with lights flashing down to the flight line and out to the parking slot where that C-130 was spooling up for the return flight to McGuire. The tower alerted the crew to stand by for a last minute high priority package.

I pulled up across the front of the nose so the pilots could see and acknowledge me. I set my handbrake, jumped out and pulled the newly re-packaged tranquilizer gun, minus one dart, from the backseat as the plane's port side crew hatch opened up. The loadmaster stuck his head out and I handed him the package. He recognized it as the one he'd delivered to us just hours earlier. A quizzical look came across his face. I leaned in close and shouted "It was never here."

+++

Oklahoma Crude

Chuck didn't have eccentricities, he was just plain goofy. He was a buck sergeant already assigned when I arrived, on a two-year accompanied tour with his wife. Anne was a thin, sad, mousey woman with large brown tortoise shell glasses and a worn, haggard look — like a pioneer woman fresh from busting prairie sod.

On the other hand, Chuck was loud and brash with an air of self-confidence and a decided willingness to engage in some of the most inane conversations for no apparent reason other than to break the silence. He was a major league bullshit artist, hailing from somewhere in Oklahoma, somewhere really rural, judging by Chuck's deportment and presentation as a man of the great outdoors.

Chuck had a car, one of the privileges of an "accompanied" tour. It was an old piece of crap, 1960-something Studebaker sedan, that often required repairs and which he hoped to sell to some other sucker when he left in a few months. One rainy night I was returning to the base from town patrol and saw Anne outside changing the driver's side rear tire. She was soaked and struggling with the lugs in the downpour and I figured Chuck was out somewhere, because no husband would let his wife change a tire in the rain. I got out of the car to offer help and asked her where Chuck was. She told me "He's sleeping and needs to rest so he'll be strong for work the next day." I got back in the car and left her to that task because you cannot fix hard-broke stupid.

I later saw that car at a squadron party and noticed Chuck had welded a metal folding chair to the right front bumper. I'd never seen anything like that before, so I asked him about it. "Why, that's my pig hunting chair!" came the casual reply. He then proceeded to tell me all about hunting pigs in Oklahoma. So now Chuck hunted pigs in Oklahoma and Mike from Iowa had sex with them. These revelations made me think things were seriously disturbed in the middle American states and those poor pigs couldn't catch a break. I asked if he planned on going pig hunting on the island, adding I wasn't aware of any roaming about and the only pig I'd even seen was served salted and smoked at breakfast each morning. He told me that he was "checking it out" but I do not believe any kills were ever recorded.

Riding with Chuck for eight hours was rarely interesting but sometimes entertaining. He spent twenty minutes one day explaining a cloud formation to me. "See that opening in the sky? That's called a 'sucker hole' because if pilots get suckered in, why, it'd close right up behind them, and well, they got suckered and vanished." My first thought was "Huh?" Then I remembered AFRTS ran a program having something to do with the Bermuda Triangle the night before. He also tried to impress me with his geopolitical awareness by reading the occasional passage from Chairman Mao's "Little Red Book"then looking thoughtfully out the window while I offered no comment.

It was a Saturday night and a bunch of us went over to the club after we got off work at ten and were able to join the crowds that packed the building, including the restaurant and snack bar towards the rear entrance. The club would stay open until two, so we had plenty of time.

Most people dressed nicely for a Saturday night out since it was the highlight of the week. It was a chance for wives to dress up, and go out after a long week with the kids, have a nice dinner, and dance. For single guys, it was a chance to have a few drinks, tell some war stories, play pool, and maybe get a chance to dance with one of the WAFs or a willing wife. Chuck's big moment happened just as the Azoreans, our house band, was coming off a break. They had one song in their playbook, *Yellow River*. Released in 1970 by Jeff Christie, it rose to number 23 on the US charts and received absolutely no play in Australia owing to an emerging "pay for play" scandal down under. The only words the band knew were "Yellow River," which they pronounced "Jell-Oh Reev-Er" and they mumbled the rest of the lyrics, which was OK as most people were drunk and didn't care.

They were preparing for that second set when Chuck appeared out of nowhere and leapt on the stage, seizing the microphone from the stand while announcing with an authority usually reserved for military coup leaders saying, "Hey, shut-up everybody! My name is Chuck and I'm gonna dedicate this song to my wife, Anne, seated back there." Portugal was then ruled by the current evil dictator, Macello Caetano, successor to the late evil dictator Salazar, and a close associate of the current Spanish dictator, Generalissimo Francisco Franco, so people in the Azores understood a strongman and knew it was best to do as they were told.

Given Chuck was wearing a white dinner jacket with bow tie after Labor Day, all heads turned rearward to see how the charming Anne might be costumed for the big evening out, and sure enough, she was wearing what might have been her prom dress from some years earlier. It was a light blue chiffon number that must have been packed under some weights when shipped over with the household goods, because the chiffon had some permanent creases at odd angles. Her eyes were hidden behind the large lenses of her glasses, giving her a decidedly "barn owl" look, so nobody could tell if she was happily excited or horrified as she grabbed her face with both hands and just shook for a bit.

Chuck, emboldened by the tepid response of the crowd, looked at the band and said, "Okay, boys, hit it!" Sadly, the Azoreans, who already spoke little English, were likewise frozen by indecision after just having their gig hijacked by a big old bobble-headed American in a white dinner jacket they assumed was pretending to be the dining room head-waiter, Oh, Senhor! Many in the crowd also sat stunned, but it only took a few seconds for the catcalls to start. My favorite was "Shut the fuck up and let the professionals play!" This was obviously shouted by some new arrival who didn't know the Azoreans or their limitations.

Everybody looked at Chuck, who was looking towards Anne somewhere in the darkness. Leaning slightly forward in a "crooner's stance," his imagined edginess was enhanced by beads of sweat forming on his large forehead, all while holding his drink in his left hand, like the singer Dean Martin used to do. This, of course, led to some spillage, but the drummer was game so he ignored Chuck and started tapping out the beat, which as it turns out was the correct response. After some moments, the rest of the band decided it was best to just continue playing and let the crazy American have his way.

For the next two minutes, an off-key Chuck belted out a rousing rendition of "Yellow River" done at 3/4 time. That, in and of itself, would have been OK, but loving the spotlight, he chose to try to work the crowd. The minute Chuck stepped off that stage, a couple of unconsidered things occurred. First, everybody in the room knew Chuck was a cop, because he was a big mouth, and anytime he and Anne came to the club there was always some sort of loud disagreement between the two and, if anybody asked them to be quiet, Chuck would bellow, "I'm a cop, I tell you to be quiet, you don't tell me." Finally, while most people felt great sympathy for Anne, nobody liked Chuck.

Relishing his time in the spotlight, he moved off the dimly lit stage and into the darkness of the room while holding a glass in front of his eyes to shield them so he could locate his beloved. A crooning Chuck began his slide past the tables, giving a nod or a bit of a two-fingered salute to people he thought he knew, when somebody in the back decided to launch the cherry tomato from his salad into the general direction of Chuck. A solid hit was scored near the left breast pocket of that white jacket and before Chuck could respond with a snappy comeback to the heckler, another ten or so tomatoes completed their flights. Two hits and a bunch of misses. The bass drum took a hit and the crowd, emboldened by the shambling form of Chuck retreating to the stage, started tossing bread rolls and frozen butter chips. A general howl went up with loud shouts and laughter came from all corners. Chuck tossed the mic at the bandleader and made a hasty exit through the rear of the club. Another wife, somewhat sympathetic, sent Anne a couple of drinks to console her for having married Chuck, and saving all the other women from him.

+++

Stormy Weather

The NCO club was our community center. If you were off work and it was open, there was always a good time to be had, always some kind of celebration. When promotions were announced, the newly promoted would put half the difference between their old monthly pay and the new pay on the bar to buy drinks. Depending on the number of people being promoted, the amounts on the bar could exceed three hundred dollars, a sum that goes a very long way at fifty cents a shot. The club was also the place for any official business meetings, like a Commander's call, where we were all briefed and brought up to speed on all things Air Force. Our "Hail and Farewells" were conducted there to greet new arrivals and say goodbye to departing airmen completing their tour. However, the happiest of all events was a member's birthday party complete with a beautiful cake baked and decorated by our own club baker.

I was off that Friday evening and the usual cast of characters was in the club. The bar was pretty full with small groups in deep conversations and some solos at the bar staring vacantly at the shelves lined with liquors. The booths along the walls were all filled so people who came in, looked for friends and pulled up a seat.

I was parked in a booth with two other guys on my shift, Mike the pig fornicator and Mac, who was recently back from a visit to the emergency room. Mac was convinced that one of our houseboys, Moises, was gay "because he is always looking at me," which is really what a house boy is supposed to do, as most did not speak a lot of English, and needed to see if you wanted something else done. A few hours earlier, Mac stopped by my room to bum a cigarette. He was just out of the shower, wearing only a towel and flip flops. Moises was making my bed on the lower bunk and turned to look at Mac. At that moment Mac decided to check his gay theory so he opened his towel and flashed his manhood about three inches from the kneeling Moises' face. As Mac turned to me and laughed, Moises reached up, grabbed his dick, and yanked down hard while Danny howled. Turned out Moises was straight and Danny had to explain to the doc how his junk got rumpled.

We didn't get many Friday nights off, so we'd gotten an early start during Happy Hour when all drinks were a quarter. We'd been there a while, long enough to run through two bucks in quarters on the Wurlitzer jukebox that gave twelve songs for a dollar. The Zodiac model held fifty two-sided records and, to ensure harmony in a multi-cultural Air Force, the songs were evenly divided in thirds for pop, soul, and country-western.

Shake, having recovered from the shock of his impending divorce, slid in around half past five, all barbered up and ready to make the scene wearing his burnt-coral-colored, highly detailed leisure suit jacket with color-coordinated slacks and a lemon-colored polyester shirt. He saw himself as the physical incarnation of Travis McGee. He loved to make his entrance, always coming through the large double doors by the jukebox because that entrance allowed him to stop and size up the room for someone to visit with. He'd pause for but a moment, tug on his white belt to hitch up those pants, then execute a slow roll as he walked across the dance floor. He'd continue on up to the bar where he would order his first, of what would be many, Miller High Life beers. I could see the tremors in his hand as he lifted the clear glass bottle towards his lips. I'd watch as that amber liquid sloshed, foamed slightly, and vanished down the sluice that was his parched throat. By the time he finished that first long pull and drained about half the bottle, the trembling subsided and he could have performed brain surgery.

Shake sat alone at the bar when he should have basking in the glow of tributes from fellow club members. He'd distinguished himself during the recent food shortage brought about by fearsome Atlantic storms that had prohibited any ships from coming to port during the previous three weeks. This lack of resupply meant base stocks of vital commercial family commodities were being depleted. The commissary was so low on food, the dining hall was opened to feed families. The hospital was passing out disposable diapers and SIMILAC baby formula from war-time stockpiles. AFRTS was keeping the population abreast of when relief might be expected but there was nothing coming until the storms abated.

I'd been working as the rainy-day shift security supervisor exercising my mandate on an empty ramp since our one base plane was stored in a hanger to ride out the storm. All non-essential traffic was halted because the step vans used by flight line operations could be easily blown over, so I was all there was. I positioned my truck at midfield after being sure to turn into the wind when I parked so to not rock back and forth as the gusts pounded it. I looked out at the gloom as the rain beat on my windscreen and I turned the heater up another notch.

It was it shortly after noon when the Fire Chief pulled along side in his fire engine red Ford pickup truck, its solitary red beacon turning slowly. I rolled down the window and he told me a C-130 was inbound with a cargo of emergency supplies since the hospital was running low. The weather was just not cooperating and landing would be the aircraft commander's call. The chief was just getting into crash position because moments counted if a plane went down.

He reminded me of a few months earlier when an F-4 Phantom, part of a Navy four-ship flight heading to NAS Rota, in Spain, declared an inflight emergency. Fuel wouldn't transfer from the external tanks, so the pilot dropped them and set course for the island and a runway. The sun was sinking in the West when he was directed toward a runway 15 approach, coming in from over the ocean to not risk flying over the town of Praia da Victoria, which sat outside the fence line and was the county seat.

Aviators prefer to land into the wind, using it to slow the aircraft while maintaining lift. Any wind not head-on pushes the airframe and the pilot has to account for that. Those light and variable winds were currently out of the North, so he'd be attempting to land with left quartering tail wind, which meant he'd be pushed south and have to adjust for the drift. The pilot had been vectored to the island and when he made his turn on final approach he was at four thousand feet. He'd just set the trim for a three-degree glide slope when his port engine failed. He was still a few miles out and knew he only had a few seconds before the second engine failed. At this low altitude, once the power was gone that machine would have the glide ratio of a manhole cover. Knowing the plane was finished, he punched out and was taken by the wind.

I was talking with the chief and didn't see him eject because lots of low clouds were drifting in. When we got into position, we only saw the black exhaust trail of the aircraft in the distance but didn't see any landing lights. That meant the landing gear was still retracted. As it grew closer, we also saw it wasn't lined up on the runway center line. It was some distance off and just coming up to where ocean met land when that second engine flamed out and it crashed right down on a small beach accessible only by a cart path.

The firefighters got down there rapidly but there was no fire after all, 1,994 gallons of fuel were consumed by those two General Electric J79-GE-17A axial compressor turbojet engines. There was no pilot, and the canopy and ejection seat were missing. Thirty minutes later, we got a call from the pilot asking to be picked up. The wind that took him dropped him on the 18th hole of the golf course up in the hills at Cabrito which was situated in the caldera of an inactive volcano. He got out of his parachute harness, walked into the 19th hole bar and ordered a drink.

So now, looking into the gloom, I heard the throb of those four Allison T56-A-15 turboprops, a low, powerful drone buffeted and lost by the wind. I was in awe of those brave airmen willing to risk their lives in a desperate attempt to bring vital supplies. I knew there would be six pallets containing 42,000 pounds of everything from diapers to coffee grounds and I watched as the Follow Me truck and other vehicles for off-loading the cargo began to arrive and wait.

As the roar of the engines grew louder, I could finally make out the landing light pattern, lights inside the wheel wells and in the middle of each wing between the engines. The flashing wingtip beacons made it easy to see just how badly the plane was pitching and yawing as the winds buffeted it, changing direction suddenly where the warmer land air met the cold ocean water. The plane was dancing and crabbing as the pilot increased power, engines spooling up in response and he flew that plane onto the runway. Safe on the deck, he chopped power and slowed down while the fire trucks started their engines and returned to the station and their interrupted lunch.

Only the freight vehicles remained as the camouflaged mottled green bird rolled down the high speed taxiway towards the designated parking spot. I saw a Security Police pickup truck racing on to the ramp with blue lights flashing. As it drew up, I was surprised to see Shake behind the wheel. Shake hated getting wet and even had a patrol drive him up to the barracks after his shift if it was raining because it messed up his hair. I pulled along side and watched as the C-130 pulled into a parking space, was chained and blocked there by transit alert guy, and the rear cargo doors opened. The assembled supply vehicles began to move into their respective positions around the rear of the aircraft while a portable alternate power unit was connected so the interior would remain lit. An aerial porter positioned his loader to lift one of the six pallets, each with about seven thousand pounds of cargo, then place it on a waiting cargo cart. Meanwhile, Shake got out of his truck and into the rain. Squinting and lifting his left hand to shield his eyes, he ran to the aircraft and, climbing the forward hatch ladder, went inside.

I decided to see what was happening, since I was the ramp supervisor, so I boarded the plane behind him. It was noisy and I saw Shake talking to the buck sergeant load master who began walking back to the third pallet and pointed at it. Shake gave him a big thumbs up and came walking back towards me. I stopped him and asked, "What's on the pallet?" He leaned in to me and said excitedly, "Beer, Babe!"

I followed the cargo to the hanger where the pallets were broken down and contents distributed further on. I watched as the Portuguese cargo guys took razors to the heavy gauge plastic encasing that third pallet. Stripping it away revealed a pallet load of beer, and not just any beer, but Miller beer, "*The Champagne of Bottled Beer*." That beer pallet contained rows of fourteen cases, stacked seven high and each case holding twenty-four bottles for a total of ninety-eight cases weighing 1,960 pounds. That was 2,352 bottles of beer, of which Shakey had exclusive purchasing rights to ten percent.

In the midst of all the needs of the Air Force, and in his own way, Shakey had correctly identified, and arranged to receive, exactly what the Air Force needed at that particular moment on the island and more than a few marriages and careers were saved. People were happy the club had beer again, enough to last out the storm, but very few people would every know of Shake's part. I was certainly stumped as to how he did that, but was damn glad he did.

+++

Ask Not For Whom That Cake Rolls

Gloria was a WAF and had been one for almost nineteen years. She rose to the rank of staff sergeant, but could go no further, being unable to pass the written promotion exams. She was the senior admin airman assigned to the command office. She was also the oldest female NCO and, therefore, also matron-in-charge of the women's barracks, a two-story building directly across the street from our police station. She would sometimes storm into the lobby during the early morning hours, yelling and causing

Senhor Luis to wake up, while shouting that MEN were in the WAF barracks and it was quite possible that illegal sexual relations were taking place. Like the rest of the USAF, Gloria was extremely reserved about sexual matters, and consensual sex between consenting unmarried adults was not to be condoned. Gloria would come running over to the ops desk dressed in a long flannel nightgown with hair in curlers under a shower cap, demanding we come with her to arrest people she suspected of having carnal relations.

Naturally I'd have to call in a patrol to relieve me so I could attend to it. I always picked the town patrol because it took the longest for them to respond. Once they arrived, I'd spend a few minutes briefing them on how to watch the desk and then she and I would cross the street and go walking down the hallway. I talked loudly while Gloria was yelling for me to be quiet and I'd listen for sounds on the far side fire escape. When we'd get to the suspect quarters, I'd bang on the door with my nightstick yelling that Gloria was suspecting sexual escapades and for the occupant to please open the door when dressed and decent. A couple of times I heard guys going out the first floor windows, but just waited. One time a woman opened the door and through her window I could see a guy running across the field; heading back to the male barracks area. Gloria wanted me to shoot the fleeing fornicator but I explained the rules of deadly force prohibited that option. She called me useless, but I got asked to dance a lot after that.

Her thinning brown hair framed a hatchet-face made more dour by early onset wrinkles, thanks to her two-pack a day habit of Camel studs. She had no particular charms that I could see and her gender identification was dubious, but she had a secret weapon. She was the steady shore-squeeze of the senior Navy enlisted man, a Master Chief Petty Officer referred to as "Sea Dog" or "Popeye," given the enormous numbers of tattoos on his forearms.

Sea Dog and Gloria enjoyed a private reserved booth on the far side of the room and nearest the bar, so drink deliveries were never delayed, not even in heavy traffic. This particular night held no joy for Gloria. Rather, a sense of gloom prevailed because this was the night Gloria got on the back side of forty and she wanted to forget that fact. She and Sea Dog had been in the bar since they'd gotten off work at half past four and now, five hours and a considerable amount of vodka later, Gloria was deep in her cups, not knowing Sea Dog decided to surprise her on this, her natal day, by ordering a cake with

"Happy 40th Birthday Gloria!"

writ large in red frosting, and nicely highlighted against the white buttercream frosting with AF blue piping on the edges.

Birthday cake service was included with the one-time club membership fee of ten dollars, all thanks to the extraordinary profits made by all the bars and heavily subsidized by the Navy golf course's revenue-generating slot machines. At one time, all military clubs overseas had slot machines if gambling was permitted in the host country. The idea was to keep military people on base so they wouldn't chase sin off base. In 1972, the Military Airlift Command "got religion" and decided to remove the slots from the clubs at its only overseas installation and ordered them destroyed.

The Navy volunteered to drop them in the ocean for disposal, the AF agreed and signed off that the slots had been removed and transported by the Navy for disposal at sea. The Navy packed them up and, lacking any ships of their own, a few weeks later transported some crates to one of the two US Army tugboats stationed at Lajes as part of some Army Tactical Tugboat unit that brought big ships into our harbor. Warrant Officer-4 "Captain Ernie" dutifully acknowledged and receipted some crates from the Navy, took them two miles out and dropped them into the mid-Atlantic as ordered. Two weeks later slot machines, minus any visible identification placards, magically appeared at the 19th hole club house and recovered pilot lounge at the Navy golf course.

At the stroke of nine, the hallway doors threw open and in came Oh Senhor, the senior waiter, resplendent in his white server's jacket. He was pushing a rolling cart with a large and flaming birthday cake aboard, one that not only had all forty candles, but unbeknownst to Gloria, the kind that re-ignite when you blow them out.

Years of heavy smoking and a decided lack of interest in physical fitness had taken a toll which manifested that very evening. She saw the flames as the cart rolled across the dance floor but, until it made a slight left turn, didn't put together that this was *her* birthday cake, now an unhappy and unwanted reminder of a post-military future that, like this cake, was screaming towards her.

The lights came up full as everybody began singing "Happy Birthday." When the song finished, it was time for Gloria to blow out the candles — knowing if she blew them all out in one breath she'd get her wish and move from shore assignment temporary side-girl to dependent wife.

She let out as big a breath as her compromised airways could muster and got all forty candles the first time. Some polite applause began from a nearby booth and Gloria, already humiliated at being outed as elderly, was wishing Oh Senhor would take that flour and egg reminder of her mortality away, when one candle lit back up, then a few more, until the cake was again fully involved.

Not to be deterred, Gloria inhaled as deeply as her lungs would allow and exhaled, sending an additional five percent carbon dioxide and a fair amount of phlegm towards those candles. Her body was quaking as she expelled every last bit of air she could summon in a determined effort to knock out those candles. She got some, but not all, and despite her personal best efforts, the flames quickly returned.

A smarter person might have realized the trick being played, but Gloria was hovering at around a .28 percent blood alcohol level at any moment, so this concept eluded her. Instead, she pushed herself away from the table and the offending cake. Standing up, she took a long, if unfocused, look around the room at all the people laughing, not realizing it was the candles, not Gloria, they found funny. Confused and further humiliated, she sat back down. She looked sadly at Sea Dog for a long moment before brushing the offending candles aside and throwing her face into the frosting. She shook her head side to side, sending small bits of yellow-caked icing flying and smearing it all around while alternately laughing and crying.

It took an uncomfortable six minutes for the ambulance to arrive and our two night-shift med techs, Al and Ronny, to roll a gurney into that silent lounge. Even the jukebox was dark, not in any tribute to all the good times she'd had, it was just awaiting more quarters.

The two airmen, dressed in white hospital uniforms, tenderly wiped as much cake as they could off her face and then gently helped her out of the booth and on to the gurney. They wrapped her in blankets and pulled them up tight, fastened the restraint straps and slow rolled her back out through those same double doors she'd come through so many times before.

Gloria didn't finish her tour in the Azores. She was air-evacuated back to the States on the next flight out. Somebody packed up her stuff and she was never seen again.

+++

Don't Bogart That Joint, My Friend

It was early morning and I was working the desk. I looked outside and saw the light fluffy clouds sailing across the ocean and fulfilling the standard weather forecast of "partly cloudy skies, winds light and variable," so I knew it was going to be a good day. After a month of working midnight shifts, our flight had finally been rotated to day shifts and a normal life for the next thirty days. I was on my second cup of coffee and looked across the foyer into the work desk area where Senhor Luis was eating a doughnut, drinking coffee, and thumbing through this tattered ten-year old copy of Stars and Stripes he enjoyed so much and used to hide an equally dated copy of Playboy. One night he showed me the magazine centerfold where he'd pasted a slightly too large black and white photo of his fifty-four year old girlfriend's face atop the body of the Playmate of the Month, who, judging by the date on the cover, must have been around the same age now.

Luis also had a crush on five-foot-three inch Wendy, the first female security policeman assigned to the island. She was just a little taller than he was, and quite buxom, which enamored Luis to her. Sadly, his deep infatuation for her was observed and brutally rejected early one morning shortly after the glazed doughnuts were delivered. Luis grabbed one and was standing in the foyer area in front of my desk. He called softly to me saying, "Oh Senhor! This doughnut is Wendy's pussy!" as he began obscenely licking the center of the doughnut. Before I could even remark or counsel him, Wendy had walked out of the ladies room. Catching him in the act, she yelled, "LUIS! YOU DIRTY OLD MAN!" and so shocking him that he aspirated some glaze. He began coughing uncontrollably while staggering off to the men's toilet to hide his shame.

As the senior senhor, Luis was responsible for all forty Portuguese who worked as unarmed static post guards monitoring different parts of the base, except for the janitor, the guy who kept the building spotless. He was his own man and worked the night shift. It was during those wee hours that I made his acquaintance.

The building was long with the command and admin sections down the West wing, then the central operations part containing the armory, desk sergeant ops desk, and a guardmount/break room behind the desk. Down the East wing were two toilets, two rarely used jail cells on one side and our supply cage on the other. The hallway ended in a large conference room where formal briefings were held, as was the Christmas party where Willie, our brigadier general commander, once kissed me under the mistletoe.

He'd popped in to visit our holiday party and saw Rita, the beautiful young wife of a newly arrived staff sergeant, standing next to me and almost under the mistletoe. He'd just come from another holiday party with those crazy communications guys and was feeling pretty good. The lights were low, the place was packed and the party in full swing. He planned on giving her a big smooch and turned away to catch a pump of Binaca mouth spray since, "It's the only freshener that's passed the ultimate *Kissalicious* test!"

In that moment Rita turned away and stepped over to talk to another wife. Willie, having lost sight of her when he was freshening his breath, turned back around and grabbed my face in his hands and gave me my first adult kiss from a man. It was warm and I'll confess, very fresh tasting. I'm pretty sure he felt my mustache because his eyes shot wide open and his jaw dropped as he pulled away from me. I was still in shock and all I could say was, "Sir, does this mean my promotion came early?"

Now the static nature of that east wing meant that senhor janitor could devote all his time and energies to keeping the rest of the building in inspection order. He'd come on at nine and leave at five in the morning. All night long he'd slowly walk his dust mop up and down the hallways, working through the empty offices. After a break, he'd wet mop the floor, then take his lunch break before getting a waxing machine out and buffing the linoleum to a high gloss.

Speaking no English made him a quiet fellow, but sometimes a bit too free with the property of others. I'd taken the habit of bringing hot chocolate to work some nights because even though I was warm and dry, the howling winds could still throw a shiver into me and the warm drink was welcome. I kept my thermos in the break room. One evening I went back and noticed that someone had been drinking from it and the only person who'd been back there was the janitor. I lacked any definitive proof so I let it go and it happened again the next time I brought some in.

Tired of this, I went to my friend Al, the medic, and got some Dulcolax, a laxative that stimulates the muscles of the bowel wall to make them contract and push food along faster. I ground up a couple of tabs and mixed it into the hot chocolate. Senhor swept on by and a few hours later I saw him running to the bathroom. The sounds of his great gastric distress provided all the proof I'd ever need. He came out pale and clammy. He began pointing towards the thermos saying, "No bom, no bom!" to warn me the hot chocolate was no good and might be poisoned.

He never went near the hot chocolate again, but on another occasion the US Navy contributed to his delinquency. A routine customs check aboard one of their P-3 Orion turboprop anti-submarine, surface warfare and maritime surveillance aircraft, revealed some contraband. The sophisticated machine carried a crew of three pilots, two naval flight officers, two flight engineers, three sensor operators and one in-flight technician. The squadron was assigned to NAS Jacksonville, Florida, and made routine circuitous deployments to the Navy Air Stations at Keflavik, Iceland; Sigonella, Sicily; Bermuda, and Rota, Spain. They'd come in from Rota and were staying with us for a few days before heading back to the States. This gave them enough time to fly some missions and, when off-duty, go into town and trash George the Crooks, a bar frequented by all those sky pirates.

They'd go in and find something to disagree about with some of the local American sailors, who were regulars, and in the finest traditions of the US Navy, a fight would break out. We'd get dispatched down to the bar along with a Portuguese military policeman and attend to the matter. When we arrived, we'd be greeted by two civilian policemen who would tell us how upset George was. We'd go inside and George would be wailing about the destruction visited upon his humble establishment by these brutes that come with no respect for antiquity or history. He'd be saying this all this while standing along a wall with plaques and other tokens of appreciation and respect from the wide assortment of Navy flying squadrons that called his place their local while they were on the rock. It usually cost about eighty dollars to salve his wounds and pay the costs of repair which was really just wood glue, because that furniture had been broken many times in the months I'd been there.

The plane belonged to VP-49, the Woodpeckers, whose mascot with a plume of hair that always reminded me of the recently departed Spooney. Those four Allison T-56-A-14 turboprop engines allowed this bird to cruise for 2,380 nautical miles while carrying Mark-50 torpedoes, rockets, mines and depth bombs to locate and destroy Soviet submarines, if need be.

The whole mess arose because the flight manifest didn't note the several ounces of high grade marijuana one of the crew thought would be a good idea to bring back to the USA. Our sole Navy Shore Patrolman was trained as a dope dog handler and the dog had performed well this time, which had not been the case a few months earlier.

Under military law, an alert from a drug detection dog is sufficient probable cause to have a commander authorize a search of any person or property on the installation. Late one night, the dog alerted on a barracks room and I woke the general to get his authorization to search that room. I also dispatched the OBM and two patrols to make the arrests. The two startled residents opened the door to the now barking dog, all the while professing their outrage and innocence as the dog had zeroed in on some fried chicken in the trashcan, leading to our sincerest apologies.

To correct this deficiency a small amount of high grade marijuana and hashish was given to us by the Department of the Navy for use as a training aid. The handler would hide it; the dog had to find it. Being an illegal substance, it had to be strictly accounted for and weighed when going out and when returned. One night the trainer returned a significantly lighter training aid and I noticed the plastic was ripped. When I asked what happened, he just pointed to the dog who was sleeping on the floor.

Now, despite the handler's asking twice, nobody confessed to ownership of the dope, so being unable to determine who brought the weed aboard the aircraft, he confiscated it. The handler brought it to the office for disposition and eventual destruction, or maybe given to the dog since he liked it so much. I weighed the marijuana and noted it on an AF Form 52 property receipt. I had the dog handler sign off as handing it to me and I put it in the back room until Sam came to work in the morning. He was the evidence custodian, so he'd sign for it and lock it in the safe.

I was back on the desk typing up my blotter entry and incident report with lengthy narrative. I would attach the witness statement of the shore patrolman when he brought it in. Taking a phone call, I hadn't paid attention to senhor janitor as he pushed his dust mop down the hallway. I hung up a few minutes later and smelled smoke, which wasn't unusual because smoking indoors was permitted. It was the smell that caught my olfactory attention. This smell I'd known well, from my pre-USAF days of youthful experimentation, and the barracks at MacDill, as marijuana burning. Described in training as a distinct and sharpish odor, "Sickly sweet," whatever that smelled like. I couldn't quite imagine how that could be happening until I stood up and walked into the break room. There I beheld a custodian happily toking away on the largest two-rolling-paper blunt I'd ever seen. I understood why he did it, because tobacco was heavily taxed to pay for the wars in Angola and Mozambique, so any loose tobacco was prized and fair game.

I stepped back on to the desk and grabbed a pair of scissors. Walking back into the break room and snatching the joint he was bogarting right out of his greedy little lips, I snipped the lit end off and on to the floor. I ground it out while yelling "No bom! No bom!" and shaking my index finger back and forth. Senhor, clearly very high, started parroting me and began to slowly wag his index finger while lazily replying, "Em nenhum senhor, isso é muito bom, muito bom!" (Oh no sir, this is good, very good!) He was given the rest of the night off with pay and took a nap in one of the cells. Of course I had to write up the story, take a drug test and be interviewed by Sam Spade.

+++

The Snow Day

It was just gone mid-morning on April 25 when Luis turned up the volume on the large AM radio he kept on his desk. He always kept it tuned to a station that broadcast soap operas and was a big fan of one called "Maria." I wasn't really sure what sort of stuff the heroine Maria was up to, but I always knew when the show came on because I'd hear the theme from "Gone with the Wind" playing, while at every musical pause the announcer would intone in dramatic fashion, "***Maria***!" a total of four times.

Maria must have taken this day off because it was now a live broadcast with a very excited announcer who sounded like the Puerto Rican guys calling Yankee's games at Moran's. After a bit, an equally excited Luis came over and leaned on the counter in front of my desk. "Oh, Senhor!" he cried, eyes wet, "Today we make a revolution in Lisboa, and I want to know if you want me to send the men home?"

In 1967, the evil dictator, Macello Caetano, succeeded the thirty-six year reign of the evil dictator Salazar, continuing the fascist "Esado Novo" (New State). This morning that evil regime was toppled by a heroic group of young military officers, who, tired of fighting and dying in all the wars in Angola, Cape Verde, Guinea-Bissau, Mozambique, and São Tomé, started an anti-war movement. Lisbon tried to maintain some semblance of control over the armed forces, but the movement was soon coupled with an unanticipated and very popular campaign of civil resistance. Rebelling soldiers put carnations that street protesters gave them into the barrels of their guns, and sparking what the radio was calling the Carnation Revolution. This movement would lead to the fall of that old new state and the withdrawal of Portugal from its African colonies.

This news took me by complete surprise, but I wanted to maintain a sense of confidence and authority, so I pushed my chair back and looked at him saying, "No kidding, a revolution, huh? Hmmm, OK, I have to see about this. I'll let you know in a few minutes, thanks for letting me know, first time for everything, right?" Luis smiled at me saying, "Oh no, Senhor, the last time they made a revolution, we were told to send the men home with pay until it was all corrected. Everybody was very happy."

He walked back to his skin magazine to await the decision, visions of an unexpected couple of days off with pay when his wife would think he was working meant some free time to visit his sweet young girl friend. While Luis dreamed his dreams, I made my way at the quick step to the Commander's office. I knocked and without even waiting said, "Sir, there's a revolution going on in Lisbon and Luis wants to know if the guards can go home."

The major looked up and said, "What revolution? How come we never hear about these things?" I asked what he wanted me to do about the guards and he said, "Whatever you think best," while he picked up the phone to call the General to let him know. I went back to the foyer and found Luis sitting up straight in his chair listening to the bulletins being read by an excited announcer, and it looked like Maria would just have to wait for another day. He saw me and stood up, looking hopeful and smiling in anticipation of this mid-Atlantic equivalent of a snow day with pay and said, "Senhor, can I send the men home now?" I looked evenly at him and told him "No," the men would have to stay on their posts because we thought the problems would stay in Lisbon.

A frown formed on his worn tan face as he said, "The men will be very sad."

+++

Won't Have Nixon To Kick Around Anymore

President Richard M. Nixon inherited a societal mess when he came into office after LBJ and it never got better. He was the first US President to enjoy a State visit to Communist China in February 1972, a crowning achievement to his years spent in global diplomacy. Four months later, on June 17, 1972, a security guard at the Watergate Hotel interrupted a burglary at the Democratic offices. The burglars were working on behalf of Nixon's "Committee to Re-elect the President" (CREP) and pled guilty to the charges in January 1973. Shortly afterward, an investigation into "who knew what and when they knew it," was launched and over the course of the next year the scandal consumed the White House. The administration and its supporters accused the media of making "wild accusations," putting too much emphasis on the story and of having a liberal bias against the administration. The reporting turned out to be accurate and the competitive nature of the media guaranteed widespread coverage as the far-reaching political drama played out.

While the scandal evolved, Nixon undertook even more global travels, if for no other reason than to escape the drumbeat in Washington calling for his head. He was out of Washington for most of June 1974, making State visits to Austria, Egypt, Saudi Arabia, Syria, Israel, Jordan, and finally coming to Lajes to spend June 18-19. He was coming there to celebrate Portugal's return to democracy and meet the newly installed President Spinola. While this was certainly an important visit, there would be no pomp or circumstance because the layover would allow the President Nixon forty-eight uninterrupted hours, providing a chance to rest and recuperate from the whirlwind global tour and not be hounded by the liberal press in DC.

Our part in this operation was relatively straight forward. We would provide security and support for the presidential mission as directed by the Secret Service. The first advance team arrived a week before the official party. This team included agents to vet service members occupying sensitive positions while the White House communications service installed supplemental communications, a necessary move since our phone system was a 1944 Western Electric 551A telephone switchboard. It had a panel of switches and plugs. You'd stick a plug into the buzzing line's receptacle and flip the switch to answer a call. Sometimes it worked, sometimes it didn't, and the White House preferred not to take chances, as I found out the day a comm guy came to wire in a beige telephone with no dial. I asked him what it was for and he shrugged his shoulders, saying, "I don't know, I just put them in." I asked him who I could call and if I had to keep a log and he said, "No, no log. It's your phone, you just pick up the handset and tell the operator the number you want, area code first."

After he left, a white-haired older guy walked up to the counter. He asked if I was the primary desk operations controller and I told him I was. With a pleasant demeanor he asked, "Do you mind if I ask you just a few questions?" I invited him to come around to the break room and asked Shake to watch the phones.

I got us both some coffee and sat down across from him. Without introducing himself, he spent a few moments asking how I'd been enjoying the assignment, then got down to business. He asked if I kept track of politics and I confessed I didn't because the Stars and Stripes newspaper was always several days old by the time it arrived, shipped in from Germany, and besides, there was never any interesting news. When the TV news came on in the dayroom, I was either sleeping, at work, or in the club so I never saw it anyway. He then asked what I thought about the President. I told him I thought Nixon was a bad guy, but I'd sworn an oath to protect the office of the President and whoever was the current occupant. Those were the right words and I was then certified to be the operations controller for the President's upcoming visit.

He left during the now quiet part of the afternoon, after lunch but before school got out, and the phone rarely rang. I looked at the beige telephone and my curiosity finally got the better of me. I picked up the handset and after a moment the operator came on asking only, "What number, please?" I replied it was just a function check and hung up. The minute hand on the 24-hour clock made a solid thunk when it moved a notch, and after a few minutes that passed ever so slowly, I picked up the handset;

when the operator came on, I gave him a ten digit number. In an instant, I heard the ringing and was connected. I said, “Hello, Ma? How ya doing?”

It was determined that the President would occupy the Commanding General’s house during the course of his visit. White House carpenters, electricians, and HVAC technicians took the house down to the frame and rebuilt it, installing new electrical and telephone lines, putting up new drywall, painting, installing carpets, new appliances, and central air conditioning, making those quarters the first on the island with central air. The day before his arrival, a C-141 Starlifter transport arrived that was dedicated to carrying the backup for Presidential limousine and two Cadillac convertibles that were part of the motorcade, plus 18,000 pounds of Nixon’s personal furniture so he’d be comfortable in the commandeered quarters.

I’d been put on fourteen-hour shifts to provide continuity during that part of the day when something would most likely happen. I came in at six in the morning and left at eight that night. Wanting to get a sense of where everything was and to learn exactly how places were laid out, I called in a patrol to cover the desk. I then took his vehicle and drove slowly around the base, checking each place where the President would stay or visit until I finally found myself on the flight line by the hanger being used to store the Presidential motorcade.

I walked in and saw all three vehicles pulled into a semi-circle and an agent sitting sideways in the backseat of one Cadillac reading a magazine. I said hello and asked how it was going. The poor guy unloaded. “I’m not Secret Service, I’m a DEA agent and I got drafted for this job. They treat me like shit and you’re the first guy I’ve seen since I got here.” He asked if I could keep an eye on the vehicles while he went to the bathroom. When he came back, he offered to show me the President’s back up limo. It was a 1961 Lincoln Continental Presidential State car which he explained included a "heavy-duty heater and air conditioner, a pair of radiotelephones, a fire extinguisher, a first-aid kit, retractable platforms to stand on and handles to hold for Secret Service agents, a siren and flashing red lights recessed into the bumper.”

The car's Secret Service code name was the X-100 and was the same car President Kennedy had been riding in on the fateful day in Dallas in 1963. There I was, sitting in the back seat, right where Kennedy took those slugs, with a DEA agent giving me the history.

+++

Withholding All Transmissions

It was finally time. Air Force One was inbound and about ten miles out. This historic meeting was open to the public, everyone on the island was invited to see the two presidents meet. The aircraft parking area in front of Base Operations was jammed with thousands of excited, happy people, all cheering and waving. Any airman who wasn't working was on the ramp in uniform, along with their families and children. It was just the sort of thing to boost the flagging spirits of a world leader. The Portuguese were just excited to be hosting a new leader who wasn't a dictator.

We'd blocked all the intersections and access points to the flight line. No vehicles were to be permitted on the flight line once the Presidential aircraft was within five miles of touchdown. Secret Service snipers were widely dispersed in overwatch positions where they had an unrestricted view of the flight line and could "neutralize" any hostile target that presented itself.

The plane was just about five miles out and I put out a 10-3 transmission, meaning no radio traffic except for emergency traffic. The net was silent for only a minute before McSpadden, the entry control point by the Ops building, reported "Got some Portuguese guy here saying he needs to get on the flight line." I replied there was no traffic allowed per the Secret Service and "Tell him to walk or he can just *coma minha cueca*, (eat my shorts). Now get off the channel." There was a bit of a pause before McSpadden keyed the microphone and said, "Be advised, he heard that, and he's really pissed."

Air Force One landed and taxied to its parking slot in front of the Ops building. A smiling President Nixon came down the stairs where he was warmly greeted by a smiling President Spinola and an out-of- breath future Portuguese Ambassador to the United States. As luck would have it, he was also the guy I told to eat my shorts.

Phones started ringing within minutes of the two Presidents finishing their speeches to the assembled crowds and within thirty minutes I was delivering a most sincere and heart-felt apology to the Ambassador, a small price to pay to avoid an international incident with my name on it.

President Nixon, equally upset at the treatment he was receiving back home, and the mounting evidence of his involvement (thanks to his secret tape-recording system) resigned the office of the President on August 9, 1974.

I was much more circumspect in my radio transmissions after that because you really don't know who is listening.[3]

+++

[3] From mid-1979 until he was arrested in June 1981 and later convicted, Wayne Williams, "The Atlanta child murderer" roamed the countryside murdering between twenty-five to thirty-one black children and adults. This case drew national attention and then Vice President George Bush insisted on in-depth daily briefings. An adult magazine with seminal fluid and fingerprints was found near one of the victims and shipped to the FBI national lab for forensic examination. The fingerprints were in the system and belonged to a thirty-five year-old truck driver. The VP monitored the situation in real time as Atlanta SWAT teams stormed the suspect's house and later dragging him away in handcuffs. At police headquarters, he was confronted with the forensic evidence and asked to account for it being where it was found. He explained he was a good Baptist, but his wife was several months pregnant and, he hadn't had sex in quite a while, so he bought the magazine, jerked off to the photos and threw the magazine away. He also had alibis for many of the other murders and was released. The world's unluckiest man jerked off one time and the Vice President of the USA knew about it.

CHAPTER FIVE

Orders To Idaho

I'd arrived with Dale on the flight over to the Azores and he'd been serving his time as the desk sergeant on the afternoon shift we relieved; we of the seemingly perennial midnight shift, the ghouls assigned to skulk about at night, looking for any sign of theft or other villainy, of which there was quite a bit; we just weren't quite so good at catching them. This was brought home when "Sam Spade" discovered the secret to the currently rampant theft from the Commissary. Some corrupt Portuguese employees would wait for the garbage truck to come late at night and then fill the dumpsters with all the frozen food it could hold. The truck would swoop in, pick up the heisted produce and whisk it off-base for resale with nobody the wiser. We surrounded them and at the right time moved in, lights and sirens going. I jumped out of my truck to catch one thief and took him to the on-site booking officer. When I got back to my truck, I discovered one of the other thieves had just stolen my Federal brand siren from its brackets. Six months later I saw it in the window of an electronics store in the island capital, Angra de Herosimo. I took the siren from an agitated shop owner after pointing out the USAF engraving Sam Spade had wisely put on all expensive items in his other capacity as the supply clerk.

I arrived thirty minutes early, got the briefing from Dale, read the blotter, opened up the armory, did a visual weapons and ammo inventory, while looking for any rust Shake might have missed. I passed out the weapons to the arriving shift while receiving the weapons from the off-going shift. It didn't take much more than ten minutes, but OBM said arriving only fifteen minutes early made me late, so thirty minutes early was on time because I was an NCO and the desk sergeant. I'd learned this when I came in ten minutes before guardmount one evening. He announced I was late and made me write a Letter of Reprimand counseling myself and then he signed it. In fairness, when he came in "late" one evening he had me write him up and he reprimanded himself. I never really understood this requirement because neither were ever filed in our permanent jackets.

Dale was a good natured fellow from Ogden, Utah, not given to cursing or even being cross. He was excited that he'd gotten his orders but not in a good way. "I'm going to Mountain Home, Idaho," he wailed. *Airman* magazine came out once a month and had recently highlighted that base. Somebody said they had photographs of guys painting the rocks white. Since it wasn't on either coast, I considered it in the middle of nowhere and just felt sorry for Dale because he said it was nicknamed, "The air base time forgot."

Meanwhile, Dale was a "Jack" Mormon, an individual deemed by adherents of The Church of Jesus Christ of Latter-day Saints (LDS) to be an inactive or lapsed member who, despite his personal religious viewpoint, maintained good relations with and positive feelings toward the LDS Church. From Dale's laments, I found being Jack Mormon is much easier to do overseas than in Idaho, because Idaho is right next to Utah, which is home to LDS central. The hundreds of thousands of them seemed to him too interested in making sure he stayed a good Mormon. This assignment also meant being too close to his wife's family, all of whom thought Dale was a heretic because he drank coffee.

I probably should have been more empathetic, but I didn't even know where Idaho was or what Mormons were. It all sounded alien. I'd put down "any overseas" status on my assignment preferences "dream sheet" so I figured I'd be off to Germany or Italy next. I looked at Dale as he shrugged on his lightweight blue jacket and thought, "Poor bastard."

I came in the next night and after getting everything out of the way, went on the desk while Dale was putting on his jacket and he said, "Oh yeah, before I forget, you got a Holy Joe in your box." A Holy Joe is a reusable envelope that had address lines to track where the package was to go next, using a unit address. A little blue truck would then gather them up and deliver them to the different offices twice a day and that could only mean one thing — I'd gotten my orders! I'd been thirteen months on Terceira, and although it was a lovely place, it was time to move on.

I hustled to the back room, grabbed up the envelope and pulled out the forty sets of orders and scrolled down to the "Unit of Assignment" block to read the news.

FROM: 1605th Security Police Division, 1605th Air Base Wing (MAC), Lajes Field, Azores

TO: 366th Security Police Squadron, 366th TFW (TAC), Mtn. Home AFB, Idaho.

Just like Dale.

I caught his look when I stepped back on the desk and knew I was now the poor bastard.

I departed Lajes on the first day of November. My replacement was a fellow from Montana and, when he learned I was heading to Idaho, offered some advice. "I'd take the Queen's highway across Canada. They know how to deal with snow up there." Since I'd never heard anything to the contrary and he was from Montana, I went with it. I'd have nine-days travel time and was also given a three-day pass to get settled back in the USA and prepare for the move west.

In the age before internet communications, getting word back to America from overseas was very difficult. You could always sneak a call to Europe on Autovon, the military phone system, but calling the States was much harder. We were given five-minute "morale" calls back to the US using the MARS network, (Military Auxiliary Radio System) designed to provide contingency communications support for the United States Department of Defense and Military Services. It was manned by volunteer ham radio enthusiasts. This meant my parents had to be briefed to say, "*Over*" when they were done speaking and awaiting a reply. That word caused the radio operator to flip the switch so that you were transmitting. It was clumsy as my poor mother had to be coached each time by the US radio operator to say the word "Over." After a few minutes, the matter was settled by my father who got on the line and said, "Hey! How you doing over there? Over and *out.*" Upon hearing that magic word, "out," the line was disconnected. It was due to these communication limitations that I could only write them a letter informing them of my return. I told my father I'd be needing a car and to please look around and talk to our next-door neighbor, Burt, a used car salesman. He had always told me to see him when I needed a car and he'd get me a sweetheart deal.

I arrived at McGuire in the late morning. This time, a high school buddy, Bobby Latuga, drove the hundred and ten miles down to save me from the indignities I'd suffered at the hands of the New Jersey transit system the last time I returned to the States. That time I'd taken a bus the nineteen miles to the train station in Trenton. Vietnam was pretty much over so people forgot about calling vets in uniform "baby killers." I knew this because I got off the bus while wearing my dark blue service uniform zip-up jacket and, while I was getting oriented and trying to locate a train platform, some security guard yelled, "Hey! You gotta move that bus!" while pointing to a Greyhound forty-passenger bus idling at the curb. I declined his invitation and realized America had turned the corner on Vietnam.

My most recent former flight chief, Archie, the OBM's replacement, asked me to take a package to an address in Queens and deliver it to his elderly aunt; Bob was kind enough to drive me there. I dropped the small box off with Arch's compliments and ran back to the car. Bob asked what it was and I said, "Limburger cheese." His face crinkled at the word and he recoiled a bit. I looked at him, "That's the same thing the customs guy did at McGuire."

+++

The Great White North

In 1970 Ford unveiled the compact Maverick as the fuel-efficient successor to the popular Falcon. The 1971 model cost $1,971, tax not included. The body was new but the engineering team continued to use leftover gauges from the Falcon and Mustang to keep costs down. Americans wanted these cars and had been told repeatedly that known petroleum reserves were in danger of running out. These fears were further exacerbated by the 1973 OPEC Oil Embargo, a response to our assisting the Israelis during Nickel Grass. This translated into high prices, long lines at the pump, and a great deal of economic and social anxiety.

One of those Mavericks, a rather snappy low-milage, two-door version painted with what Ford called *champagne gold,* but was really more like butterscotch, had just come back on the market. Belonging to a recently deceased country doctor who'd only driven it on house calls, it became available when his son in distant Pennsylvania told Bert to get rid of it. Thus is came to be that my father and I were standing in line at the NY Department of Motor vehicles late on a Friday afternoon. Although I paid $800 for the car, my father finished writing the bill of sale for $200, only $600 below the price I'd paid. This saved me some considerable taxes, which was fair, since the car did not come with a lockable glove compartment, just a map shelf. I'd noticed the dead doctor failed to sign the vehicle title transfer paperwork. I pointed this error out to my father who simply said, "Oh yeah? Lemme see that." I gave it to him, pointed to the spot and he signed it. I told him that wasn't legal and he couldn't do that. He just smiled and said, "Whose gonna complain? The doc? The son?" It was my first lesson in practical application of civil law. I walked out with the new title and registration, ready to go north and then west.

Armed with the knowledge that the distances were vast, I invested in an 8-track player mounted on to the Maverick's transmission hump. It came with two bulky tapes of my choosing. This magnetic tape sound recording was newer technology that first came out in the late 1960s and lasted a decade until replaced by cassette tapes. When time came to make my choices, I just didn't know what to get. I'd never bought record albums because I was happy with the selections on the radio. I finally opted for eclectic, picking the rock opera "*Tommy*" by The Who, and "*The Best of Dolly Parton*" which included "*Mule Skinner Blues*" an early hit from 1970 that included her yodeling. Upon reflection these might not have been the best choices for a 3,335 mile expedition across the Canadian tundra.

Those remaining hours of liberty passed quickly, spent mainly in Moran's tavern on Friday and Saturday nights. Sunday was reserved for the folks and some of the relatives who popped by.

I'd been gone for seventy-three weeks and other than Mr. Metz finally dying, and Paulie's latest misadventure, there hadn't been much happening in that town.

Early Monday morning, knowing that the New York Thruway led to Buffalo and from there into Canada, I again left the hamlet of my birth, with all my belongings in the trunk of my car and headed down the LIE westbound and out into the wild. I made Buffalo by early afternoon and came rolling into Canada with a few hours of daylight to spare. The immigration officer at the booth looked at me after I gave him my military ID card and a copy of my orders. He glanced at them, then handed them back to me saying, "Welcome to Canada." I asked "Say, is there a Queen's highway, take me across Canada?" The cop just smiled and said, "Yup, just get on it here and go on up to Toronto. Then up Highways 69 and 17 towards Sault Ste Marie and ask again when you get to Winnipeg." And just like that I was motoring into the weak sunset as clouds and low scud made the street lights come on early.

Canada is an absolutely vast place. Its 3,855,102 square miles makes it the **second largest** country on the planet. The most populated province is Ontario, followed by Quebec and British Columbia. In between is nature, with a few larger cities like Regina, Sault Ste. Marie, and Calgary, but they are few and pretty far apart. At that time, the entire Canadian population was about 23 million while there were 21 million Californians.

By day two of my journey I was still in Ontario Province, but I'd left the really populated part. That day and for the next several days I would see what the movies always referred to as the great Canadian wilderness. Commercial radio stations were few and far between so for most of the journey I was relying on the Canadian Broadcast Company (CBC) for intelligent chat and news. If I wasn't in an area with radio reception, I always had my new favorite yodeler, Dolly, and *The Who,* teaching me the lyrics and melody by constant repetition. I'd been reluctant to play those tapes too often, not knowing how long their newness would last. Turned out it didn't last long at all.

I made my evening stop just outside of Sault Ste. Marie, at a small hotel along the shores of Whitefish Bay on Lake Superior, the same bay where just one year later the searchers all said the ore ship *Edmond Fitzgerald* might have found safety if only she'd put fifteen more miles behind her. It was a small, family-run place. In the tradition of the time, a light dinner came with the room, this owing in some part to Canadian hospitality, but mainly due to a complete and utter lack of restaurants in the region.

Up early the next morning, I got a good start on the day. As I cruised down Highway 17, I watched the low scud skies flying over a frothy and violent lake. The route hugged the shoreline and I was happy to watch ice beginning to form on the edges of the lake. The wave action made the large blocks of ice bob up and down and their mass increased with every bit of instantly frozen spray that arched over the top of those ice floes as a great lake began to freeze over.

That powerful scenery fell behind as the road turned into the forests, an unending line of trees that flowed with the road until there was just a point somewhere up ahead on the horizon, like a perspective drawing. Away from the lake, the skies remained leaden and looked to say there would be some snow sometime during the day. Up ahead in the distance, I saw two figures standing alongside the highway, one parka-clad hiker had a thumb stuck high in the air, a universal signal for "Please give me a lift." To break the monotony and since it seemed the right thing to do, I decided to pull over, imagining it was two beautiful Canadian girls heading west to make their debut in Playboy. I cast aside any doubts or concerns for potential Canadian mass-murderers, like Wayne Clifford Boden. Nicknamed the Vampire Killer, sometimes between 1969 and 1971, he viciously bit the breasts of and then murdered three women in Montreal, then did the same to one more poor woman in Calgary.

It was a bitterly cold morning. The 2.8 liter four-cylinder power plant Ford installed had enough of a challenge moving the car along at 55 mph in a headwind, let alone generate any heat for the defroster. It was freezing in the cabin so I knew those poor bastards I was now looking at were truly cold. For reasons known only to them, life left them standing in the actual middle of nowhere. The last place that had a sign pointing towards it said, “Micipicoten 140 miles.” Thunder Bay still lay over 300 miles ahead.

Sadly, both hikers were male, wearing large puffy parkas, wool caps, and full beards. They tossed their gear into the back seat and offered a hearty, “Merci beaucoup” as they crammed onto the bench seat and into me. It was at that moment I learned they only spoke French when they asked in heavily accented English, “Where to go?” I took that as meaning “How far can you take us?” Not really sure about how far I’d get that day, I could only think of the place I’d planned to hit that evening. In the interest of international relations, I summoned up my best Maurice Chevalier accent and said, “Thunder Bay” which came out sounding like “*Thun-DAR Bay-yea.*” They both nodded excitedly as I pulled away and on to the road. I don’t know what compelled me to add the accent, but I also don’t know why I bothered to pull over when I stopped because there weren't any other cars on the road.

It was but a moment after regaining highway speed and committing to sharing this journey, that I became acutely aware that one, or most likely both of them, had recently enjoyed some extra garlic for breakfast. While my usual Spooney-instilled response would have been to open the windows, it was just colder than a well-digger’s ass which gave me pause, so I elected to just tough it out.

“Tough it out” is a relatively loose use of that phrase, because after about forty miles, it was getting bad. Cold, stale, moist, garlic-infused air was circulating the cabin as small spots of fog began to appear on the upper edges of the windshield. A quick glance told me the passenger window was completely obscured. The defroster simply couldn't handle this new atmosphere and neither could I. In the conversation in my head, I’m thinking, “There’s toughing it out in the interest of international relations and being a good guy.” Then I considered my more compelling reality:

I had two really stinky French-speaking guys in my car and, even if they weren’t mass murderers, their breath was killing me, and so far today I’d already carried them farther then anybody else had.

I absently contemplated this while "Tommy" was on about pinball wizards. My salvation came about an hour later when I saw a sign announcing the township of White River, aka the self-declared "Coldest Spot in Canada." I could hardly pass up a chance to visit and perhaps have lunch, even though it was only half past ten. I feigned astonishment and said something like, "Sacre bleu! I have, how you say, 'Le biziness' in Cold Spot!" again thinking an accent would aid understanding. I pointed and gestured at the sign and when I came to the off ramp, I pulled over and bid them a fond adieu saying, "Bon chance, mon amis, bon voyage!" (Good luck my friends, good journey!) This was all the French I'd ever really learned, all thanks to reading Sgt. Rock comics. This WWII action hero had many adventures while leading a small unit all over France. I mainly remembered because he worked with Mme. Marie of the French resistance. A fierce and deadly guerrilla leader, she wore a jaunty red beret, and tight clingy sweaters, while holding a chattering machine gun in her hands. She'd always call out that farewell as Rock and Easy company moved back into the war.

The boys bravely continued that lonely hike west while I pulled off and into the parking lot of a cafe, well really, the only cafe in White River. I parked the car and because all of my valuables were inside, I elected to lock it as well. I went inside where I was greeted by a very gregarious waitress who asked what I wanted to drink. As she brought the coffee to my table by the window, she commented off-handedly, "Say, is that your car with the New York plates?" pointing to the only car in her parking lot. I told her it was and she said in a kindly way "You might want to think about just leaving your car running. Nobody will steal it, but it's pretty darn cold today and you might not be able to restart it later and if that happens you have to get towed to a heated garage while you wait for the engine block to thaw."

She spoke so plainly and so matter-of-factly that I saw no reason to disagree with her and even though America had just come through a massive oil embargo, there was plenty of petrol up north and another good reason to drive across Canada. I felt compelled to follow her advice so I went outside and started the car. I noted that the temperature gauge had returned to cold — same as if it had sat overnight and this after less then 15 minutes.

I went back inside and gazed at the frozen landscape, briefly wondering how those hitchhikers were doing, and then my order came.

I got back out to the highway forty minutes later and saw no sign of the travelers as I pressed on towards Thunder Bay. My luck held and I arrived by late afternoon. I debated about getting a room, but while the sun was slanting low in the sky, there was still too much daylight and I hadn't made as many miles as I'd hoped. I could either gut it out right now, or have to make up miles towards the end of the trip. I didn't relish that thought, so I filled my tank, bought a pack of Player's Navy filter cigarettes and departed Thunder Bay, heading west and into the increasing gloom of the oncoming evening.

I'd gone around ninety miles, the snow steadily falling, light and fluffy in stretches where it would just glide by either side of the car, or strike the windshield and melt when it hit the warm glass, to be wiped away by the rubber blades that were making a steady and never ending sweep. At other times, a break in the wood line would channel wind across the road, revealing the dark macadam as the snow screed past, soon lost to white forest floor on the other side.

All in all, it really wasn't that bad. The road was straight, the traffic almost nonexistent and I'd had a Thunder Bay radio station to keep me company for quite a while, but now the signal was fading as was my enjoyment of Carole King singing "Jazzman" for the 17th time. I started to think maybe going quiet for a few hundred miles wasn't such a bad thing.

It might have been the national economy and budget, or it might have been that Canadians know where all the highways go but, unlike the States where sign requirements are set to support the sign-making industry, the Canadians were having none of that. There was quite simply nothing to spoil the exquisite, if somewhat endless, wilderness of which they should be most proud.

The next problem for me was that I'd become aware that my fuel gauge was drifting steadily down towards the half-tank mark and I could either continue and hope to find fuel, or I could turn back to Thunder Bay. Again, the voices in my head went back and forth. I thought that surely there were petrol stations within standard fuel tank range. Of course, that didn't have to be the case either. It might be some kind of business model that depended on having folks get stuck in the middle of nowhere, needing fuel or a tow to defrost their car, I couldn't say. As the gloom intensified, just before the light was lost, I had a flashback to the movie Dr. Zhivago, where he is trying to get to his lover and is forced to make his way across the endless frozen Russian steppes, battling to survive. I saw him with red-rimmed eyes and snow frozen into his eyebrows and beard and shivered.

Ignoring the peril and noticing the fuel needle dipping below a half tank, I elected to continue shooting for the town of Ignace, still in Ontario, which I'd read was officially labeled the "The Heartland Province," although it seemed to me the "Ain't Nobody Here Province" was more appropriate.

Darkness came full on and snow flakes became little white dots swooping into the glare of the headlights and creating a tunnel effect to my eyes. I knew the road was still pencil-straight but the edge of the road reflective poles were far apart and in some spots the reflectors were covered with snow. I lowered my speed to fifty, hoping to improve my fuel economy, but that orange needle just kept dropping. Finally dipping below one quarter tank put me into that fuel-anxiety state where no matter what, you're never comfortable with how much driving time you have left. I hadn't any real idea of how far Ignace would be and I hoped to see some brightly lit up sky appear on the horizon, a sky glowing blue from the mercury vapor street lamps common to rural areas. The miles slid past ever slower as I dropped my speed to forty-five now that the fuel gauge was below an eighth of a tank.

During that time I went through the mental checklist of the survival items I had in the car. Clothing, check. I had a blue USAF flight jacket with fur parka hood, lined gloves, a knit Navy watch cap. I was also armed with a half a pack of Player's cigarettes and a zippo lighter, but no food and no water. Dr Zhivago's frosted face came back to me.

Right as I was beginning to think I was hosed, I saw the bluish glow announcing civilization and drawing closer the snows let up briefly and I saw the one-pump filling station on the left side of the highway, so I gratefully pulled in. Although just past eight, the steadily falling snow made it feel later. The pump guy came outside and asked what I wanted. I wasn't prepared for that to be the first question, because given how far away this place was from Thunder Bay, I'd have thought that'd be fairly obvious to all but the most casual observer. So instead I said, "Can you fill it up, please?" He set about the task then came around front and said, "You want me to replace that driver's side headlamp?" Sure enough, somewhere along the way, the headlamp, perhaps mourning its former owner, had died. This also cleared up the mystery as to why the road seemed so dark. I told him "Absolutely" and while he was removing the dead lamp asked, "Say, how far is Ignace?"

He didn't look up from his work. "Oh, it'd be about ten miles." I was encouraged so I asked, "Do they have any good restaurants?" He thought a moment and said, "Oh yeah, there's a good breakfast at the cafe, you'd want to try it." I was a bit confused. "Sorry, I meant any restaurants open tonight."

He looked at me "I heard you. That cafe also makes an excellent steak and it's open all night." He leaned forward while reaching down for the plug, "But you can't get to Ignace tonight, seein's there's been a lorry overturned on the highway."

It took a moment before watching all those WWII movies as a kid in New York paid dividends and I recalled lorry being the English word for a truck. I said, "Oh, that's not good. I don't think I can go back." He looked at me like I was simple and said, "Well, you can stay at the motel across the street." I turned around and sure enough, the snow squall had lightened up so I could see across the highway the small eight-unit motel with owner's house attached. "I guess you must stay there a lot when a lorry tips over on the highway." He snorted, "I hope so, I own it. Go check in."

I paid for the fuel and headlamp and drove across the highway. The parking lot was empty and I pulled in front of the door to the house, which also served as the reception desk. I rang the bell and after a few moments the door opened and I was greeted by a guy who must have been just a hair under seven feet tall, an imposing giant of a man. He was made more commanding, and more sinister, by his wild unkempt beard, shiny black hair, and dark, deep-set eyes, all giving him a resemblance to the crazy Russian monk, Rasputin, the one they had to shoot, poison, stab, and finally drown to get rid of. I looked up at him and asked about the room. He looked at me for a moment and in Rasputin's own deep voice said:

"We have a room. The price is eight dollars."
"Does it come with dinner?"
"No, you've missed dinner."
"Got a TV?"
"No."
"Got a radio?"
"No."
"Phone?"
"No."

I'm beginning to wonder about this guy and not in a good way. I'd seen plenty of movies involving remote hotels and bad outcomes, so I was gonna be ready now.

"So what exactly do I get for my eight bucks?"

"We guarantee you an undisturbed night's rest." And with that I am really getting nervous, but I needed a place to stay, so I pulled out the cash and he took it while opening the key box.

"Room number eight is available."

Available? I had to work to stifle a laugh. I haven't seen another car in hours and there aren't any other tracks in the parking lot. I thought about a movie I'd watched where the hotel killers put the victim in the last room where the bedposts would slowly retract and smother the poor bastard, and I wasn't having it.
"I'd like room number FOUR please." There, solved that problem, can't be two murder rooms!

Grudgingly, he gave up the key and lost any chance to brighten up the menu, while I walked back out into the now gently falling snow, got in my car and backed into the space right in front of my door. I opened the trunk, grabbed my overnight bag and went inside. As promised, there were no electrical distractions of any kind and it was deathly quiet. But I was also very hungry, not having eaten since breakfast at the coldest spot in Canada, so that took precedence over any any qualms I had about potential murder schemes.

I remembered seeing a vending machine in the gas station office so I walked across the empty road and went inside. The vending machine with CANDYSHOP written across the top made an inviting offer; as I closed in, I realized out of ten selection windows, eight were empty. The battling choices were down to a three-pack of imitation fig newtons or a three-pack of orange crackers and cheese, the cheese being powdered and a color not found in nature. At this point I would have eaten anything, I didn't care, so the newtons and crackers were shoved into my parka pocket. I did ask the owner if he had any magazines because the hotel did not. He told me to help myself, pointing to a drawer, then went off to tend to something in the work bay. I opened the drawer hoping to see a Playboy and was profoundly disappointed to find nothing but past issues of "*Logger's World*" magazine.

Saddened, I walked outside, back into the snow falling on the pines and muffling any sound as if it were strained through cotton. The popping and creaking of the trees in the wind, and even the scrunch of my boots on the dry snow was softer. I saw the telephone booth and remembered I'd promised to call my mother each night from the road, just to let her know I was all right. Perhaps it was the days of isolation and lack of meaningful human interaction, but this place was spooky and I was getting just a little concerned for my safety and really needed to let her know where I was.

I pushed open the folding glass door, closed it against the weather, and no interior light came on. The gas station waiting room gave enough light to see the phone on the wall. It had a handset but no dial. It did have a spot on top to catch the coins.

Heading inside, I found the guy, who was now washing a carburetor in a sink full of gasoline. "Hi! Trying to make a call, but noticed the phone has no dial," I reported. He didn't stop washing, just said, "Turn the crank twice, then pick up the handset and tell the operator the number you want."

Well, that made sense, I should have known that from the movies. I went back inside the booth and looked, but there wasn't any crank, just the flat counter for holding your change or a notepad. Again I left the booth for the garage. I didn't even get a chance to speak when he said, "The crank is under the change counter." Again I'm back outside and now I find the crank. I give it two turns and lift the handset to my ear. The operator comes on sounding distant. "How may I help?" I explain I want to make a collect call to the US and I give her the phone number. She asks, "What number are you calling from?" I think, "What number?" I'm in a booth on a phone with no dial! Where are they going to put the number if not in the middle of the dial?

I saw the rates card at the top of the phone. There, in black grease pencil was written **R 1 R 2** which I took to mean "Ring One, Ring Two" and I offered that guess to the operator who immediately thanked me and put the call through. I heard my mother answer, accepting the "collect" charges. I didn't wait for her to even start talking and said, "Listen Ma, there's something weird up here. Make a note, I'm trying to get to a place called Ignace in Ontario Province. Write that down. I'm ten miles out of town and I'm not certain, but I think they might be vampires or something."

My mother immediately dismissed my concerns out of hand, but she didn't know I was in a nation of deranged breast-biting homicidal maniacs. In her motherly way, she said commandingly, "Don't be paranoid, or you'll let your imagination get carried away." She'd bought a map for just this occasion and was tracking my progress with a pin. She located Ignace and then English River where it crossed the highway as my approximate location. I told her I'd call again the next night, and that no matter what, I loved her and to call the Royal Canadian Mounted Police if it turned out I was right. I rang off and trucked back across the street to my room where I ate those dusty little treats, then washed it all down with the coke.

With nothing to read and nothing to do, I decided to take a shower before going to bed. I let the shower run, waiting for the water to heat. I'd finally stayed in a place where the infra-red lamp in the ceiling was not just a "nice to have;" it was absolutely necessary to keep this bathroom toasty. I looked at the room's outside door, walked over, turned the lock and slid the chain. Then I remembered how in every bad movie I ever saw, that chain didn't stop anybody, or anything, bent on mayhem, not ever. Still, I wanted to improve security, so I pulled the chair out from behind the desk, figuring to prop the back up tight under the door knob, to brace it shut, like I'd often seen in those same movies. Sadly, the back of this chair was a little too short to reach the knob, let alone fit underneath to provide a brace. Leaving it there would just make the villains work a little bit harder and that was OK with me.

Still somewhat concerned about homicidal maniacs, I kept my glasses on and my eyes open during the shower, watching that room door for any sign of violence. The shampoo stung my eyes, but it was a small price to pay to not be taken unawares. Clean and ready for bed, I felt if anything untoward was going to happen, it would have happened in the shower, so I shut off the light and went to sleep. I snapped awake at half past four, my stomach aching from hunger. I opened the door and saw no foot or tire prints in the snow. Now confident that I wasn't going to be murdered during my exit, I fired up the Maverick, tossed in my bag, cleared the several inches of fluffy snow from the windows, and set off towards Ignace, figuring the cops must have cleared that lorry wreck by now.

Around five, I crawled into town and saw the cafe. It was hard to miss actually, brightly lit with a large electric sign affirming "CAFE" in bright red letters. As I entered, a wave of warm and humid air, assuring with the happy smells of breakfast being made, engulfed me. I savored the aroma of bacon sizzling and listened to the eggs frying on a flatiron griddle. It was all so inviting, it about knocked me over. I thought about the words of Saint Al of MacDill, who'd casually remarked one day on our way to an outdoor social after a Baptist tent revival meeting, that had embraced the Holy Spirit unequivocally, but for far too long:

> *"I'm so hungry if you'd put a biscuit on my forehead,*

my tongue'd like to beat me to death trying to get it!"

My intensifying hunger pangs joined me as I took a seat at the counter and told the waitress, "Orange juice, a stack of pancakes with butter and maple syrup, ham and cheese omelet with side of bacon, hash browns and keep the coffee coming please!" She considered me over her half reading glasses, "Somebody must be hungry." I told her I was, and shared my experience at the motel due to the lorry overturning. She guffawed and looked at me like I was the village idiot. "Is that what he told you? Oh dearie, you're not the first person to come in here after falling for that old story, but it has been a bit. Ha! Oh ho ho, the coffee's on me!" She flapped the towel over her shoulder and looked at the cook who looked up from his cooking more to see the tourist than anything else.

Fuller and wiser, I left the cafe and gentle, snow-covered Ignace, continuing west. I'd found out that Regina was six hundred and fifty-three miles away and, with any luck, I'd make it there by six that evening. As I pressed on, the snows surrounding Lake Superior and the Province of Ontario began to dissipate and the skies finally cleared as I approached and crossed the boundary into Manitoba, where the folks claimed to be "Glorious and Free." I drove steadily along, passing endless wheat fields now laying fallow until the next crop was planted.

As large as that province is, extensive agriculture is found only in the southern area. The most common agricultural activity is cattle husbandry, followed by assorted grains and oilseed. Around twelve percent of Canada's farmland is in Manitoba, yet the population was just under one million people and two and a half percent of them were recent immigrants from Iceland. What does that say about a place? Potentially twenty-five thousand lonely Icelandic farmers, and, as I learned on the CBC, the odd mass-murderer, because there sure wasn't anybody else on the road.

I'd listened to a discussion about violent offenders, and in particular, one Victor Hoffman, just twenty-one years old and released three weeks earlier from a mental hospital over in Saskatchewan. Seems that back in mid-August of 1967, Victor went to the Peterson family farm armed with a .22-calibre

Browning pump-action repeater rifle and murdered all nine members of the family, seven of them children, all at close range. Wildrew Lang, the hired hand, found them the next morning and had to run almost four miles to a telephone post to report the crime. Hoffman was arrested four days later by the RCMP and confessed to the crime saying he'd fought the devil and went on to describe Lucifer in great detail, as being "tall, black and having no genitals." He was found not guilty by reason of insanity and put away in the mental hospital after being diagnosed with paranoid schizophrenia. During the trial, Crown prosecutor Serge Kujawa called Hoffman "the craziest man in Saskatchewan."

So now Victor was free and with any luck he's gonna be the guy working at the next gas station I pull into.

By early afternoon, I'd just rolled past Winnipeg where "Jazzman" was still doing very well on its meteoric rise so I'd dialed in the CBC for news and talk. It was a bright clear day and the reception was perfect. The announcer had a pronounced Scottish accent which seemed fair since twenty percent of the population were immigrants from Scotland. She was keen to introduce Captain Frank, from the Winnipeg Fire Department, who was going to "talk to us today about the importance of smoke detectors."

I settled in, slouching slightly into the corner by the door, allowing me to use my left foot to depress the accelerator pedal and give my right foot a rest. I was belted in and effecting a modified gangster-lean with eyes just above the dash line like I'd learned from Scottie, the guy from Indianapolis. He demonstrated this to me while we shared a patrol in the Azores and shortly before crashing our car into a low stone wall he didn't see. Unlike him, I could see for miles and successfully avoided the non-existent traffic, all the while staring out at the never-ending sea of dark brown soil and stubble that stretched on towards infinity as I followed the sun.

Captain Frank was a kindly sounding man. He very patiently explained why smoke detectors could save lives and how little they cost. I gave his words a lot of weight and had I been living in Winnipeg and heard him, I'd have gone straight out to the local hardware store and bought a unit. I drove on as Captain Frank took a few phone calls from bored and lonely housewives. All too soon his thirty minutes were up and he was shown the studio door, as the hostess said, "Tanks again for coming round Captain Frank, and mind yourself going out that door, close it if you would please, ta, tanks very much then." After the door closed, she gaily announced "All right children, time for marionette theater!"

That got my attention.

The air waves went dead and I imagined hundreds of lonely, bored, blond-haired Icelandic-looking children on distant and lonely farms all across the prairie, happily running up the wooden stairs to their rooms, and throwing open the hand-carved toy box lovingly made by their immigrant grandfather and set at the foot of their bed. They'd toss out their other toys and treasures until finally pulling out their marionette. They'd race back downstairs while hurriedly untangling strings to be ready for the lesson while I'd smoked a cigarette waiting for the show to go on. The hostess must have just finished her smoke because she suddenly came back on asking, "Are ye ready children? Have ye got your puppets?" (Only she pronounced it "**poo-pets.**")

In my mind's eye, I could see all of these even-featured, blue-eyed, tow-headed children standing erect, holding their marionettes cum poopets, all just aquiver and at the ready like the kids in "Village of the Damned." I'd seen that movie just a few months earlier at Lajes on "Bad British Movie and free popcorn night." In that classic, the inhabitants of the British village of Midwich suddenly fall unconscious. Two months later all women and girls regardless of age are discovered to be pregnant, sparking many accusations of infidelity and extramarital sex but really they all got knocked up by space aliens bent on taking over the planet.

I snapped back when I heard a phonograph needle hitting a vinyl record and in a moment the tinny sounds of the "poopet music" came out from the dashboard speaker. I listened, hoping for a joke, but no, the "tink ta tink ta tink" poopet music just kept going on with little variation. In my mind's eye, I saw poopets kicking and flailing until mercifully, after some protracted period of time, the admittedly mildly hypnotic music stopped. With a cheery goodbye from our hostess and as the sun slanted lower on the horizon, I imagined some frustrated nordic offspring in Saskatchewan strangling his poopet and getting ready to be the next Victor Hoffman.

The next eight hundred and eighty-five miles brought me to Regina, then Moose Jaw, Swift Current, and into Saskatchewan past Medicine Hat, and finally to Lethbridge in Alberta. The landscape was absolutely unremarkable save the amazing fact that it is so unremarkable. Wheat fields and farm houses dominate the scenery and at regular intervals a small town with a grain silo, rail tracks, a gas station, and a place to eat appear. Some towns had a small grocery store, Canadian VFW hall, a motel and book-end gas stations, like they were put together from the same town master plan and leaving nothing ever to recall. Just a long stretch of highway and the sun letting you know how you were doing, and I learned that sixty miles per hour worked best for figuring arrival time that evening, one mile a minute.

+++

The Operative Word Is Mountain

After crossing the border at Sweetgrass, Montana, I reached that night's target town, Lincoln. Nestled in a broad valley and surrounded by mountains, it is a lovely, if not somewhat isolated, community. Sadly, Lincoln would later become infamous as home of mad "Unabomber" Ted Kaczynski.

Still alive in the morning, I took off sans maps because there was only one road, US Highway 93, labeled "the loneliest highway in America," and sailed on into the town of Salmon, Idaho, population 2,910. The large carved wooden sign proudly proclaimed I was also in the county seat of Lemhi County, famous for being just thirty miles northwest of where Lewis & Clark crossed the continental divide.

To celebrate my arrival in Idaho, as well as getting some breakfast, I pulled into the parking lot of a roadside cafe. It was a small affair with just six seats at the counter and three bolted-in tables made of a laminated imitation wood finish. The waitress was a large-boned woman with flowing gray hair, worn too long for a woman of her years, and given she was also the cook. She came over and asked me what I wanted. Just like that, she came up, and eyeing me with some suspicion, said, "Now, what do *you* want?" I don't really blame her for giving me the hard once over, no doubt due to me being a stranger from back east, which was justified. This was 1974 after all, and just a few months earlier, on July 20, Shirley Marie Curry, of Lowell, Arkansas, who, wanting to "solve all the heartaches and hurts," shot and killed her three children, former husband, and his stepsister. Once the waitress satisfied herself that I wasn't like Shirley, she took my order and off she went. Before the food came, I got up and looked for a toilet, but finding none called back to the waitress-now-cook and asked, "Bathrooms?" She didn't even look up, just tilted her head and nodded, saying, "Around back."

I stepped outside into the chilly morning air and followed the wooden walkway around to the back of the building and was astonished to see an real outhouse. It was just a box constructed of rough-hewn vertical boards made gray by time and nature. The hinged door had a crescent moon cut out to facilitate air movement and provide some light; it was just like in the old movies! I shouldn't have been surprised since America didn't become fully electrified until forty years earlier, when President Franklin Roosevelt established the Rural Electrification Administration (REA) under authority of the Emergency Relief Appropriation Act of 1935. At that time, only ten percent of the nation's farms had electricity.

Locally, the Salmon River Electric Cooperative was created, and by 1953 was delivering retail electric service to accounts in south central Idaho including parts of Lemhi County. These improvements fueled my disbelief at what was on offer for my biological needs. My disbelief turned to chagrin by an absolute lack of evidence of any other toilet facilities. After seeing what was alleged to be the toilet, I made a complete walk around the exterior of the building in case this was some kind of joke they played on tourists. Satisfied this was, in sad fact and truth, the place, I opened the door and went inside with some trepidation having lived in the Azores, where running water was also not guaranteed and outdoor toilets were not unknown. My only immediate concern were things that might live in that environment, in an outhouse next to a small cafe in the middle of the Idaho wilderness. An old coat hanger held a roll of the thinnest toilet paper I'd ever seen. I banged the seat several times to drive off any residents and took my chances.

I finished my breakfast and by way of directions asked the waitress if she knew the way to Mountain Home generally, and Mountain Home Air Force Base particularly. She said, "Yup, just go down this road for a hundred and twenty miles or so to Arco, turn right on to highway 20 across the desert, and follow it until you get to Mountain Home."

I heard that word "desert" and locked on it. I asked her if she was certain about those directions, the operative word in the name of the base being "Mountain." She just looked at me as if I were simple and said slowly, "Just stay on 93 and go around one hundred and twenty miles or so, turn right on highway 20 and go across the desert and follow it until you get to Mountain Home." I agreed to disagree, well, not disagree, just not internally accept this new information, because until that minute I was convinced the base was somewhere in the alpine region, above the five-thousand foot mark. I was soon disabused of that notion.

My life so far had been systematically acclimating me to reduced population densities. In 1971 New York City had a population density of about 27,000 people per square mile. In Tampa, Florida, in 1973, that number was 1,617. On Terceira Island it was 363 and most of them lived in the capital city, Angra de Herosimo, over on the other side of the island. Here and now, I was about to live in a place with only six people per square mile.

On the ride from Salmon, I passed two small hamlets: Challis, population 765, and Mackay, population 540. I was enjoying the scenery provided by the narrow valley cutting through the Rocky Mountains while still holding out hope that the whole "desert" thing was a mistake, but that wasn't to be.

The forests eventually gave way to sagebrush-choked high desert as I continued my trek down the loneliest highway in America. Somewhere past MacKay, the several cups of coffee I'd indulged in earlier gave me a persistent reminder of such increasing intensity that I found myself needing relief post-haste. I knew better than to imagine some gas station existing out here where there was no traffic. I drove on for several miles still hoping against hope for a roadside rest area, but was sadly disappointed. Seeing no alternative, I pulled off to the side of the road and returned the morning's coffee to the land. At first I was nervous, concerned that some passing motorist might see me and call the police reporting me as some exhibitionist pervert, but it finally began to sink in that I was concerned about nothing because there was nothing out there, and I could see if anyone was heading my way from at least five miles off. As I should have learned in Canada, I didn't need to worry about parking my car out of a concern for impeding the traffic flow.

I finally reached the town of Arco, which was really just a place to put a junction so travelers could turn west on Highway 20 and finally on to Mountain Home. Arco, originally known as Root Hog, was the first community in the world ever lit by electricity generated solely by nuclear power. This occurred for *about an hour* some eighteen years earlier, on July 17, 1955. Power was provided by Argonne National Laboratory's BORAX-III reactor at the nearby National Reactor Testing Station (NRTS), which eventually became the site of the Idaho National Energy Laboratory. I drove slowly through the town, not wishing to injure any of the 1,500 people alleged to be living there but I didn't see a soul. After leaving the town and heading back into the big empty I realized exactly why the US government selected this area for the first commercial atomic reactor, because if it ever blew, nobody would hear it or notice it.

What I didn't know was that on January 3, 1961, the SL-1 reactor was destroyed through an operator maintenance error, causing the deaths of all three personnel present. It was the world's first fatal reactor accident. That news of national importance was overshadowed by the international announcement that the "longest recorded strike in history, by Danish barbers' assistants, had ended after thirty-three years."

I pressed on and, by late afternoon, saw a sign warning of road construction for the next twenty miles. They weren't kidding and they weren't just patching some potholes, they were constructing a whole new road because the old highway surface was gone, replaced by a large cut exposing the hard pan. The edge was delineated periodically by a sawhorse with a blinking yellow light to guide me along. I felt an admiration for the locals. New Yorkers suffer a never-ending series of months' long and terribly inconvenient roadway repairs to the already overcrowded Long Island Expressway, now billed as the world's longest parking lot. Idaho just fixed it right the first time and was done with it.

The sun was setting in the western sky when I came upon an alien landscape. Lava fields stretched for miles on one side of the highway and I thought, "This place looks like the moon." Just a few more miles, and I read the sign announcing "*Craters of the Moon*" where Apollo 14 astronauts Alan Shepard, Edgar Mitchell, Stuart Roosa and Apollo 17 astronaut Eugene Cernan, the last human off the moon, visited and explored the lava landscape after learning the basics of volcanic geology. This revelation led to a disturbing thought, "Is this what it's going to look like for the next thirteen months until my enlistment is up?"

I pressed on, passing only a few small towns, like Fairfield, a county seat, with a population of just 330. As the light began to fail, I moved out of that high valley and dropped into the eastern Snake River Valley. The bright lights of Mountain Home soon appeared on the horizon. The town was originally a post office at Rattlesnake Station, a stagecoach stop on the Overland Stage Line, several miles east and up in the mountains. In 1883, the Oregon Short Line Railroad pounded through the valley and bypassed that junction. The post office followed that iron horse downhill and west to the city's present site. Those now-displaced pioneers lamented that they were forced to leave their Mountain Home for the flats, so geography ignored, they stubbornly kept the name.

I pulled into town a little after seven, stopping to get gas at the only visible gas station, the V-1. The sign announced that they also sold propane which was good to know, never having needed propane before. I pulled alongside the pump island and the attendant came out to fill my tank. It was full dark and I had no idea how much further I needed to go, but it had taken six long days to complete the 3,307 mile trip. I asked the attendant, a guy a little younger than I was, while he washed the window "Which way to the airbase?" With a face devoid of hope for any future outside of that town, he simply nodded off into the darkness and said, "Just follow this road, you can't miss it."

I took off and after eight miles with no sign of any base, just darkness, and suspicious of the kid's directions, I turned around and drove back to town. I pulled into a bar on the side of the highway and asked the bartender where the base was and he confirmed the gas station guy, adding, "They didn't put up a highway sign, wanted to make it harder on the Ruskies. It's about twelve miles out to the base, but you'll see the lights." I got back into the car and eleven miles later, sure enough, I cleared a rise and saw the lights of the base in the near distance.

I was beat but felt pretty comfortable coming back on to a military installation where I knew there would be some decent food at the dining hall and a nice hotel room where the front desk clerk sold mini-bottles of liquor and soft drinks. All I had to do was stop at the front gate and get directions.

+++

Last tour—366th Security Police Squadron

Rat-Faced Washburn

US Highway 67 is a four-lane highway that ends at the main gate of Mountain Home AFB, aka "The Goat." That entrance is a half mile from the beginning of the base proper and it was long rumored the USAF moved the gate closer to the town to avoid paying "isolated duty pay" to all the airmen.

I came around a gentle bend and slowed my car as the gate came into view. It was a Saturday night and only one cop was posted. As I drew up, I already had my DD Form 2AF ID card out and the registration papers on the seat. He put up his hand for me to stop, so I rolled down my window and said, "Good evening" while handing up my ID card, "I'm just arriving from overseas and can you tell me where the base lodging office is, please?"

His name tag identified him as A1C Washburn. He had a thin mustache and kept the brim of his hat pulled low. He didn't say anything, just took my ID card and walked to the front of the car, specifically to the right front headlight where, with his left forefinger, made an exaggerated wiping motion across the lamp, pulled it up and walked back over to me. He examined his dirty digit a little more closely and said, "Well listen, Sarge, that headlamp is dimmer than the other and I could write you up, but I'll cut you some slack this time, just get it fixed." He handed me back my ID card and said, "I'll be watching for you."

I was surprised because I'd never heard of anything that ridiculous, but this wasn't the time to make further inquiries. I thanked him for his consideration and he gave me directions to the lodging office. The next morning I opened my room door to greet the day and get a cup of coffee from the lobby, and was immediately looking into a dust storm with tumbleweeds blowing past. Tumbleweeds! Just like you'd see in some old western. I slammed the door shut thinking, "Where the hell am I?"

I checked into the squadron on Monday and, thanks to reduced manning as the drawdowns continued, finished in-processing by Wednesday afternoon with instructions to report to work on Friday night at ten. I turned twenty-one that day and was now old enough to drink in all fifty states. The dining hall mess attendant checking meal cards noted that it was my natal day and I was later treated to a cupcake with a single candle.

I came in thirty minutes early that Friday night and met Delbert, the flight chief, and Lonny, the assistant flight chief. Delbert told me I'd be the desk sergeant and security operations controller since drawdowns and mission changes meant combining security with law enforcement. He also introduced me to my work partner, another sergeant named Andrews. Guardmount was at ten and the guys on flight began coming in after drawing their weapons from the armory around back. While guardmount got underway, Andrews and I remained on the desk, having relieved our counterparts thirty minutes earlier, after they briefed us on the evening's activities. The chief announced my arrival and told the flight to introduce themselves on their way out the door. I'd seen the duty roster assignments and was delighted to find A1C Washburn slotted for Police 3, better known as Slave 1, the unit responsible for cleaning the office and all the vehicles. Ignoring the signs saying, "Stay off the desk," he stepped up and into the desk area uninvited, while saying casually, "Hello, Sarge, welcome to Mountain Home. I'm A1C Washburn and if there's anything I can ever do or help you with, please let me know."

I liked that willingness to help, so I told him to hold up a minute and he wouldn't need to be posting right away because I needed him to do something for me. He straightened up, excited to please and ready to shine. I pointed to the bound copies of the Air Force Regulations and said, "Would you please look up the rule in the Security Police Policies and Procedures manual about the brightness of head lamps?"

He cocked his head and said, "Huh?" I pointed again, saying, "I need you to look through AFR 125-3, Security Police Policies and Procedures, and find the section dealing with headlamp brightness." Before he could answer, I pulled the volume down and told him to take it into the briefing room where he could sit at a table and set to work undisturbed.

It took him thirty minutes before he came out and said, "I can't find anything in there about headlamps." I was astonished that he hadn't put it together yet, so I asked him, "Do you remember stopping a guy last week at the gate and warning him about a dim headlamp?" He scratched his head and pondered it so I just looked at him saying, "It was me you warned and I've got to tell you, I'm not impressed." He looked down at his shoes so I knew I had his attention. I left him with the admonishment, "I'll be watching for you."

I kept that promise. I made him read those regs and each night before posting I made him tell me what he learned, especially about the base traffic regulations. Washburn remained my favorite fatigue duty guy and under my tutelage he learned how to buff floors so they glowed.

+++

Winter Of '75

As charming as Mountain Home might appear to somebody who'd been lost in the high desert for a few months, it was in fact deliberately located at the absolute end of civilization. Built during WW II and opened in August 1943, it offered two-hundred-twenty flying days a year and was far enough inland to eliminate any possible threat of enemy attacks. This isolated location was also practical because nobody much noticed or cared if a B-24 crashed in training, that was just something that happened and here there was no local population to become demoralized. The base closed in October 1945 and stayed shuttered for three years until the newly created, and rapidly growing, USAF moved back in and began training flight crews again. Thanks to the needs generated by the Korean War and subsequent Cold War, the Air Force built some nice base housing and barracks in the early 1950s. When I arrived, twenty-four years later, there'd been no significant improvements to infrastructure because, as Vietnam wound down, the future of the base was in jeopardy. No tax dollars were invested for infrastructure maintenance or construction, and so the installation fairly earned was the sobriquet: "*The air base time forgot.*"

It also turned out to be an especially cold winter and, in January 1975, the daily temperature didn't get warmer than 20 degrees. The overnight temperatures plummeted to sub-zero and the wind-chill factor only added to the misery of the people forced to be outside contributing their piece of the mission.

It was a curious observation that those folks, those people charged with protecting that installation and all its assets, the cops, are the ones so often given the least resources. In plain words, cops got all the old vehicles that had put on little mileage while living a soft, well-maintained life in another squadron. After six years, those cars and pick up trucks were past their maintenance "life cycle" and there was little attention paid to any further maintenance, other than the minimum necessary to make the vehicle run and stop, along with operational headlights. Nobody was worried about passenger comfort, so air conditioning was non-existent and a working heater just a happy circumstance.

Who were these post-draft era defenders of freedom? Part of the "All Volunteer" military, they were just guys fresh out of high school and looking for options. They finally had one that didn't include wandering around some rice paddy in a war already lost. On January 22, 1973, former President Lyndon B. Johnson, aged 64, suffered a fatal heart attack and became the last casualty of his war. Five days later the US officially ended its combat role in the Vietnam War and also ended the draft. With no war to provide vast amounts of money to the military-industrial complex, a recession began as the economy contracted.

Those new airmen were joining just to find work. The end of the draft meant the US job market for recent high school graduates began drying up in some part thanks to greatly increased competition from veterans being released early from enlistment contracts and coming back to the towns and jobs they'd left. To this mix came all those young men who no longer had to hide in university and that unleashed a flood of well-educated job applicants for entry level jobs.

Some of those volunteers were clever, some were book smart and some were just plain stupid. For those poor dumb bastards working outside, the weather was simply their particular misery. A serendipitous first assignment had thrown them into this land of ice and snow instead of sending them to Florida, land of sun and girls in bikinis. What they had to endure daily depended on where they fell in the "food chain" of rank hierarchy. I'd been brought in from the cold just a year earlier and had no particular sympathy for these new guys; it was all just a part of the winnowing process, but in any event, it beat getting shot at or developing a heroin habit.

The draft might have ended two years earlier, but the Air Force was still rife with guys just doing their time as the DoD continued to shrink. In 1971 the USAF had 755,300 airmen and three years later only 643,970 remained, a loss of almost fifteen percent, or 111,330 bodies, Spooney being one of them. By the time the last of the Vietnam era airmen's enlistment contracts were up and not renewed, the USAF would be down to force of just 570,695.

Not to be dissuaded from trying to get back into the warm, guys were always manufacturing any number of excuses to come back to the station house and get warm, and who could blame them? It was the ones like A1C Dave who went too far and that proved to be a problem.

+++

The Thin Red Line

As the operations desk sergeant, it fell to me to be the bearer of bad news when performing my required fifteen minute radio checks to make sure all the troops remained awake and alert. While I got no particular joy from announcing the time and weather while I was comfortable in shirt sleeves and enjoying the warmth, I was always grateful for the divine intervention of the OBM.

One evening was especially cold. A storm had come through dropping a ton of snow and then the winds picked up. Hovering around ten degrees, it felt more like five below with the wind chill. That wind was whipping snow and scree all over the place, much to the consternation of the airmen charged with aircraft and airfield maintenance. Maintainers assigned to the tail section had to work in relay because they couldn't wear gloves to complete the task. One would start and when he lost feeling in his fingers, he'd tap out and the next maintainer would take over, while another took up the relief position. Meanwhile, the first guy went down to warm his hands by a heater. To that mix came the unlikely combination of a functioning drunk, a sleepy partner, and an inexperienced new guy freezing his ass off on our Security Alert Team (SAT).

On any airbase there are two separate but equally important areas. Operations, which had everything to do with flying, and the Rest: support, admin people, the bowling alley, commissary, golf course, gymnasium, BX, Hobby shop, clubs, education office, and on and on, all the things you need in a small community While the rest might sleep, operations never stopped and to that end they set to the task of clearing the snow off the aircraft and keeping the ramp and taxiways clear and ready. Three squadrons were assigned to the base and all flew the F-111 Fighter/Bomber, fresh back from long term assignments in SouthEast Asia where that plane was known as "Whispering Death." Each of these aircraft contained state of the art electronic equipment that made it a very effective weapons platform. It generally scared the hell out of people because, thanks to terrain following radar, it flew faster than sound at very low altitudes so the enemy never heard it coming, hence the nickname. Each squadron was cordoned off for security purposes and only people with certain authorizations could enter those restricted areas. These areas were delineated by very bright and very RED lines painted on the concrete parking ramp. All personnel understood that they had to use an Entry Control Point no longer manned by a cop, but rather a squadron airman with a clip board.

However, if somehow, somebody forgot protocol and "broke the Red line" it was instantly assumed they were nefarious actors and every effort was made to locate and neutralize any threat they presented. This first notice of an assault on the Red line would always be designated a "Helping Hand" and at the security operations control desk an event clock started and up-channel notifications would be made to superior authorities somewhere in the ether in very short order. It was very bad if you busted time standards in garnering the facts and circumstances which either led to a national security event, or having to explain to an angry disembodied voice why your dumb ass (or your dumb ass subordinates) thought it was a Helping Hand. If in fact it wasn't just a subordinate idiot but a foreign force or crazy person bent on theft or destruction of aircraft or weapons, it immediately became a "Covered Wagon" and all hell would break loose, sirens would go off, and it would be very bad.

However bad that situation might be, there was always an even worse scenario, and that was somebody going after those nukes being stored in a SAC detachment on the far end of the base. That was a "*Dull Sword*" denoting nuclear safety deficiency involving minor damage to a nuke, or the dreaded "*Bent Spear*" which meant radioactive contamination.

In 1980, an airman conducting maintenance on a USAF Titan-II missile at Launch Complex 374-7, near Damascus, Arkansas, dropped a socket from a wrench which fell eighty feet before hitting and piercing the skin on the rocket's first-stage fuel tank, causing it to leak. The area was evacuated except for emergency personnel to evaluate and neutralize the threat. At three in the morning, the hypergolic fuel exploded and blew a W53 nuclear warhead up and out and into the night, landing about a hundred feet from the launch complex's entry gate. Its safety features operated correctly and prevented any loss of radioactive material, so even though one airman, SrA David Livingston, was killed and others seriously injured, and the launch complex was destroyed, the event was considered a "*Dull Sword.*"

On this particular evening, the snow blew and confounded the efforts of all while the SAT truck drifted slowly along the ramp. This frigid night that group of three airmen consisted of Sgt Rodney, a skinny white guy and functioning alcoholic from Seaside, Oregon, who fancied himself a cowboy called away for this four year distraction that put his life on pause. He lived in the barracks at the end closest to the exterior fire escape stairwell, in case he had to puke. This served him well since he mainly just liked to drink beer all day. Even though we had an "eight-hour bottle-to-throttle" rule, Rodney took no notice and would finish up his daily case of beer about an hour before we went on duty, while still ironing his uniform, which was always perfectly cleaned and pressed. We all knew he had four months left on his tour and was quietly marking time before he could hit the road and get on with the rest of his life, which would most likely involve a slow circular movement around the drain, a life spent searching for pleasures in honky-tonks, small town saloons and dive bars. His predilections and philosophy helped him go with the flow and it didn't matter to anybody else because he didn't drive and all he had to do was make sure he was sober enough to operate the radio if ever the need arose.

A1C Napier was a black guy from somewhere in Louisiana who spent most of the time I knew him, which was two months, espousing an insatiable curiosity and interest in the Queen hit "Killer Queen." Well, he really only seemed to have an interest in one particular lyric: "Dynamite with a laser beam." He'd just be humming that song quietly and repeating that phrase as he walked off. Like Rodney, he was finishing up his obligation to the USAF, although a bit earlier then he'd planned, owing to him not being able to pass any of the job performance written exams to get his five level and move from apprentice to journeyman. When not pondering the mysteries of Freddie Mercury's mind, he spent most of his shift sleeping in the back seat of the 1968 Chevy four-door six-passenger "crummy" pickup truck used for the SAT.

Filling in the compliment that night was A1C Dave. He was new to the Air Force, only recently having washed out of Officer Candidate School. He said he was put into security as punishment, and possessed an attitude that did nothing to endear him to us. Seeking to impress us with his fine educational credentials, he let it be known at every opportunity that he possessed a Bachelor of Arts degree from a university in Arizona. To his credit, Dave wanted to do everything right, but thought being an inflexible hard ass was the way to go. To his detriment and fairly constant sorrow, he'd just never figured out how to work with or talk to people, thus everything he did became just a little bit harder.

I was letting Dave drive on patrol one Sunday to observe his demeanor and judgment. He was operating the radar and after recording a car doing 35 mph, turned on the rotating blue lights and pulled the vehicle over. He properly and politely requested the driver's ID card, license, and registration, then returned to the truck to write a ticket for speeding. I told him the speed limit was 35 but he pointed to the school sign saying 20 mph. I reminded him it was Sunday night and school wasn't open, but he believed the 'law was the law' and saw no problem writing the citation, adding, "I don't like officers." Not wishing to embarrass the squadron any further, I voided the ticket, took everything from him, and walked back to the driver, where I apologized for the delay and misunderstanding. The driver, a Captain named Frank, was an F-111 Weapons System Officer just arriving on base. He said he understood, thanked me and left. The next week he reported in as the new Operations Officer and direct supervisor of all the cops on duty. Dave went up to introduce himself and the Captain said,"Oh yes, I remember you very well from last Sunday." It never got better and he became a regular substitute for Rat-face as my new cleaning guy.

This night the winds continued to blow and the heater, minimal when the truck was new, was clearly nearing the end of its planned obsolescent life. Napier knew the drill and wore long johns, snow pants, parka with hood, mukluk boots, arctic gloves with shells, and a knit watch cap. Rodney was likewise geared up and warmed by the remnants of that last six pack. Knowing he'd be riding around in a pickup truck all night, Dave elected to wear only his fatigue uniform, lightweight flight jacket and regular gloves, assuming the truck would have a working heater. It didn't.

The shift began at ten and ran through to six in the morning. Night shift workers were authorized to go to midnight chow, a buffet line that offered all manner of hot breakfast items. The only requirement was to be in uniform. Midnight chow ran from ten until three in the morning when they shut it down to clean for the morning breakfast operation. You had to give careful consideration to what time you went for your meal. If you wanted to wait, there was always the possibility of something happening, an accident, anti-robbery alarms, a no-notice inspection, things like that. These were routine, but ate up a lot of time. If you went too early that meant being very hungry several hours later while waiting for the shift to end. On top of all that, you had to ask permission from the desk sergeant who would then switch a two-man law enforcement patrol to move to the flight line to cover it. It was a delicate balance, but it was mitigated by the 24-hour availability of food at the flight line BX kitchen and lunch counter. The Army and Air Force Exchange Service (AFFES) had a monopoly on all non-governmental food services on base and ran two satellite shops along the flight line. They made decent enough hamburgers, hot dogs, and french fries, but guys just didn't like having to pay their own way.

Rodney requested breakfast within a half hour of hitting the flight line, needing something to soak up the beer before it soured in his stomach. Being junior in rank, the others had no vote and the team was back out and rolling again after allowing Dave just the mandated thirty minutes to warm up before getting back into the cold for the remaining several long hours. Dave was mad because he couldn't go to his house off base to pick up additional clothing, and being from Arizona, he was sensitive to the cold.

By four, it was the deep part of the night when everything inside you is telling you to sleep. At the ops desk, the second hands of the two 24-hour clocks, local and Zulu, were noisily thunking as they marched steadily on towards morning.

At that point the radio came alive with Dave's frantic voice, "SAT One to control, we have a Broken Arrow, repeat a Broken Arrow!" Andrews pulled down a clipboard holding the laminated Broken Arrow checklist and noted the time with a grease pencil. I picked up the direct line to the Command Post and alerted them. The call was acknowledged and word moved rapidly up-channel. All the other base patrol units began moving towards the flight line while the front gate was closed and no traffic permitted on or off the installation until the matter was resolved, because this was serious business. Important people in Washington DC and elsewhere would soon be focused on Mountain Home Air Force Base.

The flight chief, Delbert, was a tired old rummy just trying to mark time until he had his twenty-four years and could retire with an additional ten percent of his Tech Sergeant salary. Originally from somewhere in coal country, West Virginia, and lacking opportunity at home, he'd joined in January 1952, during the Korean War, didn't get sent there and just sorta kept re-enlisting. The food was good, the pay came every two weeks and the job was pretty easy. In fact, he'd never left the United States because he'd never been asked to. He'd been content to arrive at a base, keep his head down, and move on in four years. The price of that governmental largesse was Delbert's current duty as a flight chief in charge of the ten airmen assigned to his flight. In the ordinary course of things, this would not present much of a challenge, but Delbert was a man walking a very fine wire. If everything went OK, then he had no worries. However, when things popped off, he was confronted with the sure and certain knowledge that, come morning, he would have to sign his name to the police blotter, the official log of activities and be the person responsible. This undue burden was not welcome and only served to exacerbate his already notorious fondness for stopping at his house on base during a shift for a tuna fish and garlic sandwich, washed down by a good part of the gallon jug full of beer he kept in the refrigerator. This habit was brought to my attention by a young airman, Peters, who asked me, "Is he allowed to stop at his house and take a nap after eating a tuna fish and garlic sandwich to hide the smell of the beer he drank?"

The radio chatter provided a basis for directing the response. Andrews continued trying to raise Delbert but got no response so Lonny, the assistant flight chief, came on the net as flight chief. The patrols responded rapidly, the alleged perpetrator was taken into custody, searched, handcuffed, and removed from the area within three minutes. Meeting the time standard, the Helping Hand was terminated, but the clock was still running on the whole "good call" versus "which dumbass thought this was a good idea?" determination.

It turned out to be the latter.

Lonny pulled into the parking lot and came inside, ready to receive the prisoner. He would either question him, or if the suspect was violent, place him into a holding cell. A few minutes later, the SAT crummy arrived, emergency lights rotating, sending shards of blue and red light on our commander's office next door.

The team dropped the tailgate and pulled the prisoner out of the bed. With a lot of gear in the rear passenger compartment, they put the suspect in the pickup bed without any thought to his comfort. Rodney also had the lightly dressed Dave ride in the back with the prisoner to prevent any escape because Napier looked like a fat tick in all his cold weather gear and couldn't climb into the bed without some help. It was also as punishment for scaring the hell out of him when he called in the alarm and screamed like a girl into the radio, which was properly Rodney's one job after all. From where I stood on the elevated desk, I was able to instantly assess the direction to go on classifying this incident. As he was led into the hallway, I saw a wildly irate and handcuffed man in a USAF uniform with a line badge, which immediately reduced the threat level because to get all that gear would be a lot of work for a spy, but it was what he said to me when we locked eyes:

" Are you in charge of these fucking idiots?" I nodded and he yelled, "I had to cross the red line, I'M THE FUCKING SNOW PLOW DRIVER!"

Thus ended the Broken Arrow.

Andrews brought the blotter up to date and we both listened as the poor, now uncuffed, bastard railed on Lonny, while being offered coffee and chance to warm up. "It wouldn't have been so bad, but they watched me clearing the other squadron's red line. Tell me, just how stupid do you have to be to become a cop?"

+++

Welcome To America

Chào mừng đến với Mỹ!

It was middle of spring, just when the weather was becoming milder, that I received short-notice TDY orders to report to "*Operation New Arrival*," a task force created to process the tremendous number of refugees who fled Saigon as that capital fell to the North Vietnamese Army. It was April 30, 1975.

Each branch of the Armed Forces was tasked with creating a site where refugees could be sheltered and processed while they were vetted. There they'd be prepared for a trip through the looking glass after getting yanked from their society and culture, and beamed into an alien American society in less than forty-eight hours.

The USMC set up at Camp Pendleton, California, and opened on April 29. The Army used Fort Chaffee, Arkansas, opening May 2, and then another one at Fort Indian Gap, Pennsylvania, opened on May 28. The USAF selected Hurlbert Field, a small special operations training area inside the sprawling Eglin AFB complex, an area roughly the size of Rhode Island. Set in the panhandle of Florida along the "*Redneck Rivera*," a popular spring-break vacation spot, our camp opened on May 4, 1975.

When combined, in a little over ninety-days these camps relocated, supported, and sheltered more than 130,000 Vietnamese refugees until civilian agencies found sponsors and were able to resettle them.

Their serendipitous arrival for assimilation was timed neatly because on April 1, President Gerald Ford decided to take America's mind off the human tragedy that was the rapid extinction of the country of South Vietnam. To do this, he sought to combat the stagnant job growth and creeping inflation at home by kicking off the official Bicentennial Celebration of 200 years since the revolution. He launched the American Freedom train from Wilmington, Delaware, on a twenty-one month, 25,388 miles tour of the lower 48 states. It was a time of patriotic fervor and celebration of all things that made America great, and even fire hydrants and mailboxes were painted as Revolutionary War figures. All this served as a generational renunciation of the last decade's all-things-long-haired and hippy, while also marking the birth of razor-cut, sculpted, and lacquered hair worn with those pastel-colored leisure suits of the wildly optimistic and cocaine-fueled disco era.

Now dispatched as element leader, I'd be taking four other airmen along with me to this camp: Dale, my buddy from Portugal, and three other airmen. As luck would have it, Dale and I were bumped to first class for the ride from Boise to Denver, and that was the happiest part of the trip for the next several days.

A massive operation requires an intense amount of physical and logistical support. The USAF RED HORSE heavy construction unit stationed at Eglin was tasked to prepare the site, including water and sewerage, concrete slabs for kitchens, hundreds of wooden frames and plywood floors for the GP large tents described as providing "all weather sectional housing with window assemblies." Sixteen feet long and sixteen feet wide, each held ten cots per side and there weren't any windows, not that there was anything to see. The tents were in rows with only a few feet separating them and that area was interlaced with ropes and tent stakes. The logistics folks had to identify and bring all the support materials: food, clothing, portable kitchens and the like, and of course, flowing in from everywhere were hundreds of short-notice teams like mine. This was an "on the fly" mission responding to a national directive. We lacked sophisticated communications systems, so sometimes messages didn't get passed and troop arrivals were missed. We were sent to the Northwest Florida Regional Airport in Niceville, population 4,155, shortly before midnight and were lucky to catch a transportation guy who took us to some crummy motel on the other side of town with only one room with two double beds and a couch. I had only one contact number and nobody was answering when I called from the airport, so any changes to our sleeping arrangements would have to wait until morning.

The motel was newer but the experience of sharing a motel room with four strangers was not improved by that musty odor particular to motel rooms in the South, a condition caused by the excessive humidity that could outstrip the capabilities of the best air conditioners, and handily defeated our worn wall unit. The knob designed to control the temperature had been snapped while somewhere in the "not ever comfortable" range and now just rotated freely, while the fan only offered a choice of either screaming high or dead slow. For the next several days, we shuffled off to work our shifts. As rooms became available at a series of contract hotels all along the coast, we lost bodies. I finally had my own room at the aptly named Marina Motel in the center of Ft. Walton Beach, where US Highway 98 met Florida Highway 85. This weather-worn motel might have been perfect for a remake of the Hitchcock thriller "*The Birds*" but was also just a short walk to the clear blue waters of the Gulf of Mexico. Even better, it was two blocks to a twenty-four hour diner, with a bunch of bars in between. The motel had a pool and the owner, enjoying no vacancies and jacked-up rates, didn't care if we cooled down with a drink there after a shift ended.

The refugee relocation center was thirteen miles away and each day a USAF blue shuttle bus took us out of town and down a two-lane unstriped blacktop road to the camp. There were two access control points, one for all cargo and official vehicles, the other functioning as the "tourist" gate for camp visitors looking to sponsor families. Each had a small booth for shelter if it was raining.

The paint was barely dry on the signage when the first of many blue busses began arriving with their forty refugees, each packing everything they owned into two suitcases. Each bus was greeted by an NCO with a clipboard to call out the new arrivals' names, while a major wearing a green flight suit made the rounds welcoming people. He'd been waiting for retirement at Somewhere AFB and picked for this job because he was a short timer. He greeted each non-English speaking refugee saying something personal to welcome them like "Wow, nice suitcase" or "How did you enjoy the flight?" and happy to receive no answer.

For some reason that I've never determined, it is an institutional habit of the Air Force to task a person with a pronounced southern accent to read off any list of names, with a marked preference for easily frustrated guys from west Texas, like the NCO who was now holding that clipboard and standing before the assembled jet-lagged refugees.

In Vietnamese culture, a person's name begins with the family name, then middle name, then first name, the opposite of the American pattern. So John Quincy Adams would be Adams Q. John. The military personnel specialists back in Guam who were creating the new American identity papers didn't know this and by default applied the American format so now Nguyen (family name) Van (middle name) Nam (first name) became Mr. Nguyen V. Nam, which caused that major to be astonished at how "many people named their kids Nguyen," while the guy reading the list continued to mispronounce Nguyen as "Newgun" which added to the confusion, since the name is properly pronounced "Wynn."

Although I'd been sent down as an operations sergeant, I'd run afoul of the superintendent Senior Master Sergeant over the delay in arranging permanent board for my team. I'd complained to him every day until I finally got him to find my guys a place to settle. He'd then taken a dislike to me for making him do his job, banishing me to foot patrol duties instead of chaining me to the desk in the operations tent, which was fine by me.

We'd received all sorts of briefings but my favorite included the phrase, "Be respectful of religion and ancient Vietnamese cultural practices and customs" because it meant, "You will see some really strange shit, so don't freak out, just call for a senior officer and translator."

There were also stories of entrepreneurial success and how one man's trash is another's treasure. One refugee had been the General Manager of the Saigon AAFES, the Army and Air Force Exchange Service, which ran a bunch of US-style department stores throughout Vietnam. Believing government assurances that everything would be fine, he had little time to prepare for his departure. When the time came to run he filled his two allotted suitcases with hundreds of thousands of piasters, the currency of South Vietnam. Despondent upon arrival when learning the notes had become worthless as he was traveling, he tossed the two suitcases and some kids found them. After scrounging some construction paper, they took the notes to the laundry ladies who pasted and glued the notes in the various denominations onto the paper, making hundreds of souvenir displays that they then sold to sentimental airmen and visitors for two bucks a copy.

One of those ancient customs was converting assets into gold, in the form of a gold taels, a Chinese currency unit called Hán-Nõm, and using the Chinese system of weights and currency. Each tael weighed 37.5 grams, or 1.2 troy ounces of 999.9 fine gold beaten to just slightly larger than a stick of gum and stamped with dragons and ideograms. The US had recently lifted a restriction on private ownership of gold and the metal was being sold at $183.77 per ounce or $6.48 per gram. Deak & Company, the largest store front gold dealer in the area, had a shop on base and paid $5.75 per gram, so each tael was worth $215 and came in different denominations, five and ten. The taels were usually kept in a bundle of ten and it seemed like every refugee had at least one bundle.

Safety being paramount, the USAF contracted with banks in the nearby town of Niceville and rented safety deposit boxes, but the refugees had been through a lot recently and weren't fully convinced this whole move was on the up and up. This fear was well-founded as destiny brought them to a hot and humid place, a sandy area surrounded by thin loblolly pine forests with no other humans in sight and helicopters flying over continually and bombs going off in the distance.

What they didn't know was Eglin is a giant research and test facility and some of those things tested included a 15,000 pound BLU-82 "Daisy Cutter." Dropped from the rear of a C-130 cargo plane, it was used to instantly create a 600-meter kill zone and helipad. One night I watched an old lady wander past my gate heading towards the road and I finally sent a kid to bring her back. He told me later, "She heard the bombs and thought it was her old village, she wanted to go back."

That fear and mistrust of banks was slowly overcome by the occasional theft of somebody's life savings. It was hot and humid late one afternoon and I was partnered with an airman named Bags, in from Randolph AFB in Austin, Texas. We were walking patrol down one of the main avenues, passing by a row of mildly nauseating "Porte-Potties," those gray fiberglass toilets that find homes on construction sites globally and certainly reigned supreme in this camp. We were accompanied by my self-appointed personal translator, ten-year old Phat, a shoeshine boy, most recently of Saigon, now called Ho Chi Minh City.

Pronounced Fat, it's a popular family name in Vietnam and Cambodia with no special meaning. He had charisma, spoke excellent English, and had been able to get himself and nine other family members on to the airlift and across to America, which was no small undertaking, so I knew this kid was an operator. The day after I arrived, he walked up and said, "My name is Phat and I like you. I'm going to be your translator free of charge" and from that day forward he was. When I worked an entry control point, he would sit out there with me and if I had a foot patrol he'd walk with me. I'd prowled the donated clothing trailers and found a three-piece boys silver gray communion suit. I took it and him to the sewing ladies and in no time at all, for only two packs of cigarettes, had it tailored to fit his smaller frame. I found a snappy looking Cuban style straw hat and a pair of girl's black and white saddle shoes to finish the ensemble. He was one styling kid and I suspect a multi-millionaire today.

We walked on and soon came upon a crowd in front of the medical tent where one Mr. Newgun was getting in a big argument with several other Newguns over who would be seen next. Phat filled us in, explaining that angry Mr. Newgun, an older man, was not willing to wait in line behind so many other younger Newguns, some of whom had small children with who knows what malady and why should he be put at risk? As the argument grew louder, I became concerned for safety and order so I walked into the group and said, "OK, let's knock it off, what's going on here?" while Phat translated.

Angry old Mr. Newgun looked at me and speaking pretty good English said, "I will go before them! In my country I am a general and I do not take a knock it off order from a sergeant!" He spat those angry words out while Phat dutifully translated him back into Vietnamese for the crowd. I figured it was best to just be frank, so I said, "That may be so old man, that may be so, but over here you're just an unemployed guy who wasn't a very good general or you wouldn't have lost the war, so please wait in line." This was met, after the appropriate time delay for translation, with laughter and hoots of derision from all the onlookers.

We continued on for a bit, passing the single women's area and heading towards the shower tent facilities the engineers had thrown up, when we heard a great commotion behind us. A Vietnamese guy was running towards us, yelling and pointing behind him. I looked back and didn't see any obvious signs of danger, the only vehicle moving was one of those "shit-suck" trucks that clean the sewerage out of the Porte-potties.

This Mr. Newgun was about five and a half feet tall and slight. He began gesturing for us to follow him while he breathlessly told Phat, who told us, his immediate tale of woe. He'd managed to liquidate his business back in Saigon and converted it all into five-tael units and had a ten-pack bundle he carried everywhere with him, even when sleeping. He'd just arrived in the camp and put the pack in the back pocket of the new trousers he'd been issued when he came here. The pants were a bit baggy on him so when he finished his business and stood up in the cramped confines of the fiberglass ensconced bathroom and picked his up trousers, the packet with over ten thousand dollars in 24-karat gold fell out and disappeared into the impenetrable and toxic pale blue waters, which was actually a small amount of water with dark blue dye added to hide the appearance of solid waste. The depth would depend on how much usage the stall had received between cleanings.

Newgun brought us to the offending toilet, pointing at it while gesturing at us. Phat said, "He says you can get the money for him now, please." I liked the "please" part, but Bags and I both responded by shaking with laughter. I told Phat to tell him, "Buddy, you need to understand, we aren't doing that. Nothing on my badge says anything about shit-squeezing in the search for your lost fortune!" and added, "You got that, Phat? You can translate it?" Phat was a man of many words, because as those words left his mouth, he also pantomimed squeezing which had an immediate effect because the already sallow man took on a decidedly greenish hue. Around the back was an access panel where the honey wagon operator would stick in the hose that emptied the holding tank and was working it's way toward us. I pointed this out and Phat told Mr. Newgun to go for it. Newgun danced lightly side to side, like a guy with a full bladder but really just choked with indecision and hesitation to undertake this especially horrific chore, just like any person would. The honey wagon was now only four toilets away and across the avenue, but the sounds of the hose being taken up spurred him into action. He rolled his shirt sleeve way up his scrawny bicep, almost to the shoulder, knelt down and began prospecting.

Gingerly at first, he seemed to be skimming the surface, until the wagon operator put his truck in gear and pulled one potty closer. Newgun's face screwed up into a look of absolute revulsion as he not only increased the depth of the search pattern, but also the size of the area to be searched. For the next several moments I watched while he squeezed and squeezed but never found the prize. What he didn't know was 1,875 grams of gold weighs slightly more than four pounds and, falling from the height of his pants pocket, those four pounds smashed through the less dense fecal materials and settled on the bottom. Meanwhile, the honey truck loomed ever larger.

After a few minutes of intense concentration, the type rarely seen in anybody other than trauma room doctors and nurses, he finally struck gold, literally, and triumphantly pulled the waxed paper bundle out of the muck and mire, holding it up for all to see before vomiting.

A kind lady brought over a plastic bucket with some soapy water she'd been washing her baby's diapers in and helped Mr. Newgun clean his arm while I idly wondered how Rabbi Abe would have handled *that* hand-washing. His property now restored, Newgun ran off to wherever it was he had his cot, a wiser man.

With that show over the small crowd of on-lookers dispersed and only the three of us remained, having a cigarette. Phat smoked and I'd staked him to two cartons. I figured any kid who could get his family out of chaos of Saigon right before the end was old enough to smoke. Of course, he sold most of them to his pals at an inflated price. He was then able to find an inside man, a refugee trainee-cashier at the AAFES store, to provide him with those cheap and untaxed smokes that he then sold to locals through a sponsor he'd met. As we smoked, the honey-truck driver finished cleaning a toilet and walked up to us. He asked what was going on and why was that guy down by the access door? I told him the story and he just busted out laughing saying, "Why the hell didn't you guys ask me? Something like that would have clogged my hose and I'd have gotten it out."

+++

Ancient Rituals

The camp grew rapidly and the engineers were able to make significant improvements. There were plenty of showers and laundry machines and honey wagon loads enough that it became necessary to install a small wastewater treatment facility. These ponds required a significant amount of space, but there was plenty to be had on this abandoned WW II airfield, and construction began at one far end of the camp. A space of ten acres was cleared and on two of those acres the first stabilization pond, five feet deep, was built, providing secondary biological treatment, which meant straining out some of the bigger pieces beforehand. That requirement necessitated building a deeper, facultative lagoon, eight-feet deep to accommodate a "substantial increase in solids loading" coming from the camp. A pipe delivered wastewater to the facultative lagoon where gravity did the initial separation. From there it flowed into a stabilization pond where gravity again did the job, removing the rest, before transfer to a final holding pond. The now reasonably clean water was sucked up into a large impact sprinkler and shot into the air to fall back onto the sandy soil where it would be further filtered as it leeched into the groundwater.

The location was remote and I was walking with Bags when we decided to go check the plant. It was a nice walk and a good break from the noise associated with five thousand people living in close quarters. It was still and very hot as we walked down the sugar-sand trail deeper into the pines and scrub, with only some birds for company, until we rounded a corner. Passing a large earthen berm, we heard laughter and shouting. A little bit further and we came into view of a wastewater treatment facility under siege.

Today it appeared that many families Newgun had decided to take a break from the oppressive heat and humidity by hitting the newly discovered pool and spa, having watched a Florida travelogue about the Everglades just the night before at the camp movie. My jaw dropped open as I saw many happy families tossing children hither and fro and everyone splashing about in all three effluent ponds. It was a good thing that nobody went pearl diving in the facultative lagoon, although one engineer later opined, "It shouldn't be a problem, the Mekong River is way worse." For more than a few moments, Bags and I just stood dumbstruck. I finally took the radio off my belt and called the office, telling Dale I needed to have him get a hold of the base commander, a full colonel, and have him come down to the sewerage treatment station. Dale asked what was up and all I could think to say was "some kind of ancient Vietnamese custom, but he's gonna want to see this."

We walked back fifty yards to just where the track came into the final curve and watched the Air Force blue M-151 jeep come bounding towards us at a pretty good clip. Colonel Cherry, the diminutive F-105 fighter pilot turned base commander, hopped out from the driver's seat and walked up at the quick step. We saluted as he approached and said, "What have you guys got?" I repeated what I'd told Dale and added, "You've just got to see it for yourself sir." He quickened his already quick-step and we covered the remaining distance in short order. He was a few feet ahead of us when he stopped dead in his tracks and yelled, **"Sweet Baby Jesus! Now what the fuck is this?"**

Not waiting for us to answer, he turned to his interpreter, Newgun, and told him to get those people out of the pool and do it right smartly. Newgun yelled as loud as he could for a man with no voice projection, and Vietnamese is a language of nuances often lost in the process of shouting. I'd seen footage from February 1966, when then Vice President Hubert Humphrey visited Vietnam and addressed their leadership in Vietnamese hoping to say, "Vietnam for one thousand years!" He enthusiastically shouted out the words but got the inflections wrong and was reported to have said, "The ducks fly upside down!" At least that's what I thought because none of the country clubbers were paying Newgun any mind. Since this was now identified as a civil engineer bio-health issue and not security, we saluted smartly and returned to our patrol.

Two days later, Bags and I were again partnered up and decided to see how things had gone at Le Chez Newgun Resort and Spa. We came down the trail and sure enough there was still the sound of much laughter and frivolity made more surreal by an AM radio dialed into a local country and western music station. Reaching the ponds, we noticed the solution. The Civil Engineers had planted three two-by-six posts in the ground in front of each pond and hung a bright orange life preserver from a galvanized roofing nail.

The facultative lagoon had an additional sign saying, "No Diving" in English and "Không lặn!" in Vietnamese.

+++

Come And Meet The Locals

Once we'd succeeded in organizing the camp, the next phase was orientation to all things American. Much of this would be done by volunteer hosts organized by the many different churches and charitable groups from the local area. They sponsored refugees out of the camp to give them a look around their small slice of America. This was not something that always went smoothly. Dale had a family emergency so he was sent back to Idaho. The NCOIC who disliked me was fired for lying to the two-star pilot who was the AF Chief of Security Police. My new boss assigned me most days to the operations desk and I was there one Sunday afternoon when the phone rang. It was the police chief from nearby Niceville who reported, "I found one of your Vietnamese who escaped wandering around out here, so I picked her up and what do you want me to do with her because she's yelling up a storm and I can't make a word out."

It took me a moment to get the gist of what he was telling me. In order to not make the camp look like some sort of prison, the boundaries had been delineated by a single stand of bright yellow nylon rope because these were refugees, not prisoners, and they were free to leave any time they wished to. I explained this to the Chief and asked if his arrestee had a laminated card with our phone number and a larger three digit number. The protocol provided that when a sponsor came, the gate guard would give the refugee the numbered card with our phone number. The sponsor provided all their details and a contact phone number and that information was put on a board at the Operations Desk.

The Chief said he was holding that card right in his hands, the first thing she'd given him before he arrested her, because that's how he knew where to call. I asked him what the large number was and, when he told me, I looked over at the refugee sign-out board and asked him where he found Mrs. Newgun. He told me he picked her up near a beauty salon. I asked if he knew the name of the assigned sponsor and he replied, "She's the mayor's wife." About that time the other phone rang, so I told him to hang on and took the call. A very upset mayor's wife told me, through her sobs, that she had come out of the salon and her guest was lost. She complained that she walked all over but couldn't find her charge. Exhausted, she had returned to the salon and was just worried to death. I told her the Chief of Police had found her guest and would be coming her way shortly. I hung up and told the Chief he might want to wander his prisoner back to where he found her, making sure to sit her in the front seat after taking the handcuffs off.

One other cross-cultural communications failure occurred when I was at the other entry control point for visitors or sponsors picking up their guests. Phat and I were leaning back on our twin gun-metal gray government issued folding chairs and watched a 1973 light yellow Lincoln Town car approaching. Sporting round headlight covers, a bulldog hood ornament, oversize white wall tires, and displaying **1ww** plates from Miami, I knew a player was rolling up. I'd seen that car and others like it many times in movies like Super Fly, Super Fly T.N.T, Shaft, Shaft in Africa, Across 110th St, and a trend of other black experience movies that started in 1970. I also received mentoring from an admin guy named Ratio who was my first roommate at MacDill. When Super Fly played at the base theater, he saw it and decided the player's life was for him. I had come back from work to see him doing sit-ups on the floor, and asked what he was doing. He told me, "Getting into shape to be ready for my ladies."

Ratio decided to moonlight as a pimp. On his first effort to recruit, he happened to proposition the Korean-born wife of a Tampa police captain, who told him she'd think about it and get back to him. She told her husband who then stuffed a detective into the trunk of her car so he could listen and record the next time Ratio made his pitch. Ratio got off work on a Tuesday afternoon, was arrested later that evening. I never saw him again, but some airmen from transportation came by and packed up all his stuff. From living with him just that short amount of time, I got to learn an awful lot about what he thought about women and how he understood pimps got women to obey, so I knew what a pimpmobile was and how a pimp thought, dressed, and acted. I hated pimps, they were nothing but thinly disguised, but gaudily-dressed modern day slavers.

A strand of yellow nylon rope served as a vehicle barrier. As the gangster-leaning driver pulled up, I saw the imitation TV antenna he had mounted to his roof. He lowered a heavily tinted window and I noticed the raspberry-colored shag rug he'd had stapled along the inner rear wall on either side of the tucked and rolled white faux leather seats. I also noticed the "diamond in the back" covering on the rear window fulfilling all the outward accoutrements required for a genuine pimpmobile. He wore a pale yellow linen suit and thin white linen shirt opened at the neck and providing a view of a considerable number of gold chains. His hair was Jheri-curled and he wore it slicked back. I also took note of a pearl earring in his left ear lobe and concluded no way this guy not a player.

He offered a dazzling white and toothy smile as he extended a slender arm towards me, saying, "My man! Where do I go to get me some ladies?" He leaned forward, adding conspiratorially, "I need to increase my stable," before settling back in his seat again. It might have been the way he dragged out the "s" in *ladies* that made him seem oily, but his cavalier attitude in disclosing his motives made it an easy decision for me. I declined his proffered hand, not being distracted by all the ostentatious jewelry he thought important to display, choosing instead to look him straight in the eyes. I explained this wasn't an orphanage and we weren't going to be signing out any girls to him today, or any other day, and he really needed to leave the area. At that point, suspecting I just needed a financial incentive, he opened up his jacket for his wallet and I saw the imitation pearl handle of a .22 caliber pistol tucked into the waistband of his pants. I drew my .38 caliber S&W revolver with real wood grips and took a shooting stance, the barrel just three feet from his lightly tanned face, which was starting to lose some of its color. I told him clearly and directly that he'd best be back on down the way he came and never return lest I find myself being asked later, "Who's the dead guy in the Lincoln?"

+++

Saturday Night At The Movies

Protecting our charges from the indigenous predators was just one component, as we were also charged with helping the refugees make an informed and intelligent decision about where they wanted to live in their new country. The educational mechanism for this momentous decision was showing travelogues, movies that gave an illustrated lecture about those places visited and experiences to be had by anybody lucky enough to live there. Just after sunset every evening, right after the Malathion-loaded mosquito truck finished fogging the camp, refugees would gather, sitting on three aluminum baseball bleacher sections. A 16 mm film depicting life in one of the fifty United States would be put large on the silver screen. From these nostalgic and hazy relics from the late forties and early fifties I learned that Michigan was famous for some eleven-thousand lakes, welcoming towns with sloping beaches where happy factory workers from nearby Kalamazoo could enjoy their weekends waterskiing on Lake Michigan.

It was very pleasant the night the state of Vermont was promoted as the evening's feature destination. The bleachers were full of refugees and many more brought folding chairs from the nearby dining tent. The twenty-year old A1C film projectionist was additionally trained as a geospatial intelligence imagery analyst. He was responsible for analyzing overhead and aerial imagery developed by photographic and electronic means attached to an SR-71 Blackbird, the fastest spy plane ever produced. He'd only recently graduated tech school and was assigned to the 9th Strategic Reconnaissance Wing, at Beale AFB outside of Marysville, in northern California. This highly trained analyst was selected for this job while he was in a secured vault reviewing some critical imagery for the daily National Intelligence estimate and missed the Friday meeting when the tasking requirement was announced. His selection was an easy one since none of the NCOs wanted to go to Florida in the summer and he was the junior guy.

I was chatting with him while he fed the film into a Bell and Howell projector. Once the film was threaded and ready, he flipped the switch. The projector lit up and the opening theme music slurred as the take-up reel pulled the film taut. In moments, through the deep and warm tones produced by Super 16 mm color film, the audience was transported to a snow-covered land. Once there, some no-doubt direct descendant of Ethan Allen, the famous American Revolutionary War hero, and leader of the Green Mountain boys who led the attack and capture of Ft. Ticonderoga, and thus forever ensuring America would have an adequate supply of number two pencils, was now going to harvest maple syrup.

His on-screen descendant wore a red and black checked woolen cap with matching jacket while tramping happily about in the spring snow. We saw him tapping into one of the thousands of maple trees and then draining the sap into a small metal bucket. His two identically attired children captivated the audience by boiling the sap, turning it into maple syrup. Vermont resounded with our newest Americans because they had been learning all about maple syrup on their pancakes and waffles every morning.

For small people, they ate a lot, which was not surprising given the food insecurity they'd experienced up and until they arrived in our camp. Now, three times a day, smiling USAF cooks would heap all manner of biscuits, pancakes, waffles, eggs, bacon, sausage, steak, country ham, country fried steak, fried chicken, hamburgers with baked, mashed, hash brown, or French fried potatoes, and all of it served with the option of plenty of gravy and lots of maple syrup. The hard plastic slotted trays we'd received from the minimum custody federal prison camp on nearby Eglin airbase were challenged daily with the astonishing amount of food being carried by some of these skinny refugees. Thanks to all that food, plus copious amounts of apple pie and ice cream, most plumped right up and more than a few developed gout.

The main attraction that night was a 1973 film, "*Don't Look Now*" with Donald Sutherland and Julie Christie. What that airman didn't know, because he just threaded the film, was that this movie was about to become notorious for having the most realistic sex scene ever put on film. Sadly, none of us would get to see that particular scene because a few minutes into this prurient tale of two people suffering the death of their daughter, we see them in their bathroom where Julie is casually talking to Donald while slowly stripping off her clothes until she is standing naked and displaying FULL FRONTAL NUDITY, including pubic hair!

The assembly went wild and made a sound somewhere between a giggle and hoot, because adult nudity was uncommon in their culture. As if one naked blonde lady wasn't enough, Donald Sutherland casually took off all his clothes showing FULL FRONTAL MALE NUDITY with a flaccid penis! It was all right there on that silver screen, a first for me, and the USAF, and seemed a great way to welcome our newest Americans to the still on-going sexual revolution. The crowd erupted with some new kind of sound and I couldn't tell whether it was disgust, derision, or support, but I did catch a glint of light reflecting off a bobbing silver eagle pinned to a green fatigue cap that I knew covered the head of a no-doubt pretty-angry USAF Colonel. I took that as my cue to leave so I tapped the airman's shoulder while saying, "Good luck."

I was several yards away and nearing the back of the bleachers when I heard him starting to yell, "**Shut that goddamn movie off...**"

+++

Do I Stay Or Do I Go Now?

November, and my enlistment contract was up on December 6, 1975. I'd taken the Weighted Airman Promotion Examination (WAPS) a few months earlier, as soon as I was eligible for promotion, and with only three and a half years in service I'd been selected for advancement. Eligible candidates receive points based on a number of criteria, including time in service, time in grade, awards and decorations, Enlisted Performance Report (EPR) points, Promotion Fitness Examination (PFE) points, and Specialty Knowledge Test (SKT) points. Candidates with the highest numbers of points, up to the promotion allowance in each career field, are promoted. Reading all the applicable regulations gave me a leg up on guys who never opened a book and simply waited for promotion based on time in grade and time in service plus medals.

I received a letter of congratulations from my commander along with two Staff Sergeant chevrons. I was supposed to sew those stripes on in December, but my commander elected to hold the promotion until after I re-enlisted, if I chose to do so.

That was a mighty big carrot for me to chase, because promotion meant a $52 a month pay raise and I'd be making $538 a month with no expenses. Promotion and re-enlistment also meant I'd move into career airman status, therefore eligible to be an assistant flight chief or assigned as a full-time investigator, both good career moves, yet I was uncertain about taking the bait. I knew I could make Tech Sergeant the first time I was eligible in twenty-three months, then Master Sergeant two more years after that when I'd be twenty-six. From there it'd be an easy cruise to twenty years or beyond if I made it to chief. I wondered if it'd be worth staying in, given how the culture was changing from the Vietnam mindset, a culture created over those thirteen years that the conflict raged. The military was changing from a "didn't want to be here so party hardy because death is in the air," into a Cold War warrior mindset with the unbelievable thought of nuclear Armageddon never far from anybody's mind, but not seriously considered as possible. The USAF was entering into the all-volunteer doldrums of a pretty-much peacetime Air Force looking for work. The drunken good times of "gone for 179" were ending and new recruits arrived spun up about the menace of the Soviet Union and Warsaw Pact. They possessed a SAC nuclear warfighter mentality not previously seen in the Tactical Air forces in Europe. The new reality was harsh, because, unlike in Vietnam, on a nuclear battlefield there were no "rear areas" to relax and recuperate. Everything, including the recreation facilities were targets because "close don't count except for horseshoes, hand grenades, and nuclear weapons," so the mindset became "you better drink your asses off tonight because we might all be obsidian tomorrow." The last of the Vietnam era, fun-loving, airmen would be eligible for retirement by 1993, and their influence would wane considerably as that time approached.

Against that background, and while I struggled with those issues, there was also the siren's call of college. Public Law 93-508 authorized an education assistance payment of $270 a month and my contract promised me forty-eight months of that assistance. Tuition at nearby Boise State was $110 a semester for full-time students. I'd taken one three-credit night class on Alcohol and Drug abuse while stationed at MacDill through the University of Tampa and received an A for the course. A sergeant who worked at the base education office lived on my floor at Lajes and he talked me into taking a battery of tests, a part of the College Level Equivalency Program (CLEP). He told me if the score was high enough an applicant was awarded college credits. Thanks to comic books, science fiction and John D. McDonald, I managed to earn six science credits and three in math. I was especially surprised about the math credits given the four points out of one hundred I'd scored on that ninth grade math test Mr. Luchowder gave me all those years ago, and who might have been proud if only he'd known.

Now, despite an abysmal SAT score from a few years earlier, I was a matriculating student from the University of Tampa, with a 4.0 GPA, nine college credits and a shoo-in for any school. My suitability as a student was improved when the draft ended as did a national interest in attending college. Admission standards were relaxed because those schools had grown and gotten used to having all those tuition paying students seeking shelter from the storm in Southeast Asia.

The command staff made a pretty good run at encouraging me to re-enlist. My commander surprised me by inviting me over to his office for coffee and a chat about my future. The OIC rode around with me on base patrol explaining the benefits of staying the course and having a career. My First Sergeant invited me to take a ride with him and chat, which was great until he pulled into the personnel office parking lot where he claimed an errand inside, so I went with him. Once inside he said, "Why don't you wait for me in there and I'll be back in thirty minutes." I looked at the sign over the doorway marked "Base Retention NCO." Subtlety not being his long suit, I took a meeting out of respect, but no commitment.

I returned to the barracks unconvinced either way and struggling with this decision. I currently enjoyed a dead-easy life, one I understood and was well trained for. The Air Force was a good employer; one that paid a good salary, gave me one-month paid vacation each year, free room, food, medical and dental care. In return, all I need do was show up on time, in a clean uniform, wearing well-shined shoes, and prepared to work until the job was done.

I also couldn't ignore the ever-present and controlling military culture where strict adherence to the rules and regulations was demanded, with draconian punishments for infractions. I had such an intense fear of ever being late for work or an appointment that I'd sometimes wake up in a cold sweat with my heart racing, thinking I was late. I also had to suffer, without complaint or redress, a substandard supervisor like Delbert.

With those thoughts, my mind turned to college and the emerging disco era I experienced when I drove up to Boise on a day off and visited Boise State University. I saw students lounging about between classes, drinking coffee and invested in wide ranging discussions. I'd met several female students previously when we drove the fifty-five long miles to Boise on that rare Friday night off and spent the evening drinking and dancing in a discotheque across the street from the campus. Those women were all uniformly cute, smelled really nice, and enjoyed dancing closely. The suggestion of a college free-love sexual relationship weighed heavily given the aversion the USAF had about any matters sexual and the flat prohibition on having anybody of the opposite sex in your room.

This was my dilemma.

With fifteen duty days until my discharge, time for making my decision was drawing near. Earlier in the month I'd received an offer of employment with the Central Intelligence Agency. I took the interview at the hotel attached to the disco we frequented. I met with an older guy in a rumpled suit who'd flown in from Aurora, Colorado. Upon meeting, he said, "I know you were expecting James Bond, but I'm not and neither are you." Now properly oriented, he explained the job was providing security and training to indigenous security forces at a CIA electronic intelligence collection station in northern Iran, near Turkmenistan. This included being the "last man out" and responsible for the destruction of everything classified. The job was straightforward and paid $34,000 a year, which was insanely big money, but I wasn't ready to go back overseas to a place more remote than Lajes. I took a pass which was just as well, given one of those stars on the Wall at Langley was the guy who took the job and was there two years later, on Jan 7, 1978, when the Iranian revolution started and he didn't get out.

I'd be asked to make my re-enlistment decision within the next five days, right before Thanksgiving. I continued to work my shifts and get input from others around me. My desk partner, Andrews, encouraged me to bail, having elected to take his leave when his hitch was up in January. He'd had enough of the life and was eager to get back to his home near St. Anthony, in eastern Idaho, and work on the family ranch. He pointed to guys who had re-enlisted for four more and would be my peers for the remainder of my career. One jarring example was a grossly overweight and incompetent buck sergeant. He was being promoted after six years based solely on his time in service and time in grade because his job knowledge was close to nonexistent. My belief was evidenced by a very angry wife who came storming into the office waving a pink DD Form 1408 Armed Force traffic citation alleging she'd been doing 50 mph in a 25 mph zone, a serious infraction which would result in the immediate suspension of her on-base driving privileges. This was no small thing, given how large the base was, and how distant to town. She told me that, when stopped by this patrolman, he told her she'd been speeding and doing fifty. She denied the charge and asked him how he figured that speed since she was doing twenty-five. She quoted him as saying, "I had to do fifty to catch up to you, so you had to be speeding." I called him in and he confirmed her version of events and how he calculated the speed. I voided the ticket and apologized profusely. I also took his citation book away.

With all of these considerations it was Monty Hall who finally helped me make up my mind. Monte was the original host of the "*Let's Make a Deal*" game show on every morning at eleven. The format involved selecting members of the studio audience dressed in outrageous or crazy costumes as a "trader" making deals with Monty. They'd be offered something of value and given a choice of whether to keep it or exchange it for a different item, one hidden from view until that choice is made. The trader never knows if they are getting something of greater value, or a terrible prize referred to as a "zonk," an item purposely chosen to be of little or no value, like a stuffed donkey pulling a broken two-wheeled garbage cart.

Monty was also a Major General in the USAF reserves which suggested a person could have both worlds, but it certainly seemed like education was, in fact, as I'd been so often admonished by AFRTS, the key to success. I'd been a fan of the show since I started watching it in my Florida hotel room, thanks to working only afternoon shifts at the refugee relocation project.

Today I was in the day room watching the large console television. I came to realize this day room was my own new and improved Moran's bar, a place where big money crossed the card table twice a month on payday Friday nights, the bar stocked good beer and liquor and only charged enough to cover the booze costs plus bar snacks. There was a community lounge across he hall where the large color television usually was tuned to comedies and not the Yankees. This was the same day room where our Superintendent called a barracks meeting and said, "I know some of you guys smoke pot and aren't planning on staying in, so I'm asking you to treat it like alcohol and no smoking eight hours prior to duty. Okay?" I thought about all that, and about some of the new guys currently billeted on the floor, who confirmed my suspicions that we were only lacking a Mr. Metz.

At that moment, some guy in a yellow chicken suit traded a fair amount of cash for a shot at the "Big Deal of the Day." He had to pick one of three choices behind curtains and if lucky could be rewarded with a brand new car or exotic vacation package. The crowd was shouting out numbers and he picked curtain number three. Monty showed him behind curtain number one which was a nice prize, but not the big deal of the day, so now the chicken man had a fifty-fifty chance. His curtain drew back and revealed a goat chewing bobby socks while a slide whistle announced the Zonk, so blind folks could also enjoy his humiliation.

As Monty said goodbye to us, my decision needle moved towards new horizons, one that would include college and nice-smelling smart women who liked to dance close. When the day came, I took a pass on re-enlisting, sold back my forty days of unused leave, packed my car and shortly after midnight on December 6, 1975, fired it up and said goodbye to the USAF. I was off to see what came next.

+++

I shall be telling this with a sigh
Somewhere ages and ages hence:
Two roads converged in a wood, and I –
I took the road less traveled by,
And that has made all the difference.

— Robert Frost

EPILOGUE

The Road East

I left at four in the morning to get in as many miles in as I could during the day, the national speed limit now being 55 mph as a result of the fuel crisis in 1973. After completing the great Canadian trek just a year earlier, I did some research and found out I'd be shaving over eight hundred miles and several days off my ride by using the US Interstate highway system. As dawn came, I left the largely barren high desert of central south Idaho and travelled into the even more desolate high country of Wyoming. Only 332,000 people were living there in the tenth largest state, almost four people per square mile, but that ratio really drops if you adjust for the 112,000 living in Cheyenne and Casper. Any way you slice it, the state is a mighty lonely and windswept place. By day's end, and after twelve hours, I saw the lights of Little America, a restaurant and motel attached to the world's largest gas station, then bragging of over 100 fuel pumps. The next town was only thirty miles away, but according to the billboards, this place was a lock for good food and a good room and, given how far apart things were, I decided to stay.

After refueling my car, I checked in and went to the room to drop my gear before going to dinner. Opening the door, I found a king-size bed covered with a maroon faux velvet coverlet and mirrors on the ceiling. The bathroom was very nicely appointed and had mirrors on the walls. The decor made me wonder if I could just call the desk and order a hooker, but I settled for watching a showing of "*Tora, Tora, Tora,*" a classic about the attack on Pearl Harbor, the date being the anniversary of that attack thirty-four years earlier.

I went into the restaurant and ordered my dinner. While waiting I read the story of the man who built this oasis in the wilderness, it being written on the paper place mat and thus unavoidable. I was amazed to discover that fifty years earlier, as a young cowboy herding cattle, he'd spent the most miserable night of his life right on this spot, shivering as a storm blew and he swore nobody would ever have to go through that ever again, and this place was the end result of that vow.

The next four days passed in a succession of stark landscapes carved by the wind, as I drove across Rockies and down into the Plains. The barren landscapes gave way to agricultural areas and the odors from the stockyards of Denver remain firmly etched in my nostrils decades later. Cows need corn and nearby Kansas was happy to produce and provide it. I was impressed when the first exit in Kansas proclaimed "Home to Astronaut Steve Hawley" and less impressed later, after passing hundreds of miles of corn fields, brown and denuded of corn. I felt a brief stir of excitement when one sign announced the exit for Oakley and the amazing "*Prairie Dog Town*" where I would be able to see the world's largest prairie dog, and, as a bonus, could gaze upon the wonder of a six-footed steer. I took a pass, happy to be driving into the lengthening afternoon shadows and steady cross-wind out of the North. I learned this because I'd been holding the wheel across these straight roads with my pinkie and when the car went under an overpass blocking this wind, the car immediately veered to the left, telling me I'd been unknowingly compensating for it, and I wondered if this would effect the wear on my tires.

I was passing by Russell, Kansas, a place with no highway sign and apparently no fame, when I saw a billboard announcing an opportunity to see the "*World's Largest Ball of Twine*" in nearby Cawker, only one hour away. The sign assured me it would be "fun for the whole family!" But I was pretty certain it'd just be a ball of twine and wondered just how starved the good folks were for entertainment.

I turned north out of Kansas City and reached Des Moines, Iowa, home for pig porkers, for no other reason than I knew it was in the general direction of New York. I spent the night just short of my goal in Stuart, a small town along the interstate whose sole claim to fame was having its First National Bank robbed by Bonnie and Clyde on April 16, 1934.

Driving across the heartland again exposed me to the joys of daytime AM radio. Most stations were locally owned and lacked power to go but a few miles and serving only a small community, but some stations were "clear channel" and given the highest protection from interference from other stations. These would provide any disaster, war, or other critical news if directed by the federal government. While most rural AM stations went off the air at midnight, clear channel stations existed to ensure the viability of cross-country or cross-continent radio service, and they delivered.

It was early afternoon as I came towards Chicago. The Bay City Rollers had released their massive, and only, hit "*Saturday Night*" which opened with them spelling the word Saturday rather loudly and repeating it several times. While assuring an entire generation would never forget how to spell Saturday, it also would have been a fine addition to the Azoreans' play list. The DJ must have been drinking more than was good for him, because he made it clear-channel clear to all that he was a fan by playing it and when it finished, yelling, "One more time!" Then commencing to play it three more times before the station went into a commercial break and the news came on.

As the Chicago station faded into the background I started dialing around and found the next station in Toledo, Ohio, where the people were also fans of the Bay City Rollers.

By the time I hit Lewisburg, Pennsylvania, I hated them.

It didn't change

My mother was happy to have me back after a four-year absence with only a few visits. I'd taken a seasonal job as a delivery guy for Rudy's delicatessen while I planned my next move. The holiday season in New York is a great time to be a delivery guy because people are feeling generous and the tips are great. People were surprisingly generous because besides delivering their food order, we also provided a service where we'd stop at the nearby liquor store and pick up their order of holiday spirits.

The season was in full swing, but there would be a break on Christmas Eve and Christmas Day, and I planned to spend the

Christmas Eve with my friends at Moran's and catch up. It was a little after one when I got back from the last holiday deliveries and found my mother in the kitchen making sauce for the lasagna. Like most families, we also had a turkey or a ham, but lasagna was simply a must-have item. This would be complimented by my grandmother's home-made ravioli. Now in her late seventies, Grandma had been making raviolis for as long as she'd been in America. She didn't make a lot of them, and those one hundred raviolis would have to feed the sixteen adults and eight kids who came to the dinner. The raviolis had grown smaller as she grew older and many hands had been scarred by errant forks in the scramble for those tasty pasta pockets of cheese and meat.

Almost absently, my mother said, "I need you to go into the City to pick up Grandma." I said I would but didn't give it any thought, because it was only thirty miles to her apartment in lower Manhattan. I asked when, and she told me to be there "right at three o'clock, that's when I told her you'd come." She looked at me, "Listen, she's almost deaf and won't hear you knocking on the door, so don't be late."

I left a little after two and drove west down the LIE enjoying the view as the spires of Manhattan drew large. I threaded my way along the Brooklyn-Queens Expressway, across the Williamsburg Bridge and on into Manhattan. I drove the few short blocks to her tenement at 91 Baxter Street, and in what could only be attributed to a Christmas Eve miracle, I was able to find a parking space on the street directly in front of the building. It was just after three.

The ethnicity of the neighborhood had changed in the sixty plus years since my grandparents took up residence. The Italians left, out to the suburbs, and the Chinese moved in. The marble stairs had a worn spot from the countless soles that had shuffled up and down them over the many decades. I pulled myself up the last flight, wondering how my aged grandmother made her way up and down them twice a day.

I was late and so my grandmother took her attention from the door and turned it to the black and white TV set in the corner by a window where her soap opera, *The Secret Storm,* was coming on. The show debuted in February 1954 and Granny never missed an episode if she could help it, and I could hear it while walking up to the front door. I knocked using the firm triple-tap I'd learned at the academy, but with no results. I balled up my fist and began pounding on the door. Still no response from inside, a door opened down the hall, and a young Asian guy stepped out and was eyeing me suspiciously. I explained that I was her grandson sent to bring her out to Long Island for the holiday. The look of suspicion left his face and he smiled broadly, telling me, "I'll call her."

I heard her phone ring and a few moments later Granny opened the door and motioned me to come inside while she went back to her program. A commercial came on a few minutes later and she greeted me, asking if I wanted something to drink. I told her we needed to get a move on, it was getting dark and there was bound to be traffic on the LIE heading west because I'd seen it building on my ride into the city.

Not to be deterred from watching the episode, she pointed at her suitcase and told me to put it in my car then come back up to get her. I did as she instructed and really began to appreciate her daily fitness regimen as I climbed those worn and sagging marble steps a second time.

When her show ended, I hustled her down those stairs as fast as anybody can hustle a seventy-eight year old Italian lady, and into the car. We spent the next thirty-minutes negotiating Bayard Street which was full of Chinese restaurants and other shops all packed with people getting ready for the big rush the next day. Large segments of New York's Jewish population enjoy Christmas Day by eating Chinese food and seeing a movie. I saw numerous pairs of men carrying poles supporting an ungodly number of ducks which had already been prepared in some other industrial kitchen, and were now being brought to the smaller restaurants that would serve them as Peking duck to hungry diners.

We slowly drove back on to the Williamsburg Bridge and undertook a slow crawl all the rest of the way out to Syosset, finally pulling into the driveway at half past nine that evening, owing to the holiday traffic. I'd been unable to smoke, out of respect for my grandmother, and those six hours of riding my brakes while being illuminated by harsh red brake lights worked to convince me that I really didn't belong in New York anymore. I wasn't eager to resume being just one more schlub among the many millions, and there was no reason to stay, certainly not after living in a place with only a few people per square mile. As I walked my grandmother up the steps and into the house, I realized I couldn't live here anymore and this would be my last Christmas in New York. Syosset had remained pretty much the same as when I left it a few years earlier, but in the course of seeing all those other places, I had changed.

I began to formulate my plan to make my move back to the West.

The Gap Year

I decided to make the application to Boise State University and was accepted for the fall semester. I spent the spring traveling around Europe on a rail pass. Being a poor ex-serviceman meant planning my trip destinations to all be at least eight hours apart so I could visit a city and then board the overnight train to the next city and sleep on a "couchette," a bed made by pushing two of the chairs together in the cars. Etiquette demanded the first in the car sleep closest to the window so others could also lay out and sleep. Our sleep was sometimes interrupted when the train crossed an international frontier and border guards would come aboard and check all passports. I'd wake up and find myself in the company of perfect strangers all fumbling about to produce the necessary documents and then trying to settle back in for a few more hours before arriving in the next city.

After touring Europe on the "poor guy plan" I again loaded all my worldly goods into my car and made my way back across the USA to Idaho and began my studies at BSU. During the spring break, I took a trip to Oregon to visit my old dorm chief and Mexican travel buddy Danny, who'd also left the USAF and taken a job as a Sheriff's deputy in Clackamas County, just outside of Portland. I liked what I saw and wondered if there were job openings. Oregon was undergoing a contraction in

State spending due to a recession and growing unemployment because Oregon hadn't developed new industries to augment the economy when the logging and fishing industries tanked in the early seventies. The state was further handicapped by a mindset that didn't want any newcomers "Californicating" Oregon and so the economy went stagnant and the unemployment rate began to tick upwards.

Meanwhile Danny had kept an eye open and it was in early September, right after I'd spent that summer tossing packages and emptying forty-foot trailers at a rate of twelve-hundred pieces per hour at the UPS hub in nearby Garden City on the night shift, that he called. He told me there was an opening in a small town and would I like to apply and be interviewed? In addition to tossing packages at night I also worked for a florist delivering flowers and had saved just enough to pay my tuition and books and the thought of starting a real job with regular hours was very appealing, so I set up the appointment for the interview.

What was the worst that could happen?

You've just finished Syosset Blues. If you liked what you read, you can pick up the tale after I finished up following Monte Hall's advice in, *"The making of a COMBAT JAG, and a life spent on the tip of the spear,"* recounting sixteen years I served as a JAG officer in locations around the globe. It's written in the same vignette style. The stories are all true.

Here are three reviews:

"***Before sitting down and reading this book, pour yourself a double Jack Daniels and Coke and contemplate the most atypical lawyer and military officer you've ever known, then***

exaggerate what you know about him and you'll have the author, Mike Sciales, the original "Regular Guy." I served with Mike in England and Panama and have known him for thirty years. His stories were legendary and now finally part of military lore. Two thumbs up!!!"

Bob Blevins, Colonel, USAF (Ret)

"Its a fun read!"

Robert Burns, National Security Writer at The AP

A good read. Think a bit Tom Robbins, a bit Patrick McManus, a bit Hawkeye Pierce. Highly recommended.

Wade Porter, fraternity brother

A sample follows, along with the Table of Contents.

REMINDER: One dollar from **each** sale goes to Veterans Squaring Away Veterans, a 501(c)(3) non-profit dedicated to helping those vets who fall through all the social safety nets get stabilized and catch traction in the civilian world. Learn more at VSAV.org

Now please enjoy "How Merv Griffin Ended The Cold War,"

How Merv Griffin Ended The Cold War

We got off the train before seven, as promised, but our rooms at the Templehof airport hotel were not ready, so we spent Sunday morning visiting the Egyptian Museum of West Berlin. While I enjoyed seeing the Nefertiti Bust and pondering the intervening 3,500 years, I was hot to visit East Berlin. American officers could walk unimpeded from Checkpoint Charlie through the "no man's land" kill zone, past barking dogs, bright lights, and East German Vopos, the folk or people's police. They had no authority to speak to us and we were ordered to never acknowledge them in any way. Giving us the stink eye was the infamous STASI, the Ministry for State Security, a much-feared secret police agency. One in sixty-three East Germans provided information on neighbors and friends, and those agents behind mirrored glass regularly photographed people transiting through to add to their collection of known US Military. I didn't care about any of that, I was more interested in seeing the city and enjoying the fact that while the West German mark was worth $1.89 US, the East German "Ost" mark was worth six cents.

We came through the "wall" and I was walking with another lawyer, Steve, ready to see what was on offer in East Berlin. We'd stopped at the Checkpoint, picked up our identification placard and proceeded uneventfully into this most restricted-access city. We wandered down the Unter der Linden a broad formerly tree-lined avenue, denuded during the war, and spent our time simply observing the cityscape.

We passed department stores and I noticed, that while display cases in the West would showcase high-end luxury goods, these windows enticed entry with items of more pedestrian and proletarian interest like shaving cream, green-colored shampoo, tooth paste and hair brushes. As we walked, I had the curious sensation that we were being followed. Using a shop's window-pane reflection, I could see two twenty-something guys taking more than a passing interest in Steve and me. At the next block we made a right turn, then again at the next corner. We were now off the main thoroughfare where the buildings were largely unchanged since the end of WW II. These exteriors were still sooty, with scorch marks from fire and pockmarks from bullets fired forty-four years earlier. For all the Russian talk of the modern Soviet Man and Society, the Russians were still punishing the Germans for the carnage of WWII by leaving much of the city in ruin as a reminder; besides, they knew where the nuclear battleground would be.

We stopped in front of the shell of a building and I tied my shoelace. The two guys had to walk ahead of us and went around the corner. We ambled up that way, then made the next right to get back on to the main thoroughfare. It was only about a block later that I spotted the tail back in place. They'd subbed out one guy for a woman of about the right age and the couple were walking hand and hand. The guy changed his jacket, but he hadn't changed his patterned socks which matched his shirt in the European fashion.

We smiled and waved at them, receiving only a scowl in return. We headed to the InterContinental Hotel, at the time the finest hotel on that side of the wall. When the waiter saw us come in, he pulled the "reserved" sign off a table and invited us to enjoy the best view in the house. We tried Berliner beer and the 600 year old cheese he touted. Paying the bill in east marks but leaving the tip in west marks, the waiter enthusiastically asked us to come back and visit again. Having checked out the process of going into East Berlin, we promised, despite the 600 year old cheese, to come back and bring a group the next night.

Walking back toward the checkpoint we passed a small market and I went inside. Certain staples reflect a society: I purchased a container of milk, a loaf of bread, some wurst, and a packet of cigarettes. Once outside Steve and I sampled each one of the products. The milk was watery, the bread dry and tasteless, the wurst was fatty and the cigarettes tasted like they'd been put together using the sweepings from the factory floor. This society was in a bad way.

What we didn't know was that six weeks earlier, on September 4, 1989, after a weekly prayer for peace at the church in Leipzig, people began holding rallies and protests against the government of the German Democratic Republic (GDR). With the confidence that came with knowing the Lutheran Church supported their resistance, and would do its best to protect them, these demonstrations began to accompany the weekly prayers, swelling in size as groups emerged to better organize the growing resistance.

Groups around the country rapidly duplicated the actions of the protesters in Leipzig, and the weekly rallies became known as the "Monday Night Demonstrations." A month after the initial rally, a few hundred protesters had become 70,000. A week later, on October 16, there were 120,000. The next week, there were 320,000 people demonstrating in Leipzig alone, and groups of citizens held protests at churches across the country. It was during this period that resistance groups experienced enough popular support to go public with their ideas and materials.

So it was the next night, Monday, that a group of six of us presented ourselves at Checkpoint Charlie where the MP (Military Police) warned us to avoid any public demonstrations that might occur, and keeping that stern admonition in mind we made our way across the killing zone and into the East. We were held up briefly while some papers were checked. A small booth with mirrored glass was where the Stasi would be recording our information and checking it against their data banks. A second visit in two days would be noted.

We began walking up Friederikstrasse and after a few blocks turned right on to the Unter den Linden. We'd been told by some old Berlin hands to have dinner at the exclusive Golden Goose restaurant. It offered an outstanding view of Alexanderplatz, the social center of East Berlin, with many restaurants and shops offering goods for sale to anyone with any cash other than the almost worthless Ost marks. It was late autumn, just before Halloween, and the low German sun had dropped behind the horizon shortly after five.

We turned on to Karl Liebknecht Strasse, a broad avenue lit only by an occasional lamp post. As we drew up to the Soviet Monument against Fascism, we could see lights blazing from the imposing GDR headquarters across the street. Its impressive size and brightly lit exterior was enhanced and made sinister by the more than one hundred AK-47 toting Vopo ringing the exterior, ready to repel any threat from insurrectionists.

As we drew alongside the monument, I saw a lone German in civilian clothing standing in front of us, looking across the street at the armed guards ringing the building. Recalling my best German from ninth grade language class and every World War II movie since, I began my conversation by asking him what was going on.

"Guten Abend. Was ist los?"

The man had seen us walking up and recognized us as Americans, aided by our uniforms, no doubt. Once I'd given the greeting, he cast a furtive look up and down the broad avenue and across the street before turning slightly and presenting his back to that evil building. Smiling broadly and speaking in lightly accented English, he exclaimed happily, "Tonight we are making a demonstration for democracy!" The group of us murmured appreciatively, not wanting to be so loud as to attract the attention of the Vopos our way. While we were immune from arrest or detention, this fellow was not.

At that point, we wished him well and began to move away. But before we left I leaned in towards him and said, “You know, our own experience in revolutions is that you really need a few more people to show up.” He drew himself upright and looked me evenly in the eyes and with absolute conviction said, “More will come. You will see.”

We ambled on, approaching Alexanderplatz, when suddenly, from an intersecting street we were startled to see a hundred or more East German protestors, walking with banners and carrying candles in cups, calling for freedom and democracy. Just as the German gentleman back at the monument had predicted.

As the senior officer and designated group leader, and heeding the advice of the MP at the checkpoint, I looked about to see if I could find a way to get out of the area because I knew none of us wanted to end our foray into the heart of the Evil Empire this early. It was then that I eyed the rathskeller, a basement bar, just a door away. The demonstrators were drawing abreast and the time to leave was upon us. I led the way downstairs, pushed open the heavy wooden door and we entered the dim interior of a place that was a European version of Moran’s, a small bar back in my home town on Long Island. We saw eight representatives of the modern Communist man quietly drinking the evening away. I was instantly reminded of those old Westerns where the strangers walk into the saloon and the piano playing stops. In this case, it was manifested by the simultaneous movement of all eyes upon us and conversations coming to an instant halt.

This is that part in the movies where the stranger has to decide how to reveal his intentions in the clearest possible way to avoid misunderstandings or bad outcomes. My very rusty German provided the solution and I said loudly, “Guten Abend, meine Freunde, die Getränke sind auf mich!” Buying a round of drinks is a universally understood offer of friendship, and that caused the crowd to come alive with offers of many thanks and a few shouts of “Machen sie meine ein doppeltes!” (Make mine a double!) Those fine working men shouted their orders to the now animated barman who began rapidly pulling bottles off the top shelves to satisfy the desires of our new friends.

We settled in with our drinks and I paid the two dollar tab. We knew we had a few minutes’ wait to be certain the demonstrators had left the area, so we relaxed and started chatting. The TV volume picked up again and in a few minutes I would come to understand how it was Merv Griffin who had ended the Cold War.

For whatever reasons, television signals from West Berlin were not being blocked by the GDR, whether that was a recent development or routine I could not know, but what I did hear was the unmistakable sound of the opening music to "*Wheel of Fortune,*" and I glanced to see the syndicated West German version of Pat and Vanna spinning that wheel and the happy West German contestants winning speed boats and ceramic Dalmatians.

I watched those men watching that television, those workers of the proletariat, and I saw something in their eyes, some yearning that would be explained a few years later in the movie "*The Silence of the Lambs*" when Dr. Lector told FBI agent Clarice Starling, "People covet what they see."

Finishing our second two-dollar round and having earned the good will of that entire drinking establishment, we made our way out the door, up the stairs and off into the evening.

We soon found ourselves at the restaurant and by this time it was just half past seven. As we were walking inside, we ran into two other JAGs from the conference. They were both assigned to bases in West Germany and one, Mary, spoke fluent German. They joined us, and the tuxedoed maitre d' escorted us up thickly carpeted stairs. We entered a huge open dining room and were seated at a large table set inside a bay window with an unobstructed view of the Platz. The few local diners were elderly couples in small groups of three or four. We were either early by European standards, or not a lot of folks could afford to eat there. The men wore jackets and ties and the women stylish dresses. They all looked our way and many nodded pleasantly. The diners were being serenaded by a gray-haired gentleman playing a dirge-like tune on his electric piano, but this ended as we were being seated when he broke into some snappy American show tunes from "Oklahoma" and "South Pacific."

Our waitresses were young and pretty, both spoke limited English, but their enthusiasm for the movement towards democracy was unmistakeable. One of them greeted us by sharing her name and saying proudly in practiced English: "I cannot wait for democracy! As soon as I can leave here I am going west and then if I am lucky, I will go to America and to live with my sister in Chicago."

Now satisfied that she wouldn't be spitting in our soup, we began to work on our selections for dinner. The first order of business was ordering drinks. Since most of us were having white wine we demurred to her suggestions after reminding her that, "Geld ist kein problem" (money is no problem) and how about a nice selection of appetizers?

She came to Jimmy-Jam, a wild man from a base in the UK, who fired off "I want you to bring me the best thing on the menu, what you only bring out for the big shots." He leaned back conspiratorially, "You know, without telling all of us good folks about it."

Some might say Jimmy had problems with voice projection as his volume was always set way too high. He got his nickname because of getting jammed up when the US government shifted from handing over Temporary Duty (TDY) pay in cash and instead issued government credit cards for recording and reimbursing all the credit card expenses. This required the card to only be used for government business which Jimmy came to understand did not include Valentine's Day chocolate, fancy lace underwear, and a spa day for his wife.

Confused, the waitress leaned in and said, "I'm sorry, your English is too fast for me, please." Jimmy began to pantomime shoveling an imaginary fork towards his mouth and turning up his volume just a notch in case she couldn't hear him and which was now attracting the attention of other diners while saying, "Something good!" and he gave her a thumb's up gesture and big smile. Unable to remain quiet and allow the loud American stereotype to be further denigrated, Mary, the German-speaking attorney blurted out "Bringen sie ihm ein schweineschnitzel mit spätzle und kartoffelsalat!" (Bring him breaded pork with noodles and salad) Jimmy, stunned by the rapidity of the order, sat back, cocked his head and looked at her appraisingly. "Yeah, that sounds good," he told the waitress while closing the menu he couldn't read, and turning to Mary saying, "That's good, right?" She nodded and told him it was a very good choice, so the entree was settled.

The liberty-loving waitress probably should have left it at that, but further inquired as to Jimmy's drink choice, in English. He decided he wanted some red wine, which was fine except there really was no red wine in East Germany in 1989, maybe some Bulgarian red for cooking, but for drinking, only white wine. He looked up at her and said, "I don't know, maybe have some red wine." Again, she leaned forward and said,"Please? I'm sorry?" Jimmy looked at her and said very slowly and much too loudly for the room, "I said REEEED WIIIIIINE!" dragging the vowels. The waitress was confused and looked to the same attorney who said, “Bringen sie ihn einfach ein glas, er wird trinken, was wir trinken!” (Bring him a glass, he’ll drink what we’re drinking) Grateful to be done with this big-voiced American, she nodded, finished up the order and left for the kitchen, and no doubt telling any other future immigrants what the Americans were like.

As the evening progressed and courses began to roll out, we made another judicious use of “Drinks are on the Americans!” and the place became even livelier. A later crowd arrived and people were being serenaded by a now lively piano player who was stoked by the appearance of American dollar bills in his tip jar and had amped it up to selections from *Cabaret.*

While we were chatting amiably, somebody glanced out the bay window and said, “Would you look at this!” We stopped talking and looked out and on to the Platz. The shops had closed a half hour earlier and the square was no longer brightly illuminated, but still, there was no mistaking as thousands of ordinary Germans began walking into that square from all directions. There were hundreds more banners and every single person had a candle which blended into a peaceful, but determined, mass of humanity petitioning their government and the world for freedom. As they converged and coalesced, a phalanx of helmeted Vopos surrounded the plaza on several sides. They were backed up at a distance by other officers in riot control vehicles. The protestors chanted and waited for the carnage that never came. We finished our dinner, said our goodbyes, and made our way back to the West. Ten days later that hated wall starting coming down.

I wonder if that waitress made it to Chicago.

Table of Contents

About the Author

Mike grew up in Syosset, New York, but you know that now.

After getting out in 1975, Mike kicked around Europe, traveling on a EurRail pass, returned to the States, went to college for a year but in 1977, due to being broke; and times again being what they were, took a job as a cop in a small logging town in Oregon. Over those three rain-soaked years he answered a number of interesting calls for police services -- told in a soon to be released book, "***Memoirs Of A Small Town Cop***."

Tired of the never-ending rains, and heeding the admonishment of the Beatles, "And so I quit the police department and got myself a steady job." Mike moved to Florida to complete his undergrad work, but tiring of the heat, humidity, and mosquitos with tail numbers assaulting him, he applied for, and was accepted at, the greatest law school in the state of Idaho, well, at the time, also the only law school. He spent three years amidst the wheat fields of the Palouse, studying law on occasion while also juggling the demands of being a house painter and combat engineer in an Army Reserve firefighting unit. All this led to meeting new people, having interesting roommates, and experiences, like TV's Judge Wapner, as commencement speaker, all told in another soon to be released book, "***For My Next Trick.***"

His other book, "The making of a COMBAT JAG" picks up the story in 1988, after getting a law degree and re-entering a Cold War Air Force. His "Forest Gump-like" career arc made him witness to a few incredible moments of world history and introduced him to a pantheon of interesting characters across six continents.

He got stupid in 2006, during the height of the insurrection in Iraq, and took a "safe" job in the Green Zone with the Multi-National Security Transition Command, MNSTC-I, as an unarmed contractor working to restore, or try to re-establish, the Iraqi military justice system. He lived in the US Embassy trailer park on the grounds of the Former Republican Guard palace complex, in a 110-square foot room with a deaf guy named George, who always denied being deaf.

They shared a telephone booth-sized bathroom with two other guys, the MNSTC-I public affairs guy, and a guy from Missouri who was paid $80,000 a year to drive the shit-suck truck on the Embassy grounds and empty the porte-potties. After arriving and getting his room, the shit-suck driver "ghosted," and simply never went into work. Nobody missed him, they thought he hadn't arrived.

Despite being promised differently, Mike lived in the Green Zone, sometimes called "*The Emerald City*" because of the luxuries within the walls, but worked outside those massive walls, at the Ministry of Defense, and experienced the daily lives, and many deaths, of ordinary Iraqis in the Red Zone.

After several near misses, Mike finally got blown up while investigating a report of corruption, during a briefing from a Romanian guy who looked like Count Chocula, namesake character of a chocolate breakfast cereal. This will be the final book in the series of memoirs and due out in December. "***The Thieves of Baghdad***" and subtitled, "*Confessions Of A Sleazy Contractor In The Emerald City.*"

A serious photographer, after retiring from active duty, in 2004, Mike took up motorcycle riding and has spent the last fourteen years taking photos while putting some serious miles on his GoldWing. Along with his artist buddy, Paul Hill, (paulhillfineart.com) on his Harley, they've toured huge swaths of America and British Columbia, Canada.

These books, like his life, all came about by serendipity. In 2016, while coming home from a road trip and driving down US Highway 95, just outside of Worley, Idaho, pop 257, he stopped to take a selfie because the rolling hills looked nice. He liked it so much he posted it to Facebook saying, "Got the author photo done for my book." A friend from high school commented, "I always found the dust cover photo to be the hardest part. Let me know when you have 100,000 words."

He began writing in the early autumn of 2015. He wrote the quarter-million word first draft during the, "Once every 500-

year, Snowpocalypse," that was the winter of 2016. He spent the next few years whittling, chopping and polishing.

His works are best paired with anything containing alcohol, and in places where legal, some Maui-Wowie or other herbal remedies.

If you buy his books, he'll only write more of them.

Printed in Great Britain
by Amazon

71930102R00187